INDESTRUCTIBLE HULK

AGENT OF S.H.I.E.L.D.

VOLUME 01

INDESTRUCTIBLE HULK VOL. 1: AGENT OF S.H.I.E.L.D. Contains material originally published in magazine form as INDESTRUCTIBLE HULK #1-5. First printing 2014. ISBN# 978-0-7851-6647-4. Published by MARVEL WORLDWIDE, INC., a subsidiary of MARVEL ENTERTAINMENT, LLC. OFFICE OF PUBLICATION: 135 West 50th Street, New York, NY 10020. Copyright © 2012 and 2014 Marvel Characters, Inc. All rights reserved. All characters featured in this issue and the distinctive names and likenesses thereof, and all related indicia are trademarks of Marvel Characters, Inc. No similarity between any of the names, characters, persons, and/or institutions in this magazine with those of any living or dead person or institution is intended, and any such similarity which may exist is purely coincidental. **Printed in the U.S.A.** ALAN FINE, EVP - Office of the President, Marvel Worldwide, Inc. and EVP & CMO Marvel Characters B.V.; DAN BUCKLEY, Publisher & President - Print, Animation & Digital Divisions; JOE QUESADA, Chief Creative Officer; TOM BREVOORT, SVP of Publishing; DAVID BOGART, SVP of Operations & Procurement, Publishing; C.B. CEBULSKI, SVP of Creator & Content Development; DAVID GABRIEL, SVP of Print & Digital Publishing Sales; JIM O'KEEFE, VP of Operations & Logistics; DAN CARR, Executive Director of Publishing Technology; SUSAN CRESPI, Editorial Operations Manager; ALEX MORALES, Publishing Operations Manager; STAN LEE, Chairman Emeritus. For information regarding advertising in Marvel Comics or on Marvel.com, please contact Niza Disla, Director of Marvel Partnerships, at ndisla@marvel.com. For Marvel subscription inquiries, please call 800-217-9158. **Manufactured between 11/29/2013 and 1/6/2014 by R.R. DONNELLEY, INC., SALEM, VA, USA.**

0987654321

WRITER
MARK WAID
PENCILER
LEINIL FRANCIS YU
INKER
GERRY ALANGUILAN
COLORIST
SUNNY GHO
LETTERER
CHRIS ELIOPOULOS
COVER ARTIST
LEINIL FRANCIS YU
WITH **SUNNY GHO** & **VAL STAPLES**
ASSISTANT EDITOR
JON MOISAN
EDITOR
MARK PANICCIA

COLLECTION EDITOR
CORY LEVINE
ASSISTANT EDITORS
ALEX STARBUCK
NELSON RIBEIRO
EDITORS, SPECIAL PROJECTS
JENNIFER GRÜNWALD
MARK D. BEAZLEY

SENIOR EDITOR,
SPECIAL PROJECTS
JEFF YOUNGQUIST
SVP OF PRINT & DIGITAL
PUBLISHING SALES
DAVID GABRIEL
BOOK DESIGN
JEFF POWELL & CORY LEVINE

EDITOR IN CHIEF
AXEL ALONSO
CHIEF CREATIVE OFFICER
JOE QUESADA
PUBLISHER
DAN BUCKLEY
EXECUTIVE PRODUCER
ALAN FINE

BRUCE BANNER WAS A BRILLIANT SCIENTIST THAT CREATED WEAPONS OF UNLIMITED DESTRUCTION FOR THE ARMY. AFTER BEING CAUGHT IN THE BLAST OF A GAMMA BOMB OF HIS OWN CREATION, DR. BANNER NOW TRANSFORMS INTO THE MONSTROUS HULK WHEN ANGERED OR THREATENED. THE TWO PERSONALITIES HAVE FOUGHT ALONGSIDE OTHER HEROES FOR YEARS BUT THEIR BIGGEST STRUGGLE HAS ALWAYS BEEN WITH ONE ANOTHER. BANNER HAS CONTINUOUSLY TRIED TO CURE HIMSELF OF THE HULK BUT HAS FINALLY ACCEPTED THAT HE NEEDS HIS OTHER HALF TO SURVIVE.

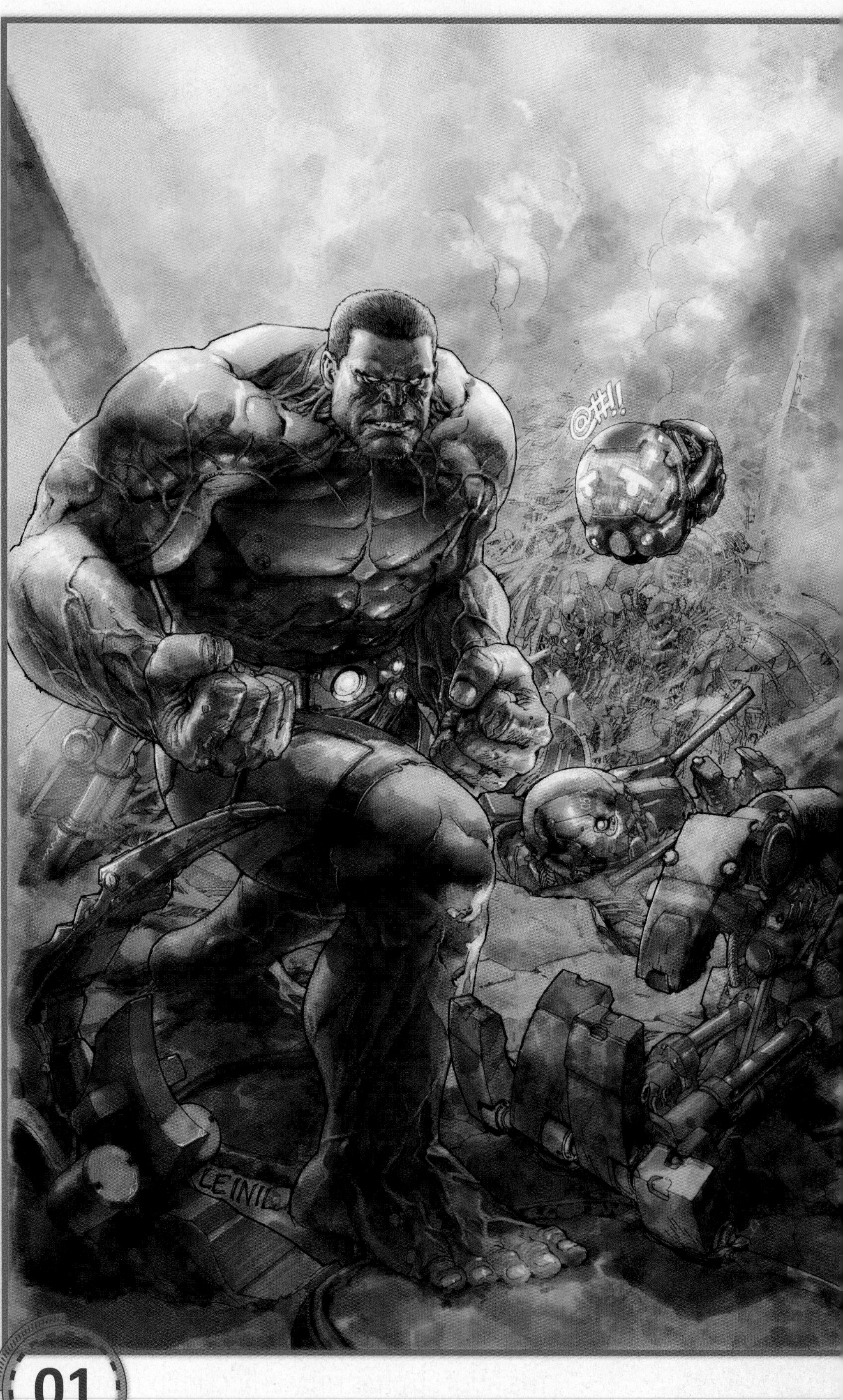
@#!!
LEINIL

01

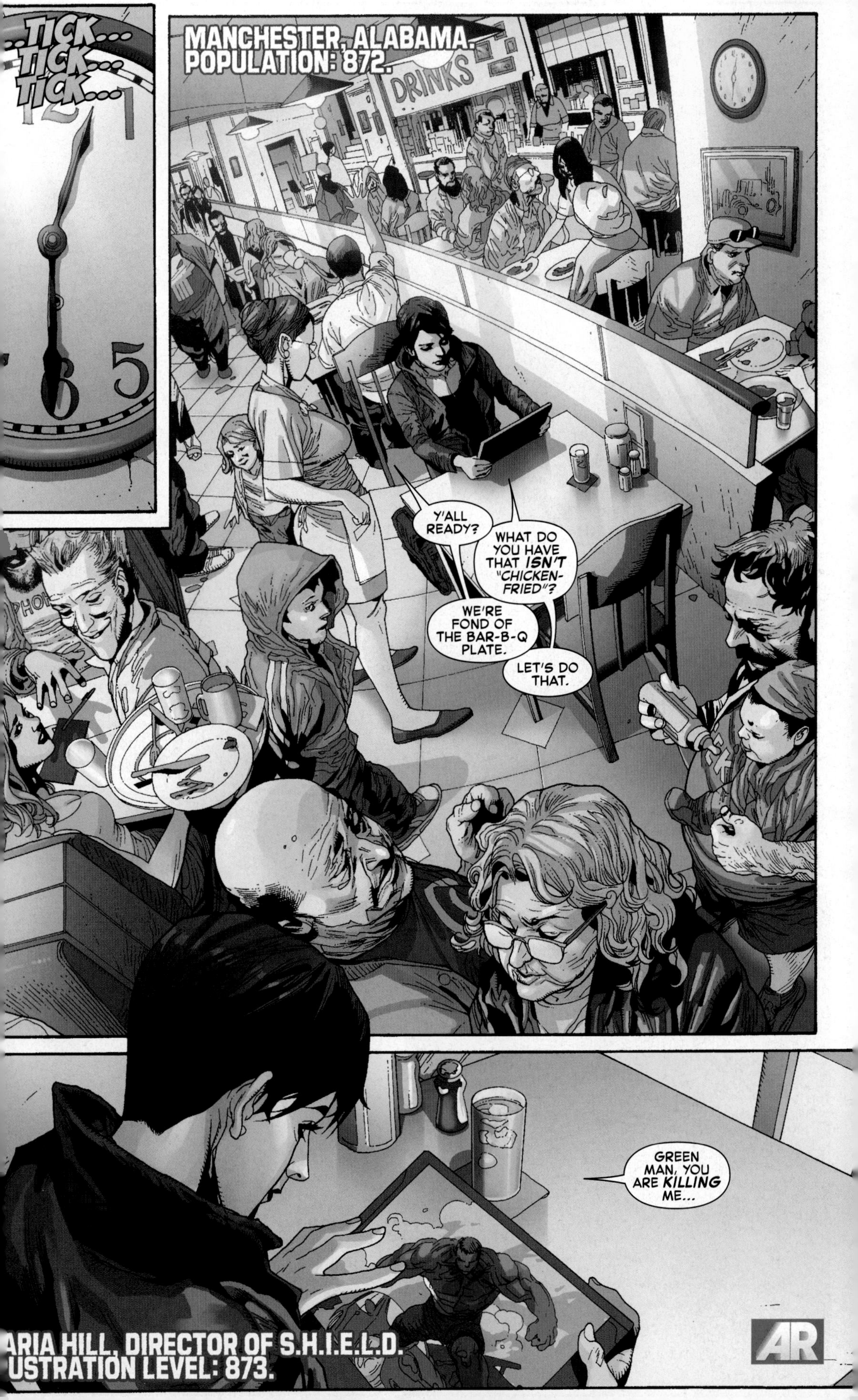

...TICK...
...TICK...
...TICK...
MANCHESTER, ALABAMA.
POPULATION: 872.
DRINKS
Y'ALL READY?
WHAT DO YOU HAVE THAT ISN'T "CHICKEN-FRIED"?
WE'RE FOND OF THE BAR-B-Q PLATE.
LET'S DO THAT.
GREEN MAN, YOU ARE KILLING ME...
ARIA HILL, DIRECTOR OF S.H.I.E.L.D.
USTRATION LEVEL: 873.
AR

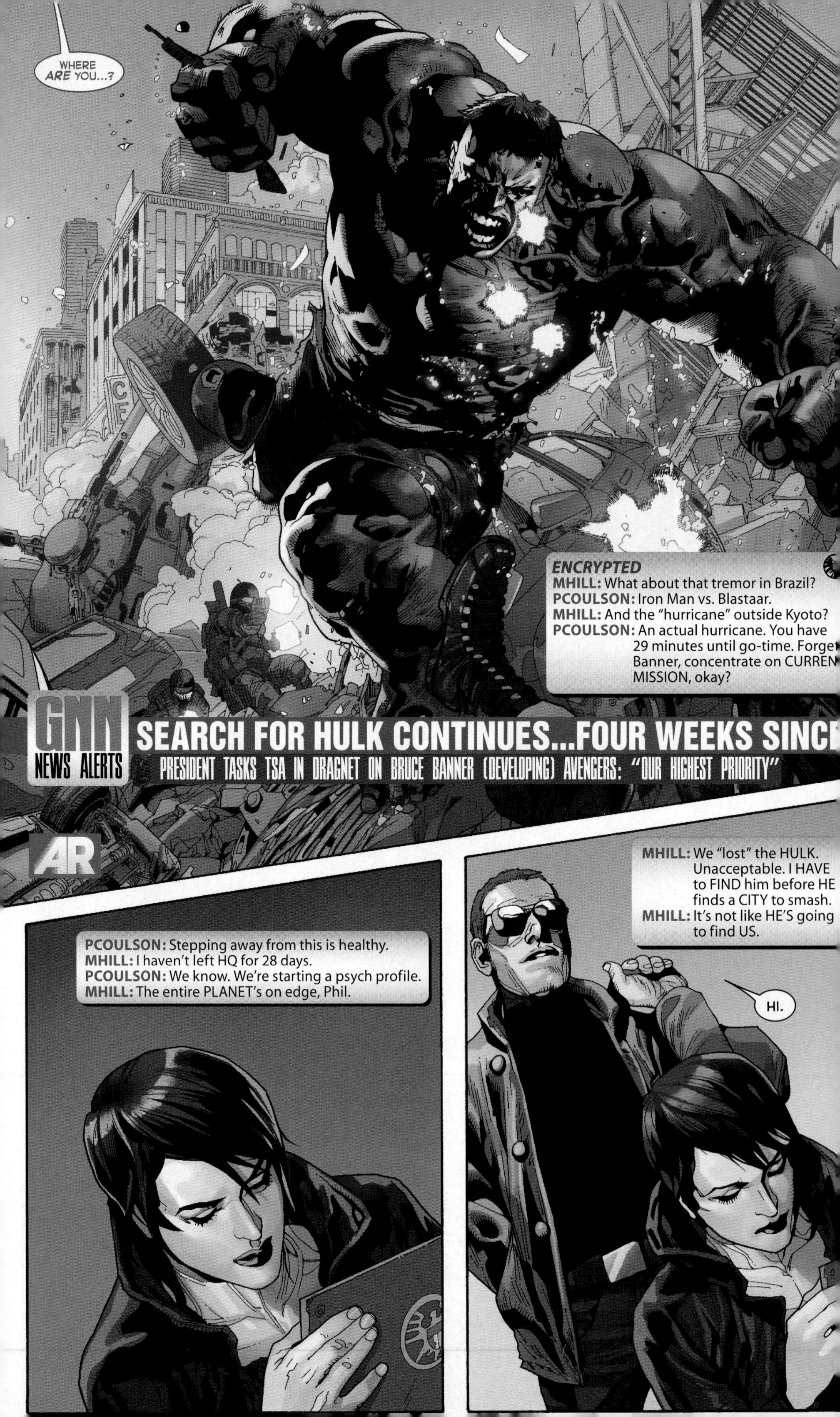
WHERE ARE YOU...?
ENCRYPTED
MHILL: What about that tremor in Brazil?
PCOULSON: Iron Man vs. Blastaar.
MHILL: And the "hurricane" outside Kyoto?
PCOULSON: An actual hurricane. You have 29 minutes until go-time. Forge Banner, concentrate on CURREN MISSION, okay?
GNN NEWS ALERTS
SEARCH FOR HULK CONTINUES...FOUR WEEKS SINC
PRESIDENT TASKS TSA IN DRAGNET ON BRUCE BANNER (DEVELOPING) AVENGERS: "OUR HIGHEST PRIORITY"
AR
PCOULSON: Stepping away from this is healthy.
MHILL: I haven't left HQ for 28 days.
PCOULSON: We know. We're starting a psych profile.
MHILL: The entire PLANET's on edge, Phil.
MHILL: We "lost" the HULK. Unacceptable. I HAVE to FIND him before HE finds a CITY to smash.
MHILL: It's not like HE'S going to find US.
HI.

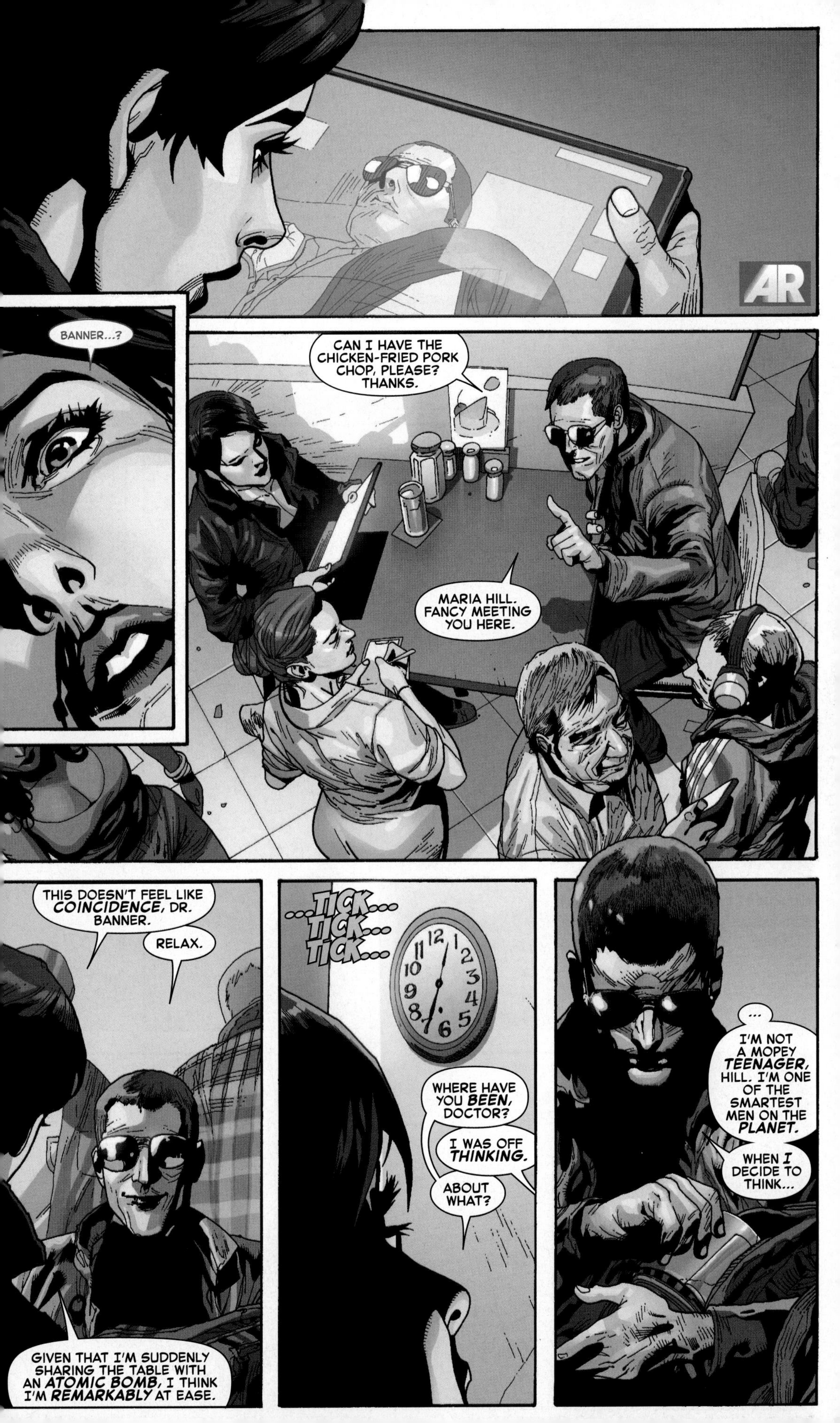
AR
BANNER...?
CAN I HAVE THE CHICKEN-FRIED PORK CHOP, PLEASE? THANKS.
MARIA HILL. FANCY MEETING YOU HERE.
THIS DOESN'T FEEL LIKE COINCIDENCE, DR. BANNER.
RELAX.
GIVEN THAT I'M SUDDENLY SHARING THE TABLE WITH AN ATOMIC BOMB, I THINK I'M REMARKABLY AT EASE.
...TICK... TICK... TICK...
WHERE HAVE YOU BEEN, DOCTOR?
I WAS OFF THINKING.
ABOUT WHAT?
...
I'M NOT A MOPEY TEENAGER, HILL. I'M ONE OF THE SMARTEST MEN ON THE PLANET.
WHEN I DECIDE TO THINK...

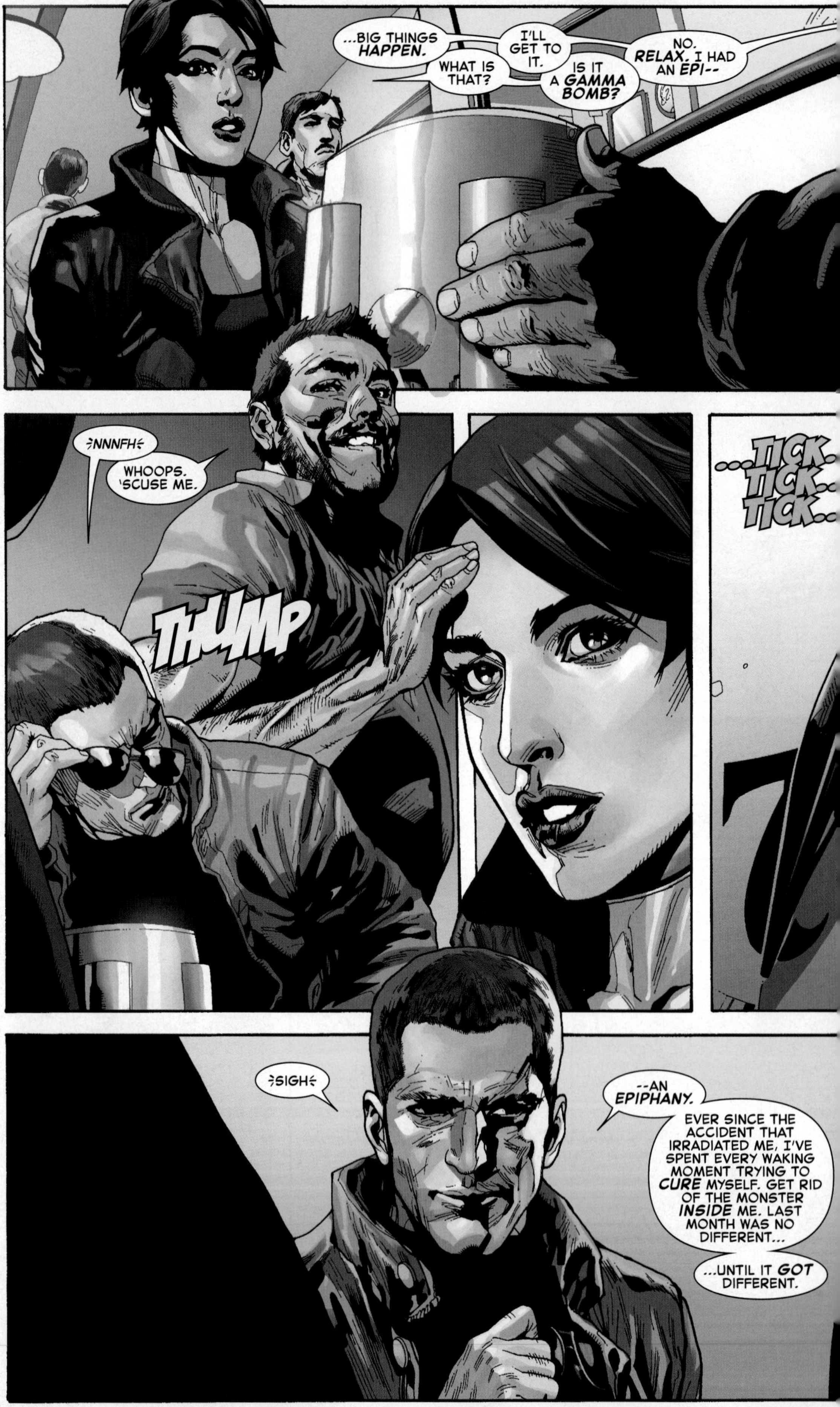
...BIG THINGS HAPPEN.
WHAT IS THAT?
I'LL GET TO IT.
IS IT A GAMMA BOMB?
NO. RELAX. I HAD AN EPI--
NNNFH
WHOOPS. 'SCUSE ME.
THUMP
...TICK... TICK... TICK...
SIGH
--AN EPIPHANY.
EVER SINCE THE ACCIDENT THAT IRRADIATED ME, I'VE SPENT EVERY WAKING MOMENT TRYING TO CURE MYSELF. GET RID OF THE MONSTER INSIDE ME. LAST MONTH WAS NO DIFFERENT...
...UNTIL IT GOT DIFFERENT.

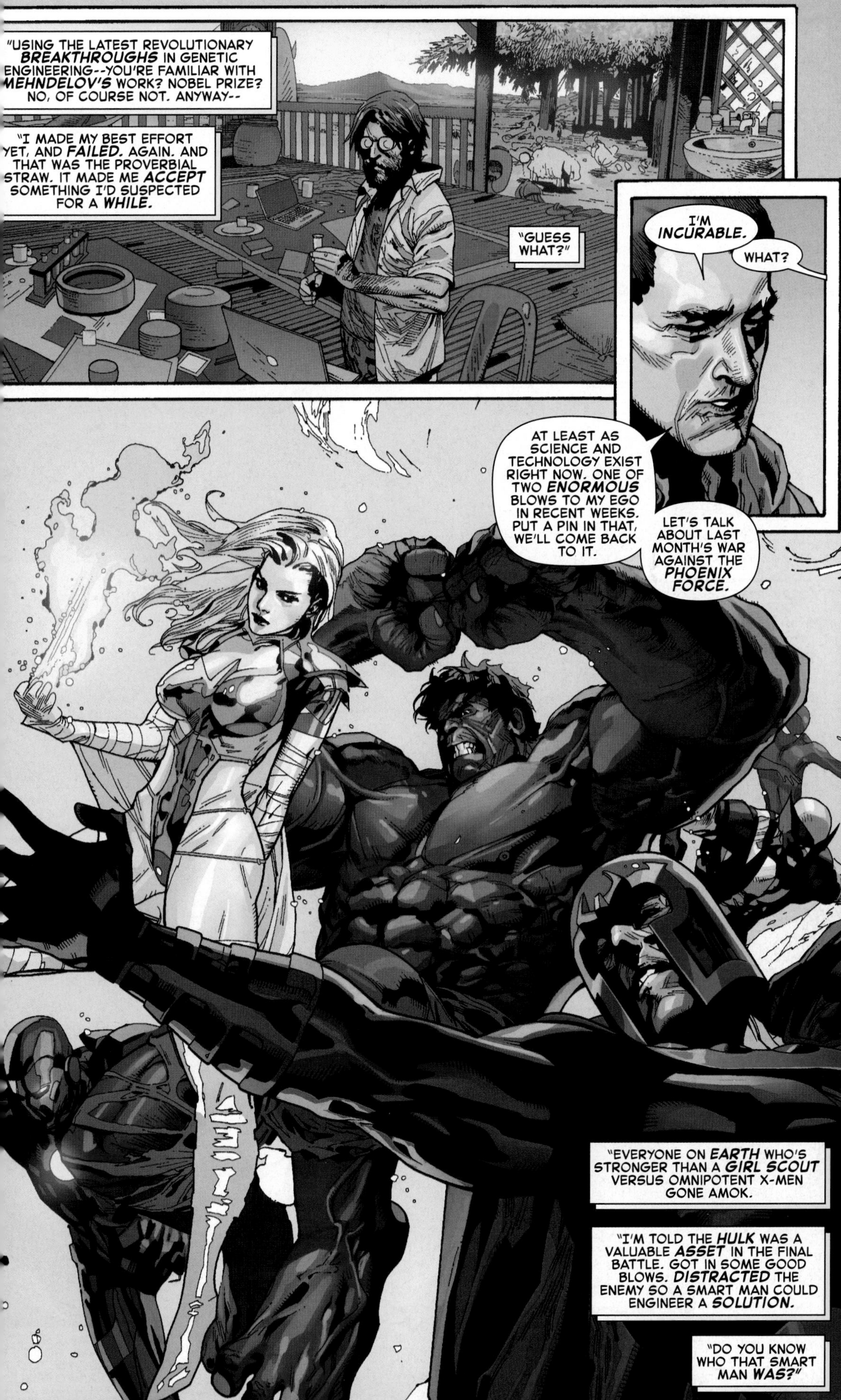
"USING THE LATEST REVOLUTIONARY BREAKTHROUGHS IN GENETIC ENGINEERING--YOU'RE FAMILIAR WITH MEHNDELOV'S WORK? NOBEL PRIZE? NO, OF COURSE NOT. ANYWAY--
"I MADE MY BEST EFFORT YET, AND FAILED. AGAIN. AND THAT WAS THE PROVERBIAL STRAW. IT MADE ME ACCEPT SOMETHING I'D SUSPECTED FOR A WHILE.
"GUESS WHAT?"
I'M INCURABLE.
WHAT?
AT LEAST AS SCIENCE AND TECHNOLOGY EXIST RIGHT NOW. ONE OF TWO ENORMOUS BLOWS TO MY EGO IN RECENT WEEKS. PUT A PIN IN THAT, WE'LL COME BACK TO IT.
LET'S TALK ABOUT LAST MONTH'S WAR AGAINST THE PHOENIX FORCE.
"EVERYONE ON EARTH WHO'S STRONGER THAN A GIRL SCOUT VERSUS OMNIPOTENT X-MEN GONE AMOK.
"I'M TOLD THE HULK WAS A VALUABLE ASSET IN THE FINAL BATTLE. GOT IN SOME GOOD BLOWS. DISTRACTED THE ENEMY SO A SMART MAN COULD ENGINEER A SOLUTION.
"DO YOU KNOW WHO THAT SMART MAN WAS?"

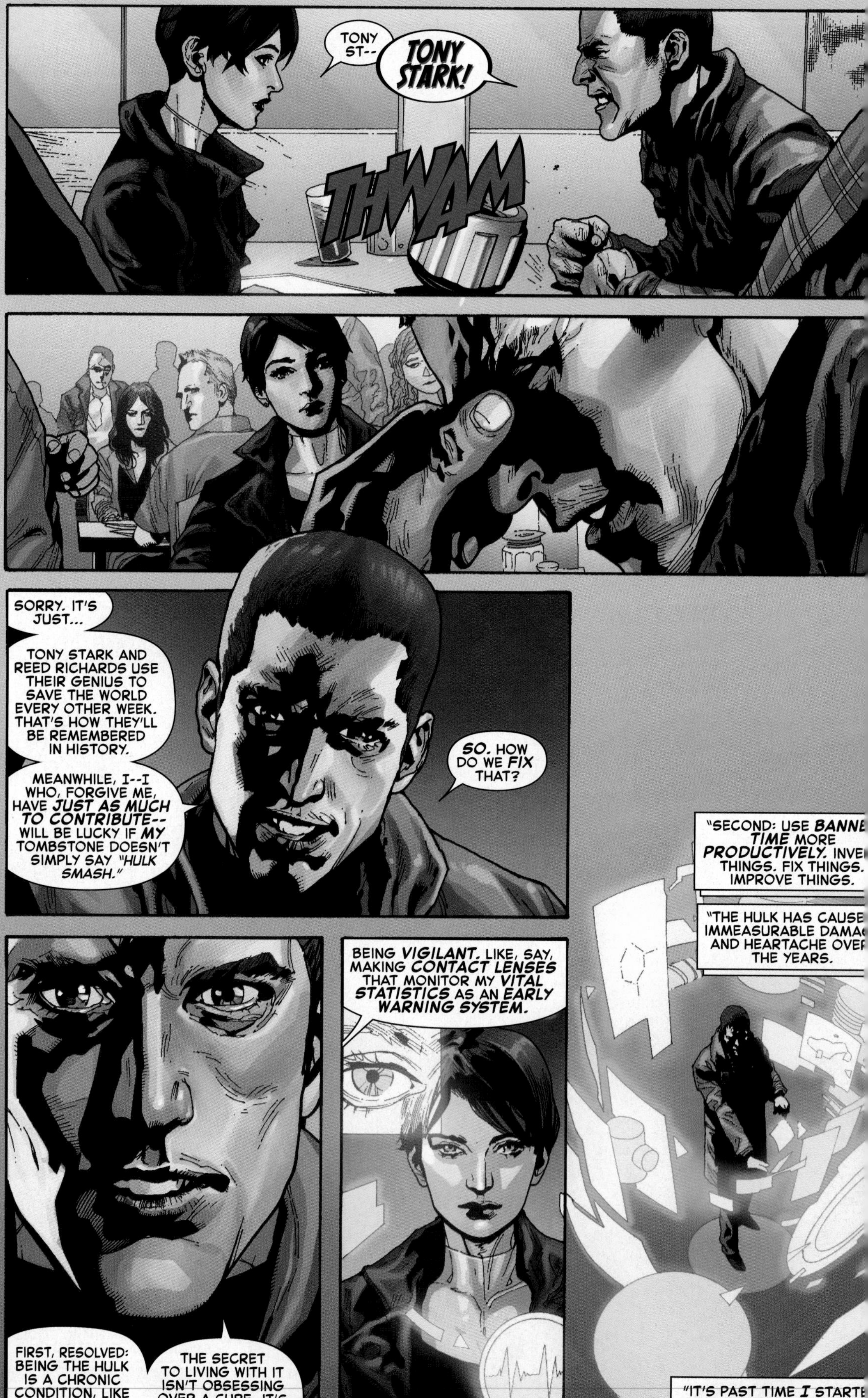

TONY ST--
TONY STARK!
THWAM
SORRY. IT'S JUST...
TONY STARK AND REED RICHARDS USE THEIR GENIUS TO SAVE THE WORLD EVERY OTHER WEEK. THAT'S HOW THEY'LL BE REMEMBERED IN HISTORY.
MEANWHILE, I--I WHO, FORGIVE ME, HAVE JUST AS MUCH TO CONTRIBUTE--WILL BE LUCKY IF MY TOMBSTONE DOESN'T SIMPLY SAY "HULK SMASH."
SO. HOW DO WE FIX THAT?
FIRST, RESOLVED: BEING THE HULK IS A CHRONIC CONDITION, LIKE DIABETES OR CANCER OR M.S.
THE SECRET TO LIVING WITH IT ISN'T OBSESSING OVER A CURE. IT'S IN MANAGING WHAT EXISTS.
BEING VIGILANT. LIKE, SAY, MAKING CONTACT LENSES THAT MONITOR MY VITAL STATISTICS AS AN EARLY WARNING SYSTEM.
"SECOND: USE BANNE TIME MORE PRODUCTIVELY. INVE THINGS. FIX THINGS. IMPROVE THINGS.
"THE HULK HAS CAUSE IMMEASURABLE DAMA AND HEARTACHE OVER THE YEARS.
"IT'S PAST TIME I STARTE BALANCING THE SCALES DOING AS MUCH GOOD F MANKIND AS POSSIBLE.

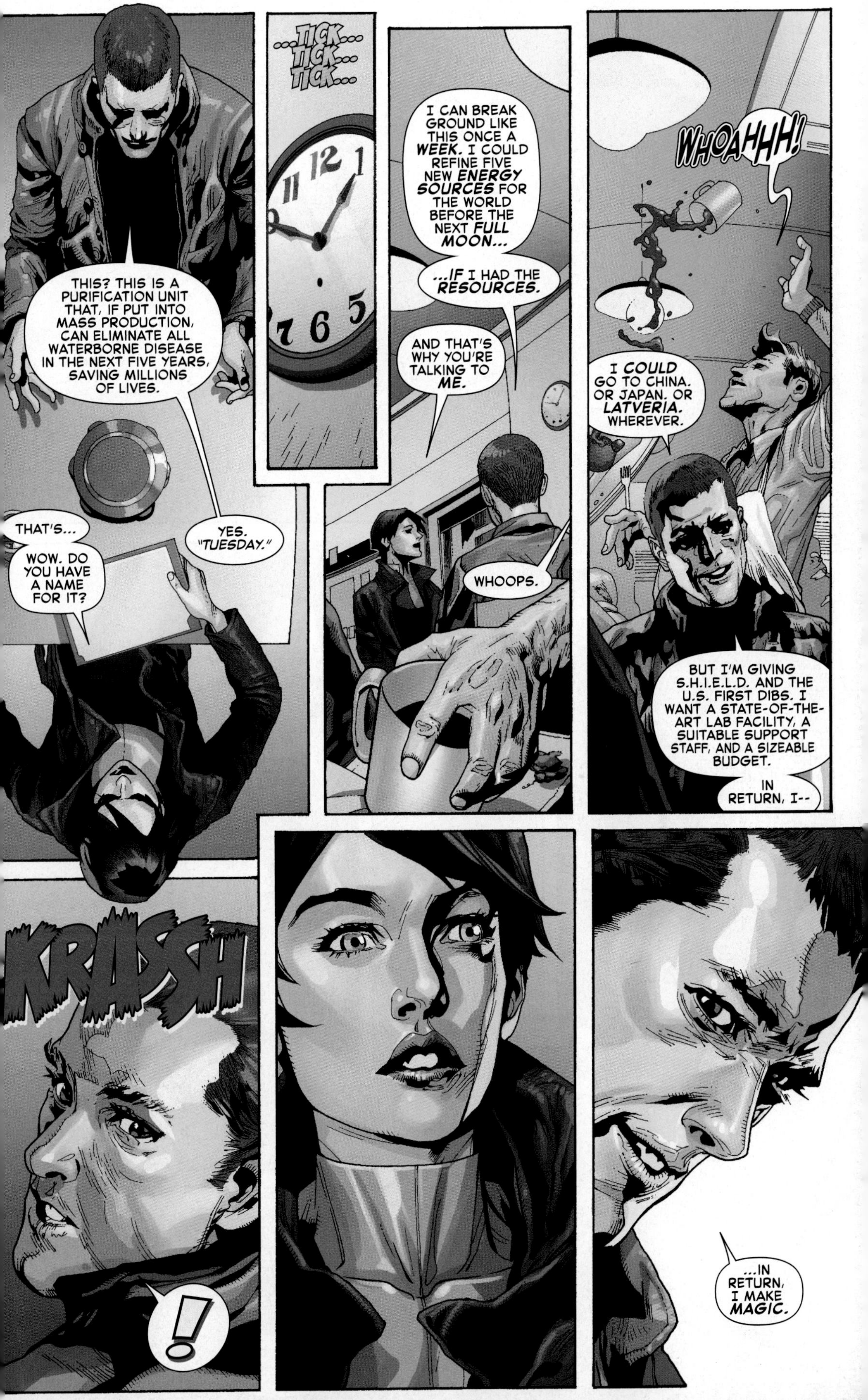
THIS? THIS IS A PURIFICATION UNIT THAT, IF PUT INTO MASS PRODUCTION, CAN ELIMINATE ALL WATERBORNE DISEASE IN THE NEXT FIVE YEARS, SAVING MILLIONS OF LIVES.
THAT'S...
WOW. DO YOU HAVE A NAME FOR IT?
YES. "TUESDAY."
...TICK... TICK... TICK...
I CAN BREAK GROUND LIKE THIS ONCE A WEEK. I COULD REFINE FIVE NEW ENERGY SOURCES FOR THE WORLD BEFORE THE NEXT FULL MOON...
...IF I HAD THE RESOURCES.
AND THAT'S WHY YOU'RE TALKING TO ME.
WHOOPS.
WHOAHHH!
I COULD GO TO CHINA. OR JAPAN. OR LATVERIA. WHEREVER.
BUT I'M GIVING S.H.I.E.L.D. AND THE U.S. FIRST DIBS. I WANT A STATE-OF-THE-ART LAB FACILITY, A SUITABLE SUPPORT STAFF, AND A SIZEABLE BUDGET.
IN RETURN, I--
KRASH
!
...IN RETURN, I MAKE MAGIC.

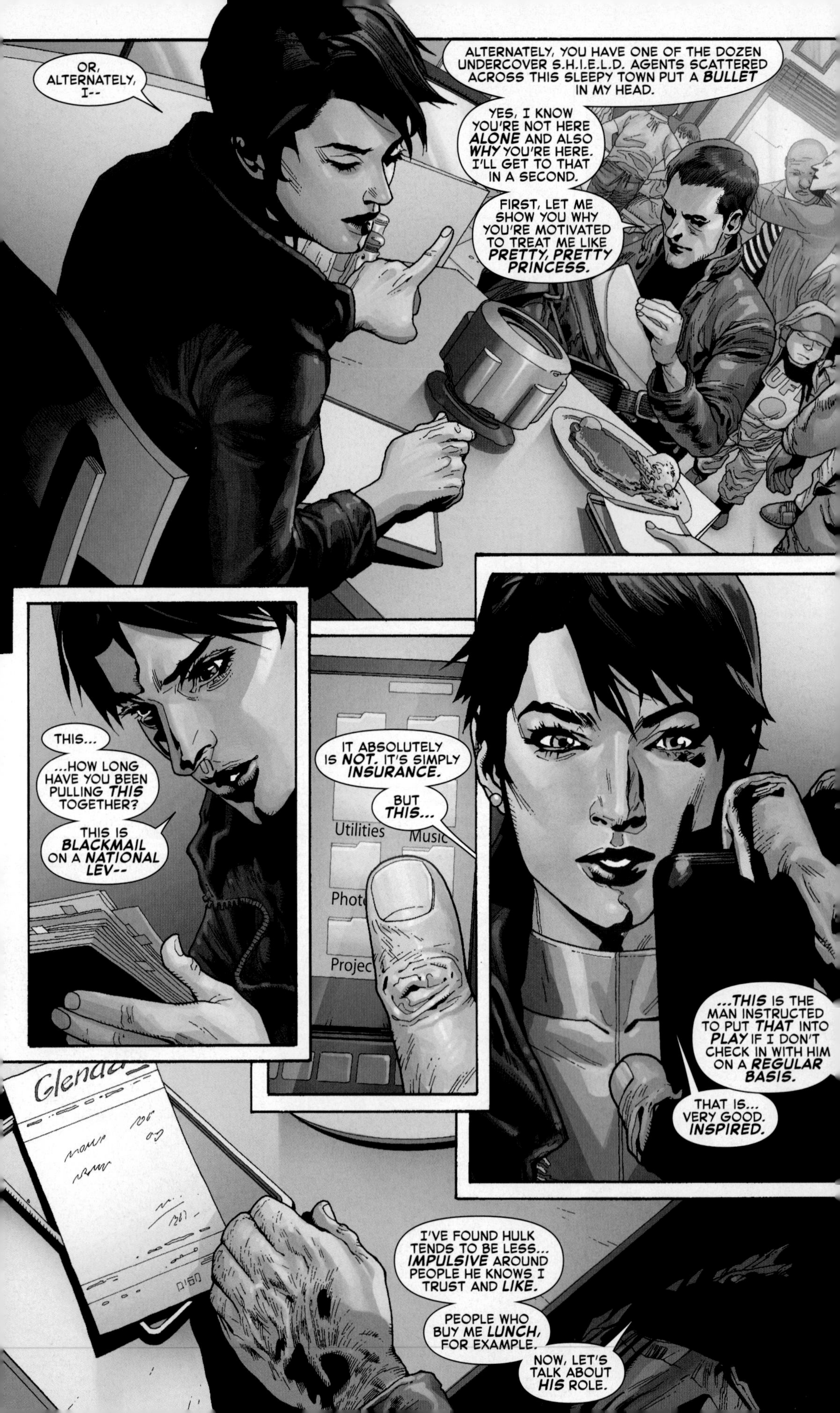
OR, ALTERNATELY, I--
ALTERNATELY, YOU HAVE ONE OF THE DOZEN UNDERCOVER S.H.I.E.L.D. AGENTS SCATTERED ACROSS THIS SLEEPY TOWN PUT A BULLET IN MY HEAD.
YES, I KNOW YOU'RE NOT HERE ALONE AND ALSO WHY YOU'RE HERE. I'LL GET TO THAT IN A SECOND.
FIRST, LET ME SHOW YOU WHY YOU'RE MOTIVATED TO TREAT ME LIKE PRETTY, PRETTY PRINCESS.
THIS...
...HOW LONG HAVE YOU BEEN PULLING THIS TOGETHER?
THIS IS BLACKMAIL ON A NATIONAL LEV--
IT ABSOLUTELY IS NOT. IT'S SIMPLY INSURANCE.
BUT THIS...
Utilities
Music
Photo
Projec
...THIS IS THE MAN INSTRUCTED TO PUT THAT INTO PLAY IF I DON'T CHECK IN WITH HIM ON A REGULAR BASIS.
THAT IS... VERY GOOD. INSPIRED.
Glenda
I'VE FOUND HULK TENDS TO BE LESS... IMPULSIVE AROUND PEOPLE HE KNOWS I TRUST AND LIKE.
PEOPLE WHO BUY ME LUNCH, FOR EXAMPLE.
NOW, LET'S TALK ABOUT HIS ROLE.

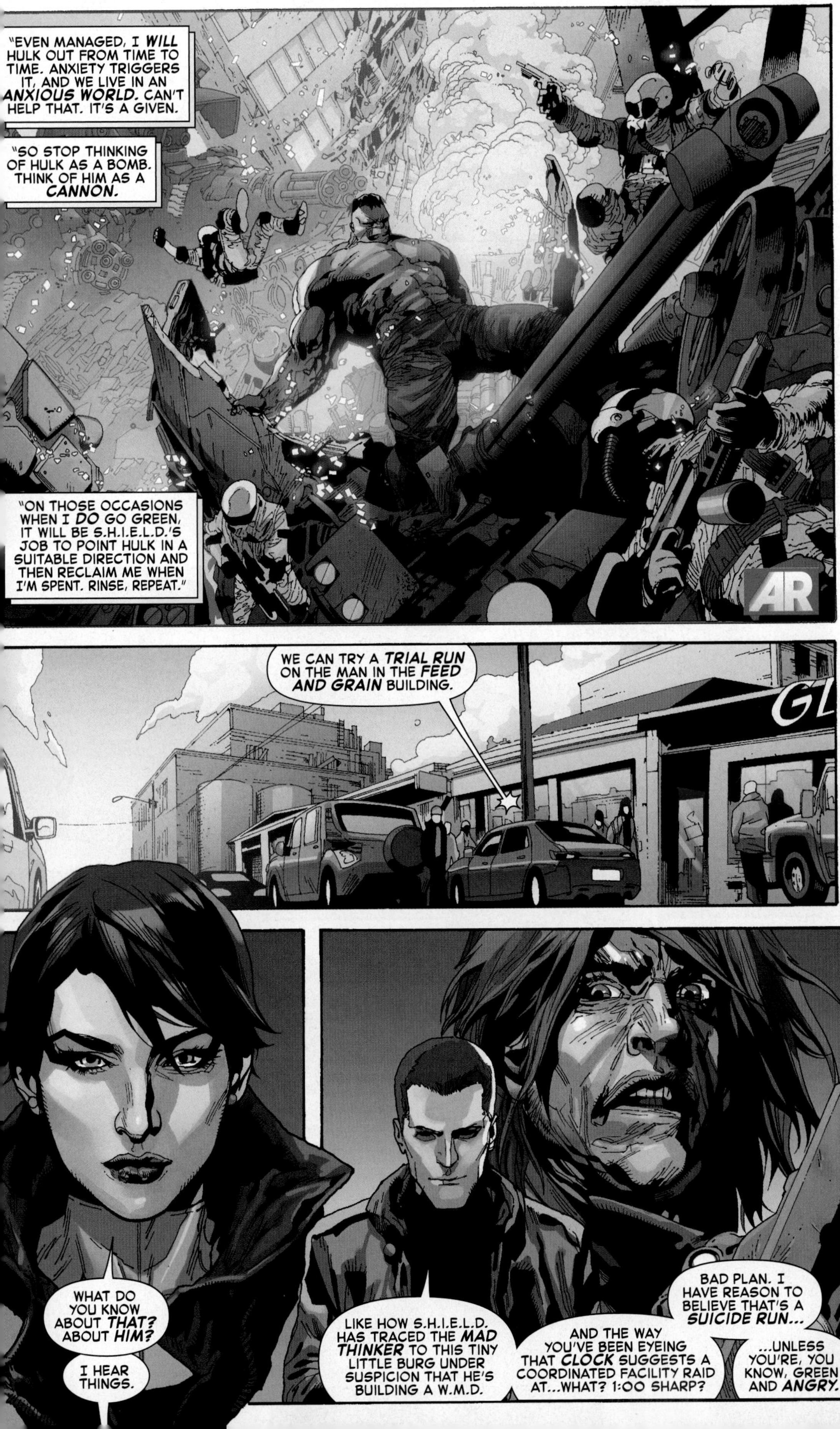
"EVEN MANAGED, I WILL HULK OUT FROM TIME TO TIME. ANXIETY TRIGGERS IT, AND WE LIVE IN AN ANXIOUS WORLD. CAN'T HELP THAT. IT'S A GIVEN.
"SO STOP THINKING OF HULK AS A BOMB. THINK OF HIM AS A CANNON.
"ON THOSE OCCASIONS WHEN I DO GO GREEN, IT WILL BE S.H.I.E.L.D.'S JOB TO POINT HULK IN A SUITABLE DIRECTION AND THEN RECLAIM ME WHEN I'M SPENT. RINSE, REPEAT."
AR
WE CAN TRY A TRIAL RUN ON THE MAN IN THE FEED AND GRAIN BUILDING.
WHAT DO YOU KNOW ABOUT THAT? ABOUT HIM?
I HEAR THINGS.
LIKE HOW S.H.I.E.L.D. HAS TRACED THE MAD THINKER TO THIS TINY LITTLE BURG UNDER SUSPICION THAT HE'S BUILDING A W.M.D.
AND THE WAY YOU'VE BEEN EYEING THAT CLOCK SUGGESTS A COORDINATED FACILITY RAID AT...WHAT? 1:00 SHARP?
BAD PLAN. I HAVE REASON TO BELIEVE THAT'S A SUICIDE RUN...
...UNLESS YOU'RE, YOU KNOW, GREEN AND ANGRY.

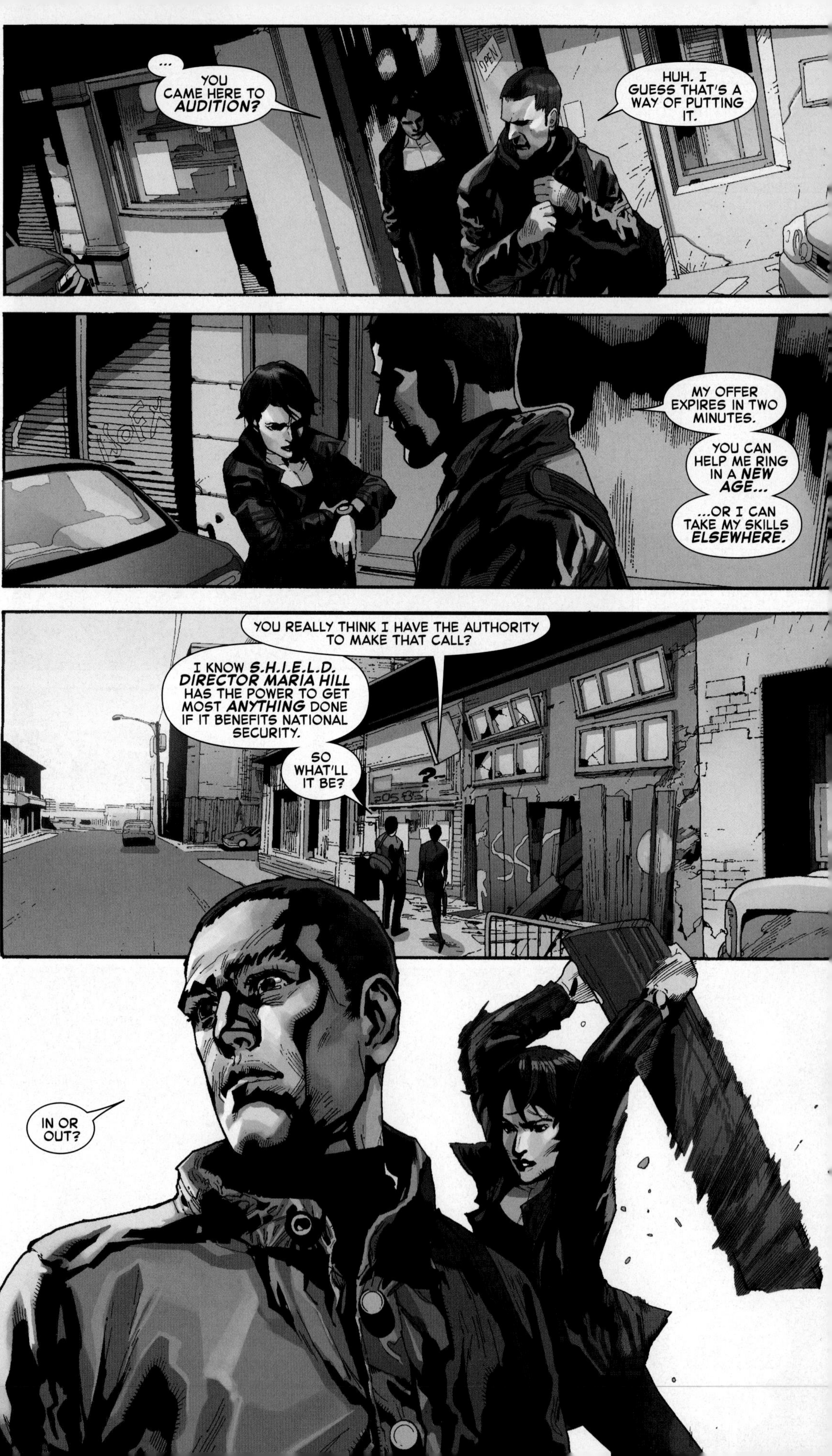
OPEN
...
YOU CAME HERE TO AUDITION?
HUH. I GUESS THAT'S A WAY OF PUTTING IT.
MY OFFER EXPIRES IN TWO MINUTES.
YOU CAN HELP ME RING IN A NEW AGE...
...OR I CAN TAKE MY SKILLS ELSEWHERE.
YOU REALLY THINK I HAVE THE AUTHORITY TO MAKE THAT CALL?
I KNOW S.H.I.E.L.D. DIRECTOR MARIA HILL HAS THE POWER TO GET MOST ANYTHING DONE IF IT BENEFITS NATIONAL SECURITY.
SO WHAT'LL IT BE?
IN OR OUT?

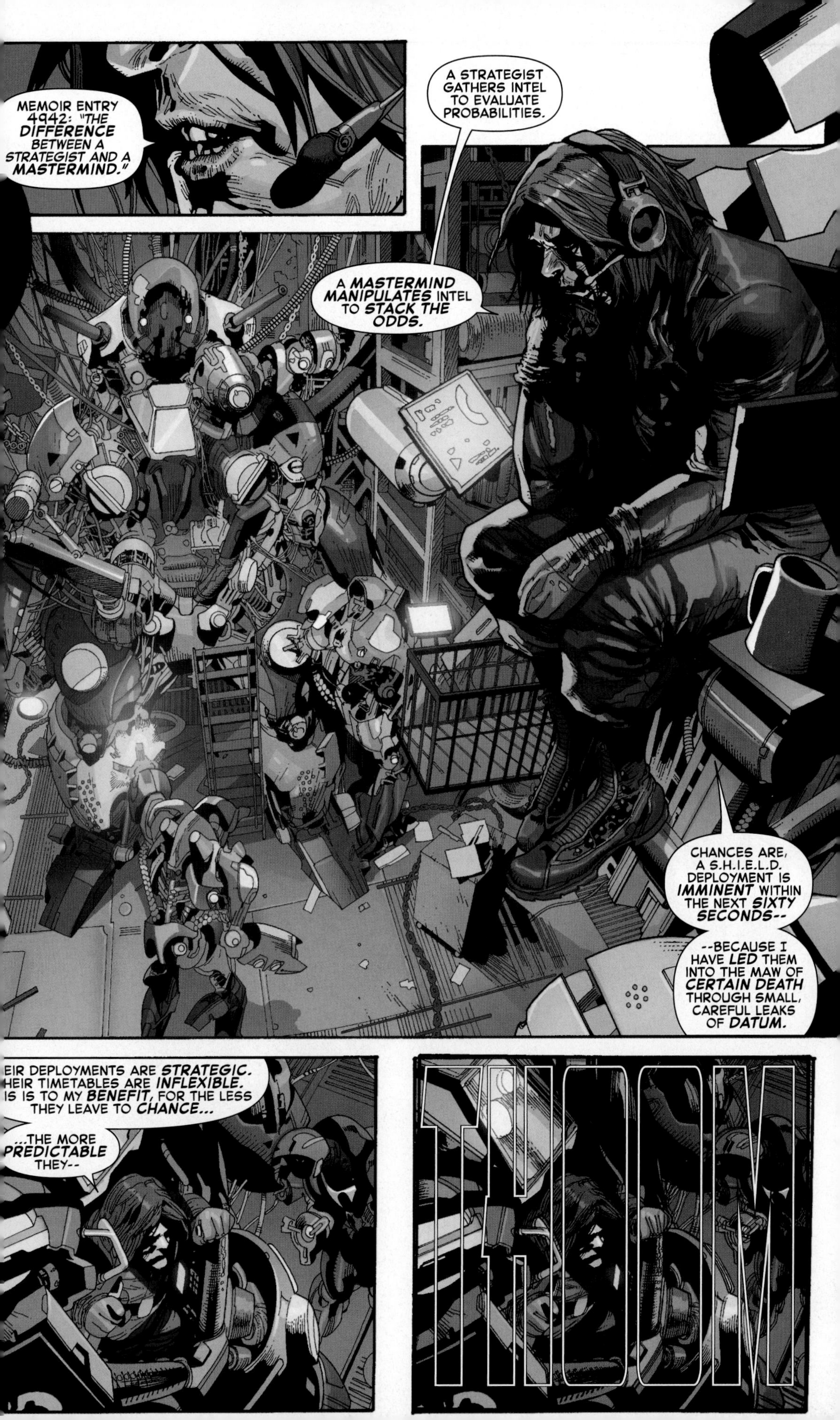
MEMOIR ENTRY 4942: "THE DIFFERENCE BETWEEN A STRATEGIST AND A MASTERMIND."
A STRATEGIST GATHERS INTEL TO EVALUATE PROBABILITIES.
A MASTERMIND MANIPULATES INTEL TO STACK THE ODDS.
CHANCES ARE, A S.H.I.E.L.D. DEPLOYMENT IS IMMINENT WITHIN THE NEXT SIXTY SECONDS--
--BECAUSE I HAVE LED THEM INTO THE MAW OF CERTAIN DEATH THROUGH SMALL, CAREFUL LEAKS OF DATUM.
EIR DEPLOYMENTS ARE STRATEGIC. HEIR TIMETABLES ARE INFLEXIBLE. IS IS TO MY BENEFIT, FOR THE LESS THEY LEAVE TO CHANCE...
...THE MORE PREDICTABLE THEY--
THOOM

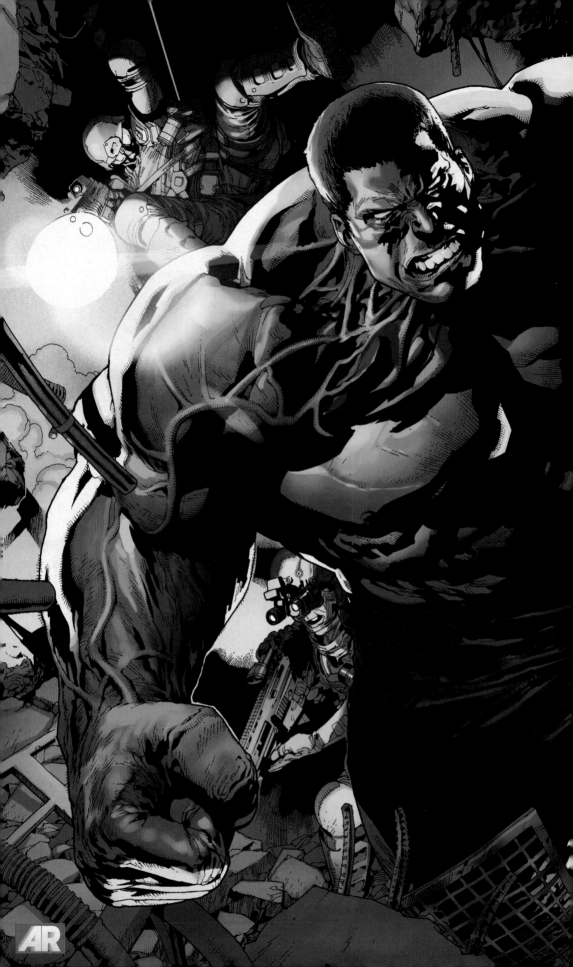

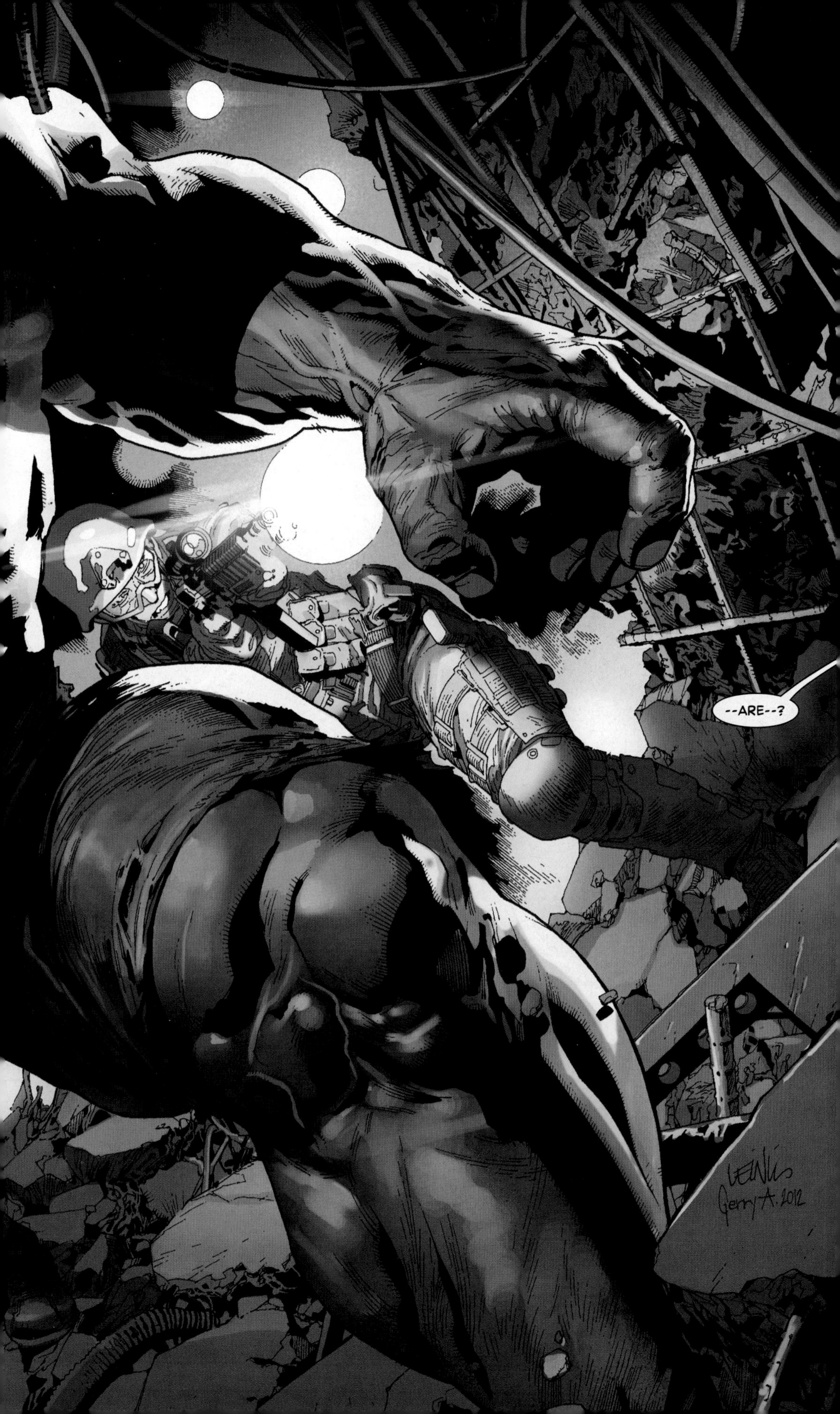
--ARE--?
Gerry A. 2012

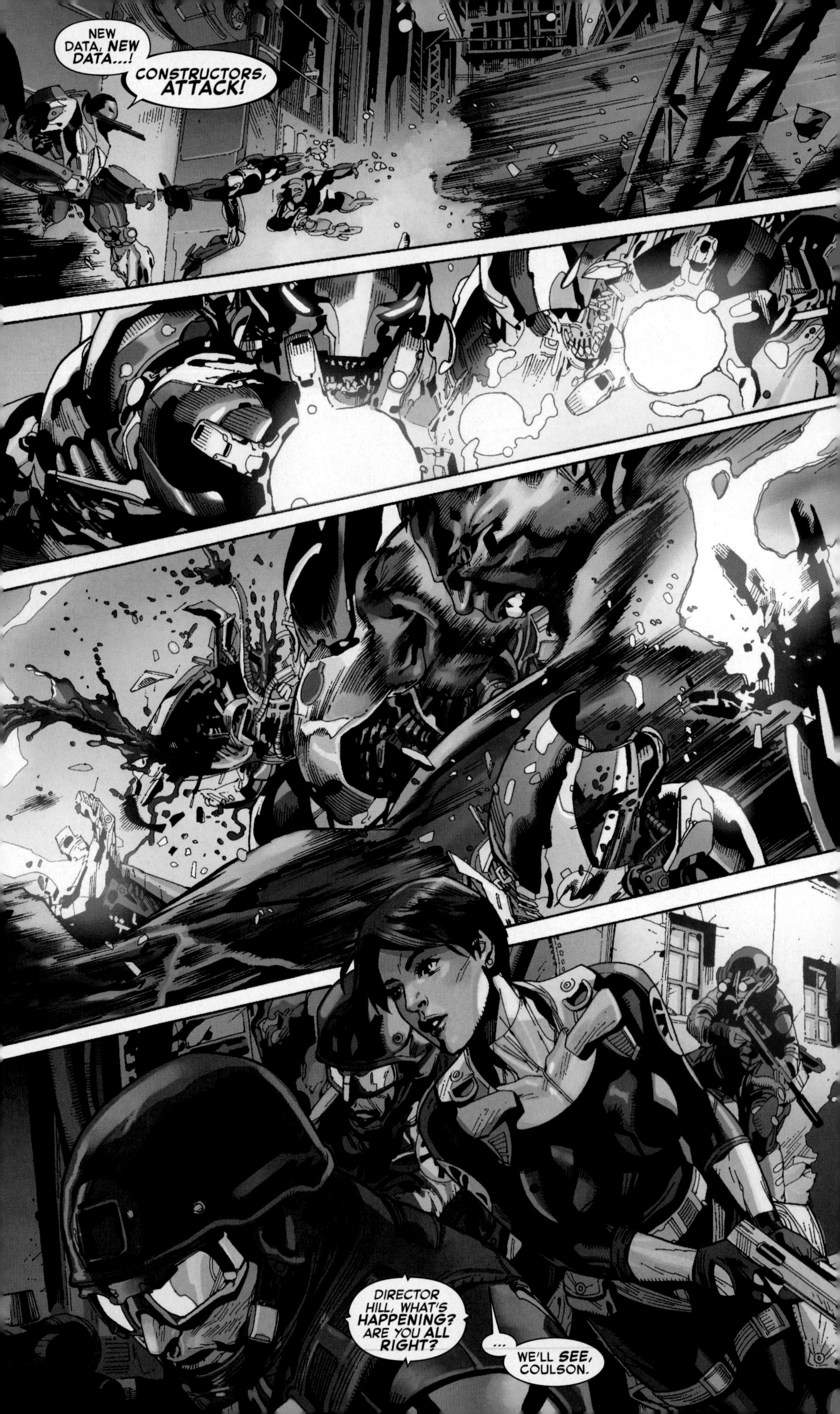
NEW DATA, NEW DATA...!
CONSTRUCTORS, ATTACK!
DIRECTOR HILL, WHAT'S HAPPENING? ARE YOU ALL RIGHT?
...
WE'LL SEE, COULSON.

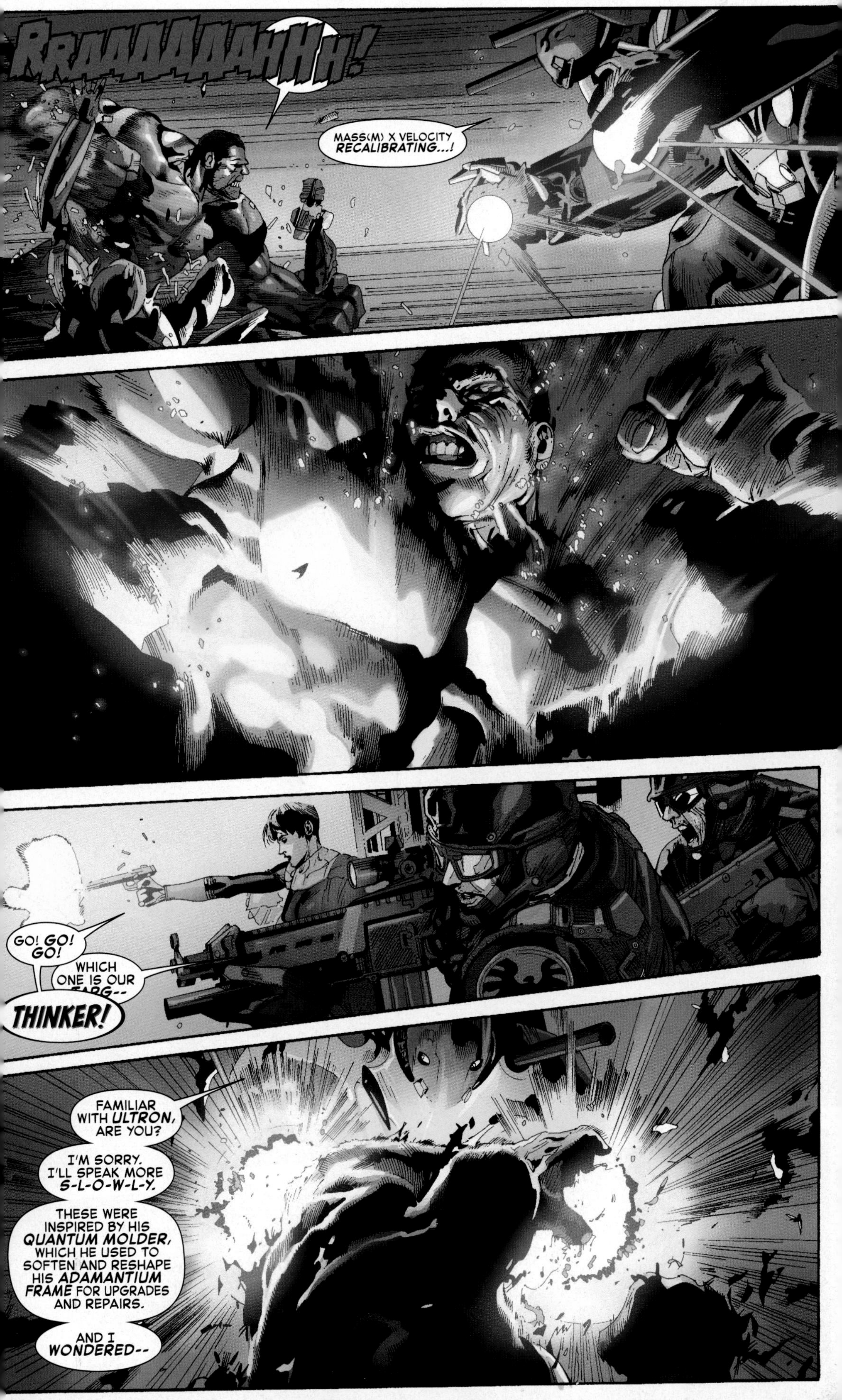
RRAAAAAAAHHH!
MASS(M) X VELOCITY RECALIBRATING...!
GO! GO! GO!
WHICH ONE IS OUR
THINKER!
FAMILIAR WITH ULTRON, ARE YOU?
I'M SORRY. I'LL SPEAK MORE S-L-O-W-L-Y.
THESE WERE INSPIRED BY HIS QUANTUM MOLDER, WHICH HE USED TO SOFTEN AND RESHAPE HIS ADAMANTIUM FRAME FOR UPGRADES AND REPAIRS.
AND I WONDERED--

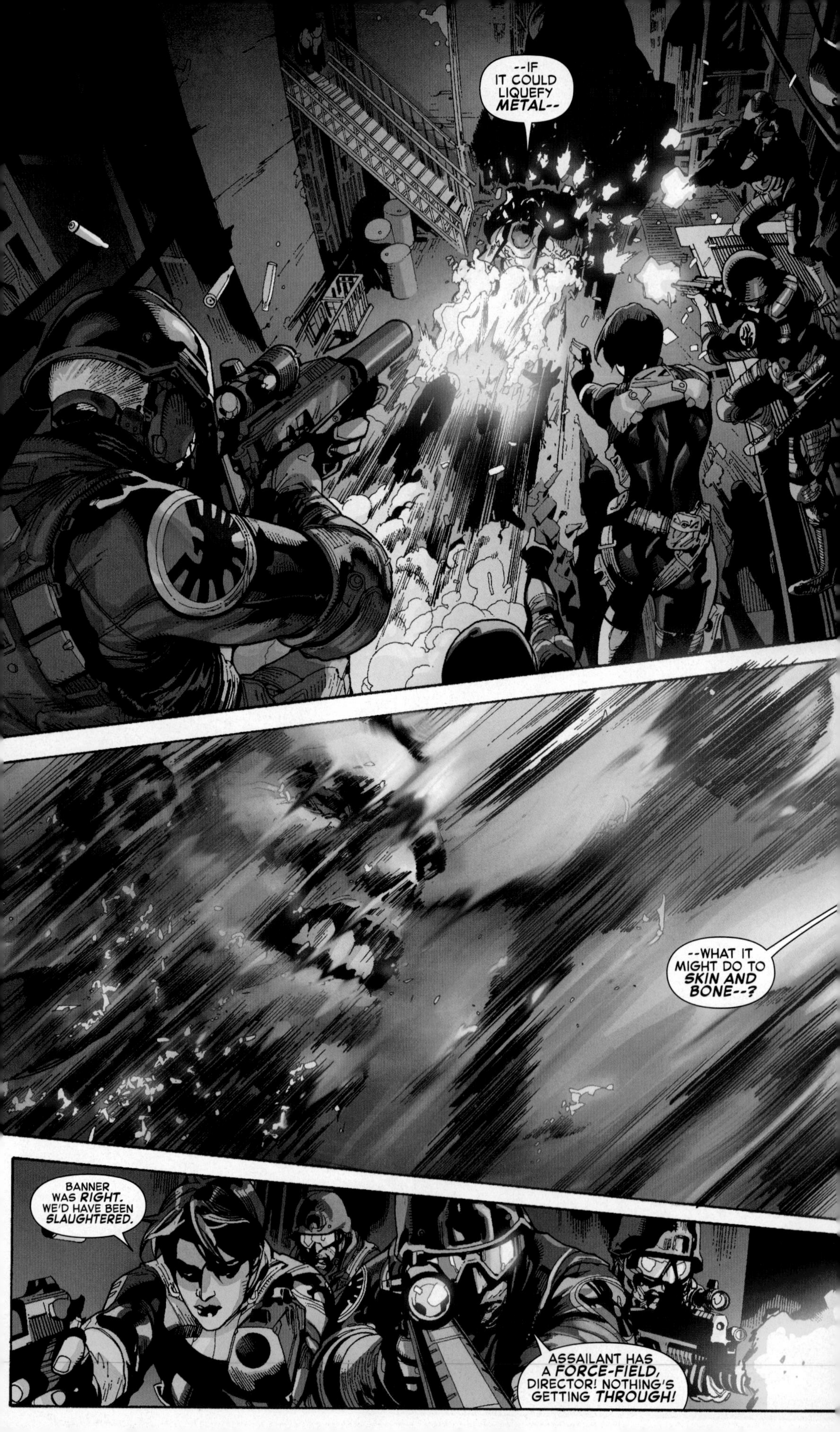
--IF IT COULD LIQUEFY METAL--
--WHAT IT MIGHT DO TO SKIN AND BONE--?
BANNER WAS RIGHT. WE'D HAVE BEEN SLAUGHTERED.
ASSAILANT HAS A FORCE-FIELD, DIRECTOR! NOTHING'S GETTING THROUGH!

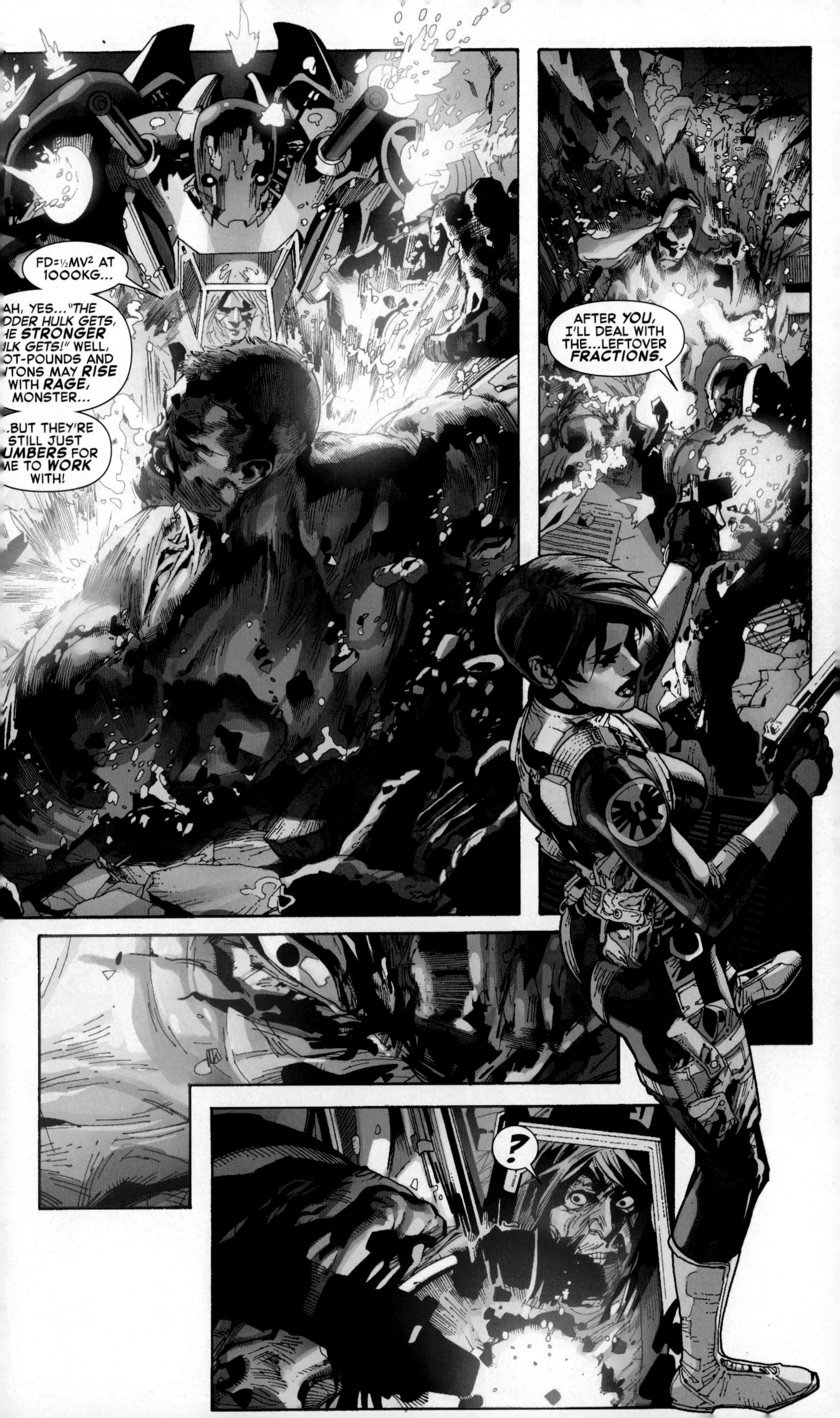
$FD=\frac{1}{2}MV^2$ AT 1000KG...
AH, YES..."THE DDER HULK GETS, HE STRONGER LK GETS!" WELL, OT-POUNDS AND TONS MAY RISE WITH RAGE, MONSTER...
..BUT THEY'RE STILL JUST UMBERS FOR ME TO WORK WITH!
AFTER YOU, I'LL DEAL WITH THE...LEFTOVER FRACTIONS.
?

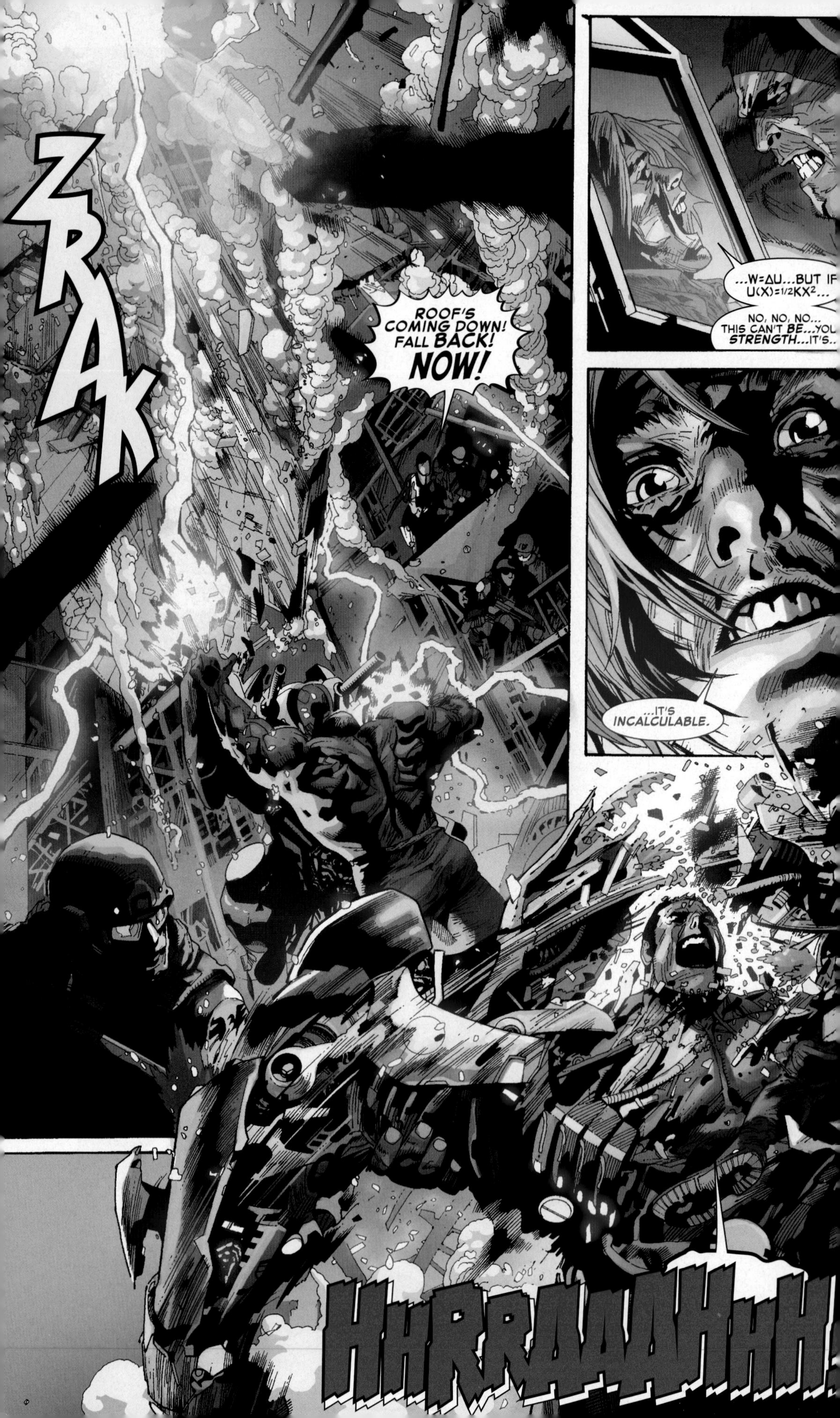
ZRAK
ROOF'S COMING DOWN! FALL BACK! NOW!
...$W=\Delta U$...BUT IF $U(X)=1/2KX^2$...
NO, NO, NO... THIS CAN'T BE...YOU STRENGTH...IT'S..
...IT'S INCALCULABLE.
HHRAAAHHH

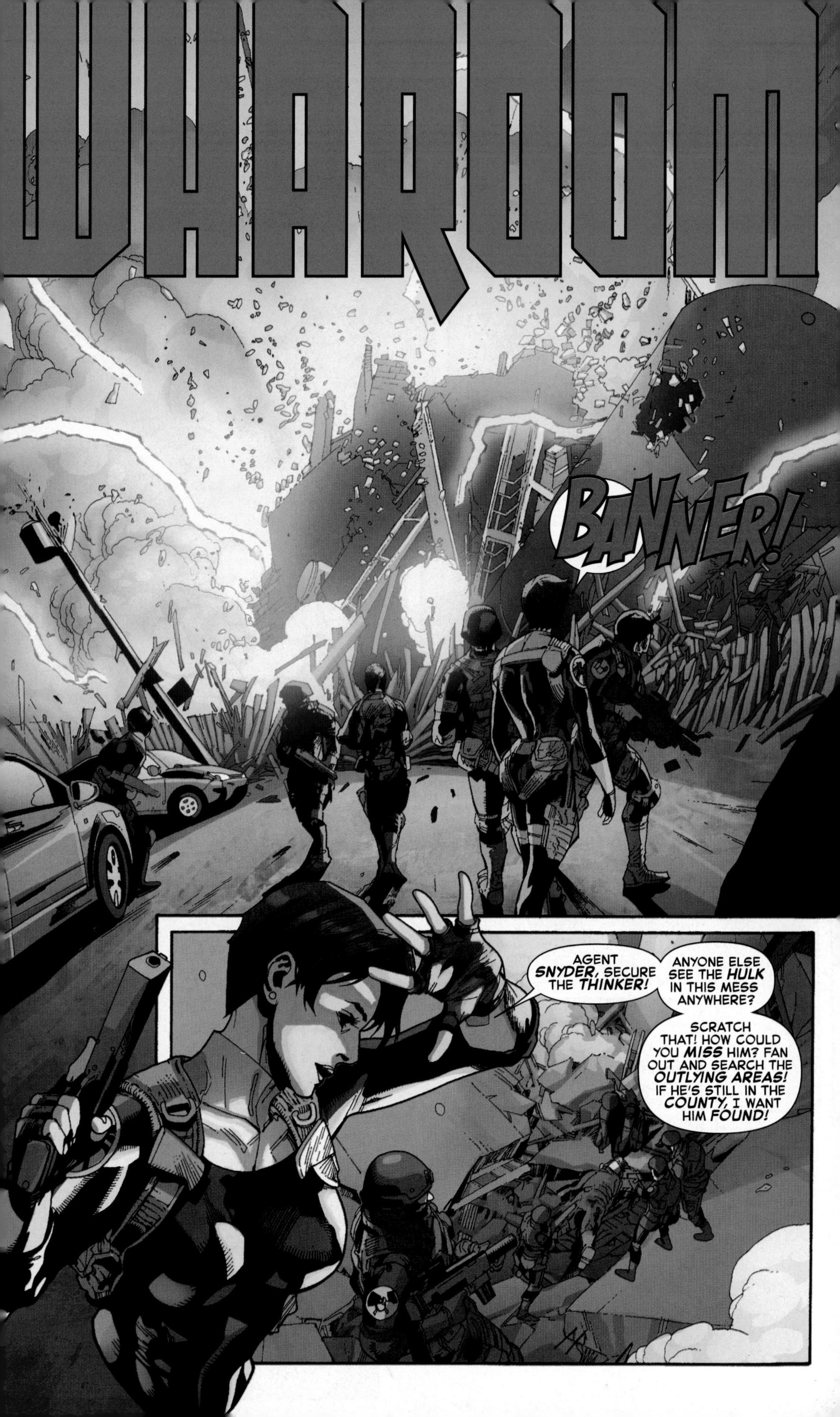
WARDOM
BANNER!
AGENT SNYDER, SECURE THE THINKER!
ANYONE ELSE SEE THE HULK IN THIS MESS ANYWHERE?
SCRATCH THAT! HOW COULD YOU MISS HIM? FAN OUT AND SEARCH THE OUTLYING AREAS! IF HE'S STILL IN THE COUNTY, I WANT HIM FOUND!

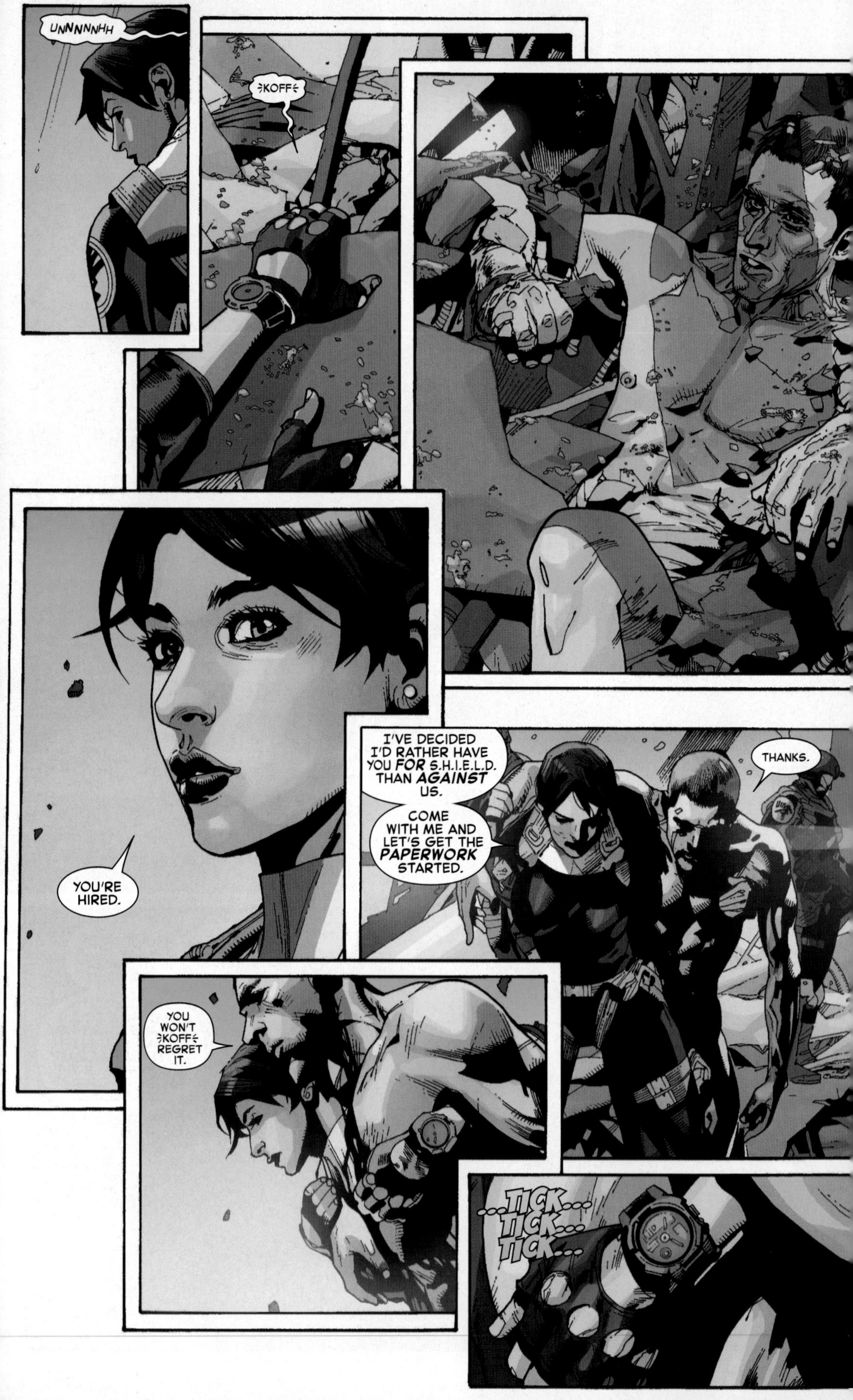
UNNNNNHH
KOFF
I'VE DECIDED I'D RATHER HAVE YOU FOR S.H.I.E.L.D. THAN AGAINST US.
COME WITH ME AND LET'S GET THE PAPERWORK STARTED.
YOU'RE HIRED.
THANKS.
YOU WON'T KOFF REGRET IT.
...TICK... TICK... TICK...

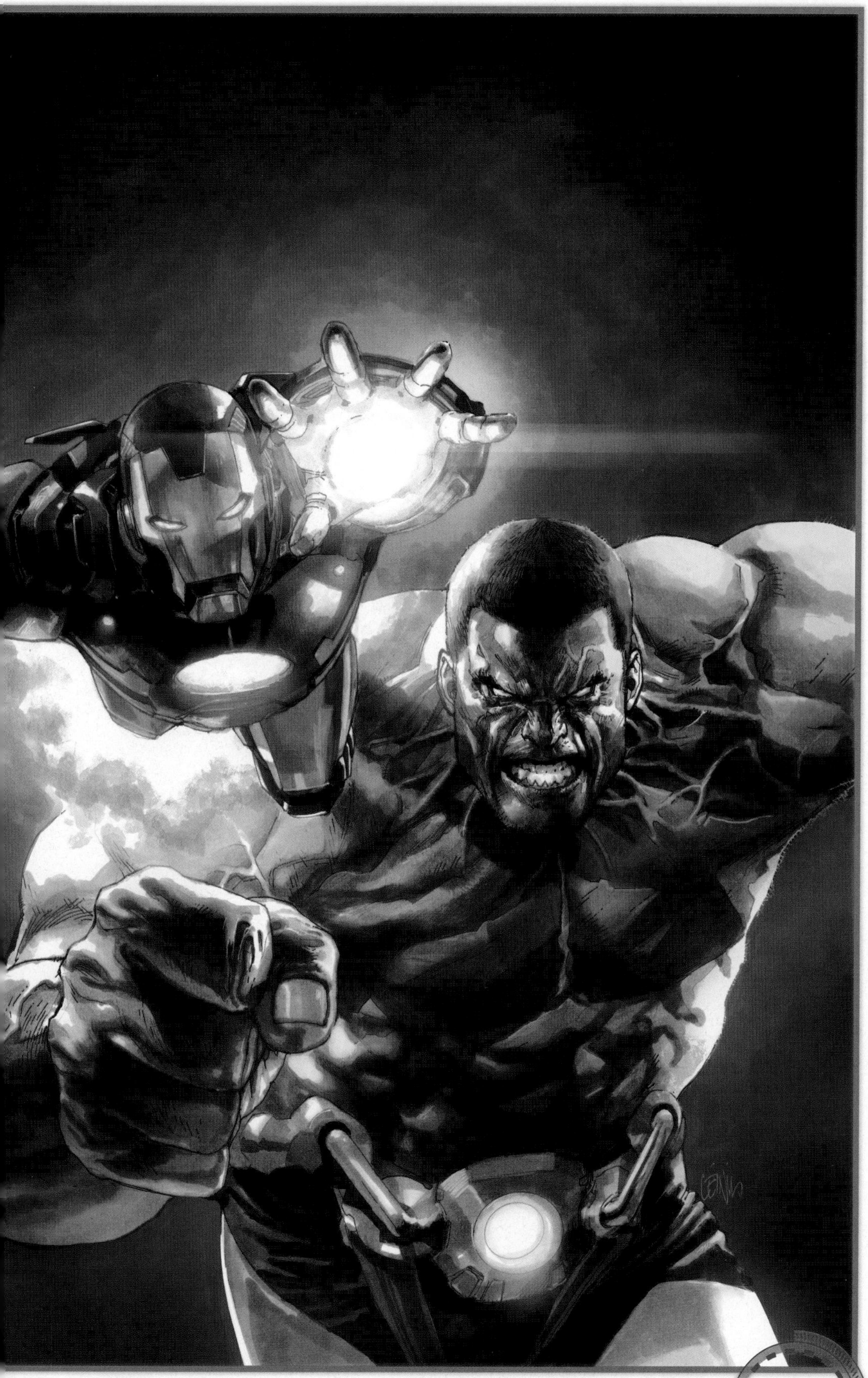

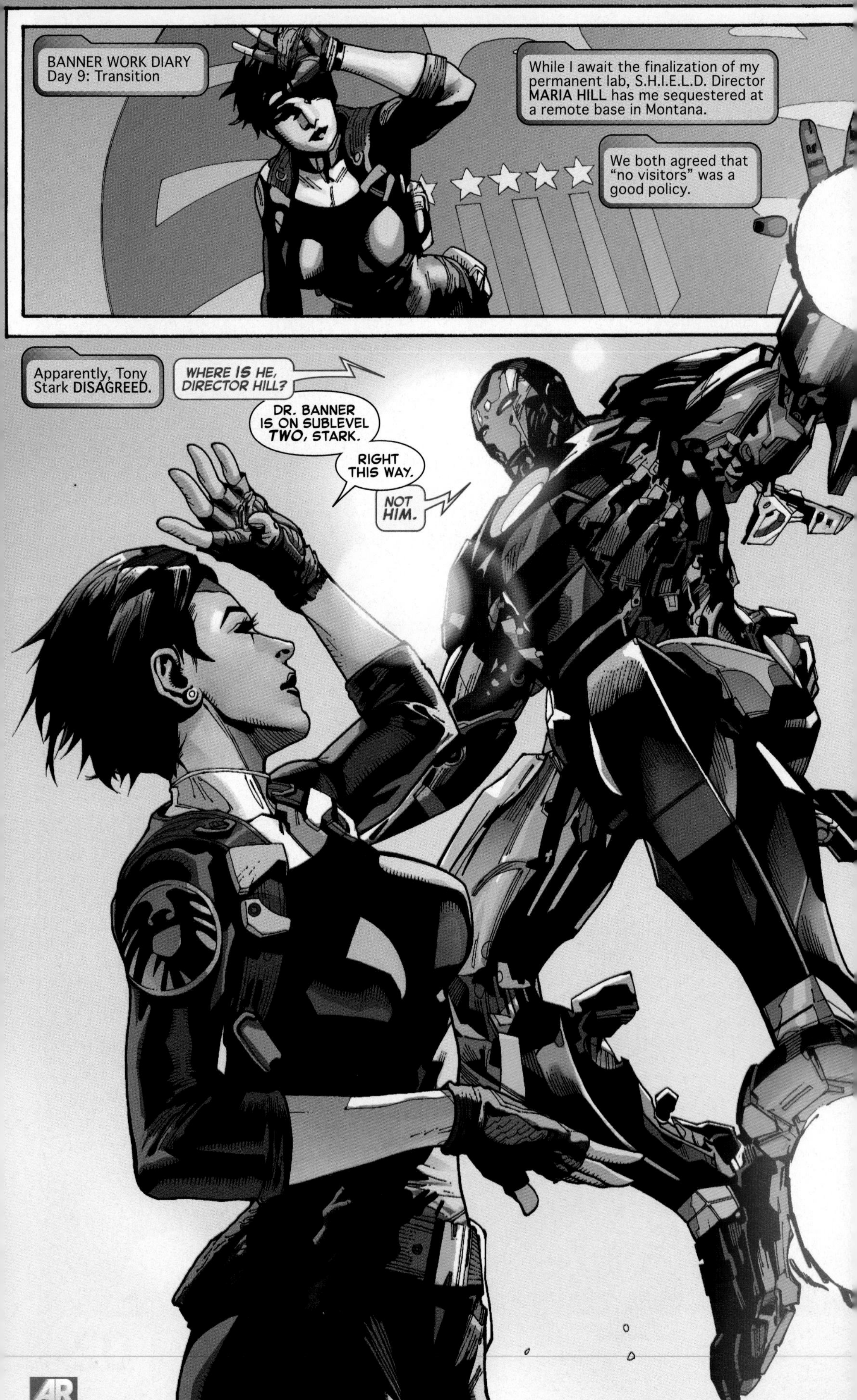
BANNER WORK DIARY Day 9: Transition
While I await the finalization of my permanent lab, S.H.I.E.L.D. Director MARIA HILL has me sequestered at a remote base in Montana.
We both agreed that "no visitors" was a good policy.
Apparently, Tony Stark DISAGREED.
WHERE IS HE, DIRECTOR HILL?
DR. BANNER IS ON SUBLEVEL TWO, STARK.
RIGHT THIS WAY.
NOT HIM.

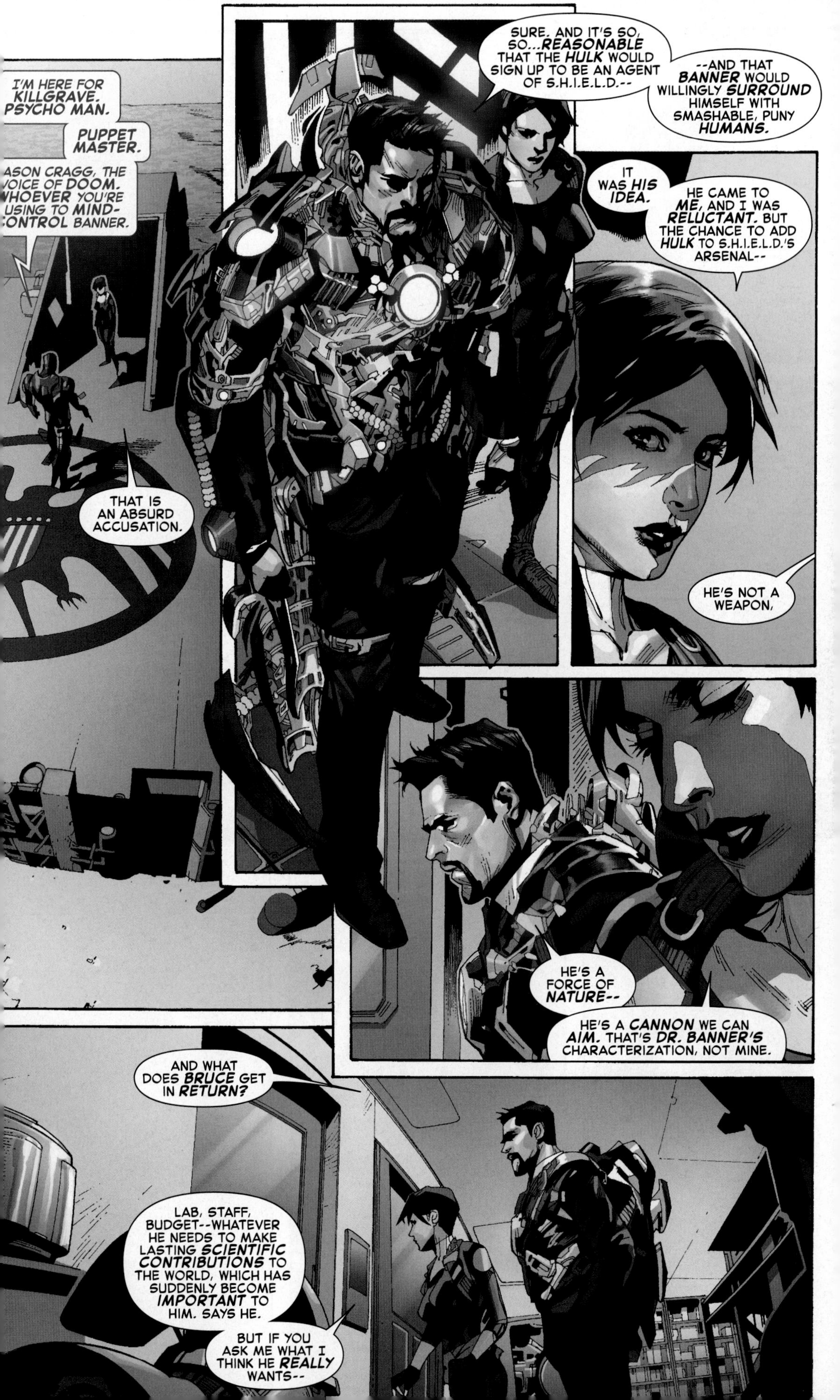
I'M HERE FOR KILLGRAVE. PSYCHO MAN.
PUPPET MASTER.
ASON CRAGG, THE VOICE OF DOOM. WHOEVER YOU'RE USING TO MIND-CONTROL BANNER.
THAT IS AN ABSURD ACCUSATION.
SURE. AND IT'S SO, SO...REASONABLE THAT THE HULK WOULD SIGN UP TO BE AN AGENT OF S.H.I.E.L.D.--
--AND THAT BANNER WOULD WILLINGLY SURROUND HIMSELF WITH SMASHABLE, PUNY HUMANS.
IT WAS HIS IDEA.
HE CAME TO ME, AND I WAS RELUCTANT. BUT THE CHANCE TO ADD HULK TO S.H.I.E.L.D.'S ARSENAL--
HE'S NOT A WEAPON,
HE'S A FORCE OF NATURE--
HE'S A CANNON WE CAN AIM. THAT'S DR. BANNER'S CHARACTERIZATION, NOT MINE.
AND WHAT DOES BRUCE GET IN RETURN?
LAB, STAFF, BUDGET--WHATEVER HE NEEDS TO MAKE LASTING SCIENTIFIC CONTRIBUTIONS TO THE WORLD, WHICH HAS SUDDENLY BECOME IMPORTANT TO HIM. SAYS HE.
BUT IF YOU ASK ME WHAT I THINK HE REALLY WANTS--

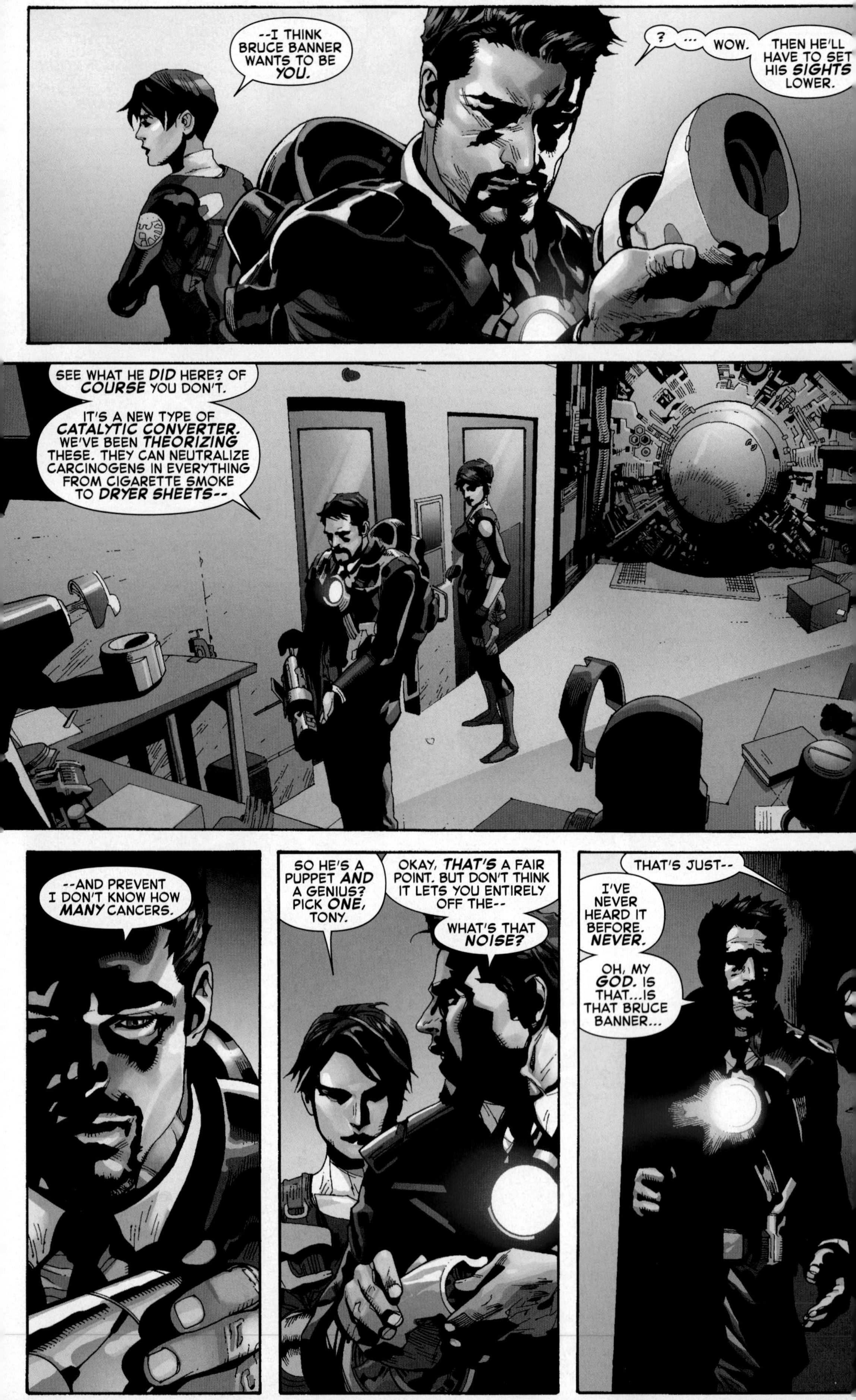
--I THINK BRUCE BANNER WANTS TO BE YOU.
?
...
WOW.
THEN HE'LL HAVE TO SET HIS SIGHTS LOWER.
SEE WHAT HE DID HERE? OF COURSE YOU DON'T.
IT'S A NEW TYPE OF CATALYTIC CONVERTER. WE'VE BEEN THEORIZING THESE. THEY CAN NEUTRALIZE CARCINOGENS IN EVERYTHING FROM CIGARETTE SMOKE TO DRYER SHEETS--
--AND PREVENT I DON'T KNOW HOW MANY CANCERS.
SO HE'S A PUPPET AND A GENIUS? PICK ONE, TONY.
OKAY, THAT'S A FAIR POINT. BUT DON'T THINK IT LETS YOU ENTIRELY OFF THE--
WHAT'S THAT NOISE?
THAT'S JUST--
I'VE NEVER HEARD IT BEFORE. NEVER.
OH, MY GOD. IS THAT...IS THAT BRUCE BANNER...

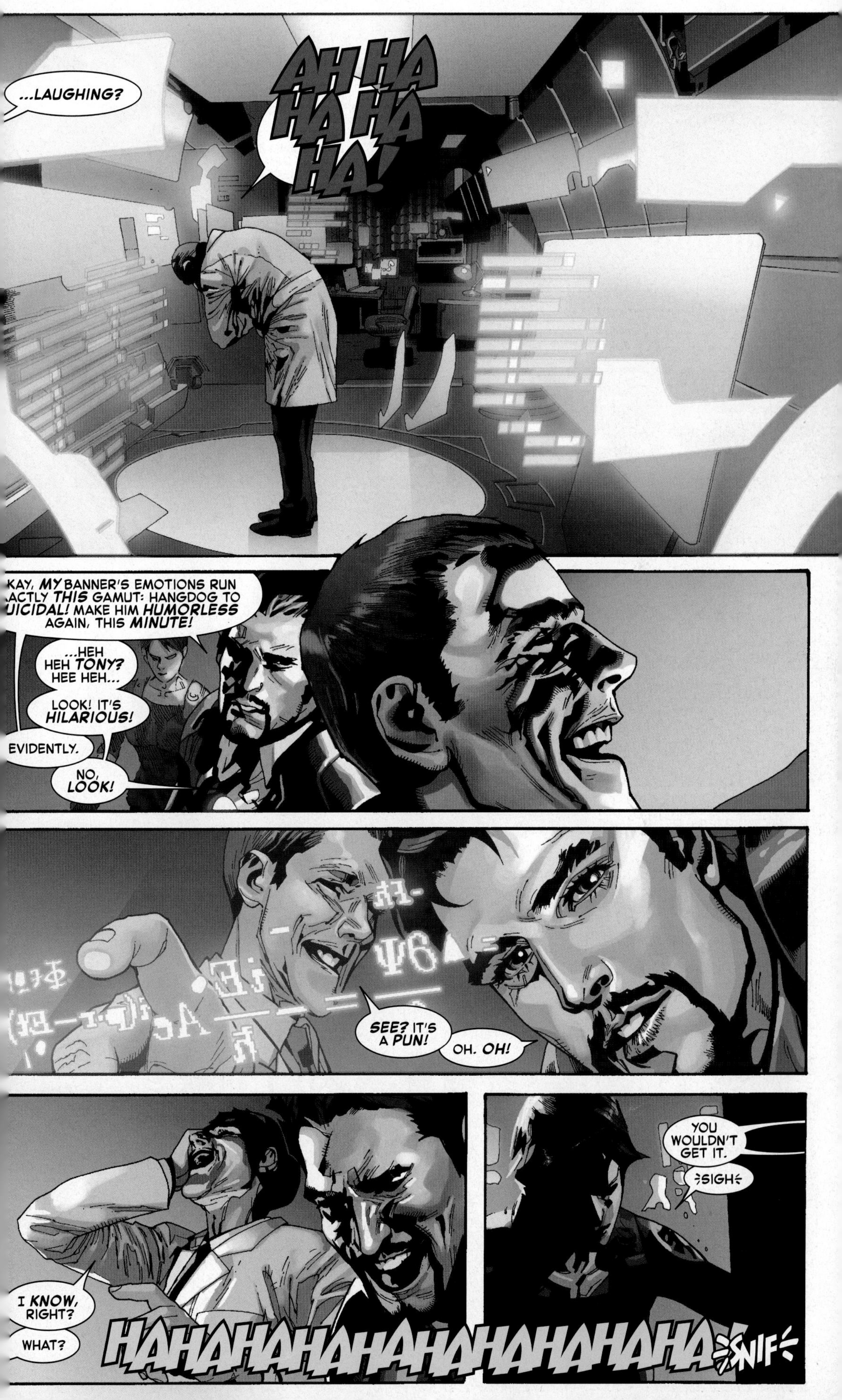
...LAUGHING?
AH HA HA HA HA HA!
KAY, MY BANNER'S EMOTIONS RUN ACTLY THIS GAMUT: HANGDOG TO UICIDAL! MAKE HIM HUMORLESS AGAIN, THIS MINUTE!
...HEH HEH TONY? HEE HEH...
LOOK! IT'S HILARIOUS!
EVIDENTLY.
NO, LOOK!
SEE? IT'S A PUN!
OH. OH!
I KNOW, RIGHT?
WHAT?
YOU WOULDN'T GET IT.
SIGH
HAHAHAHAHAHAHAHAHAHAHAHA!
SNIF

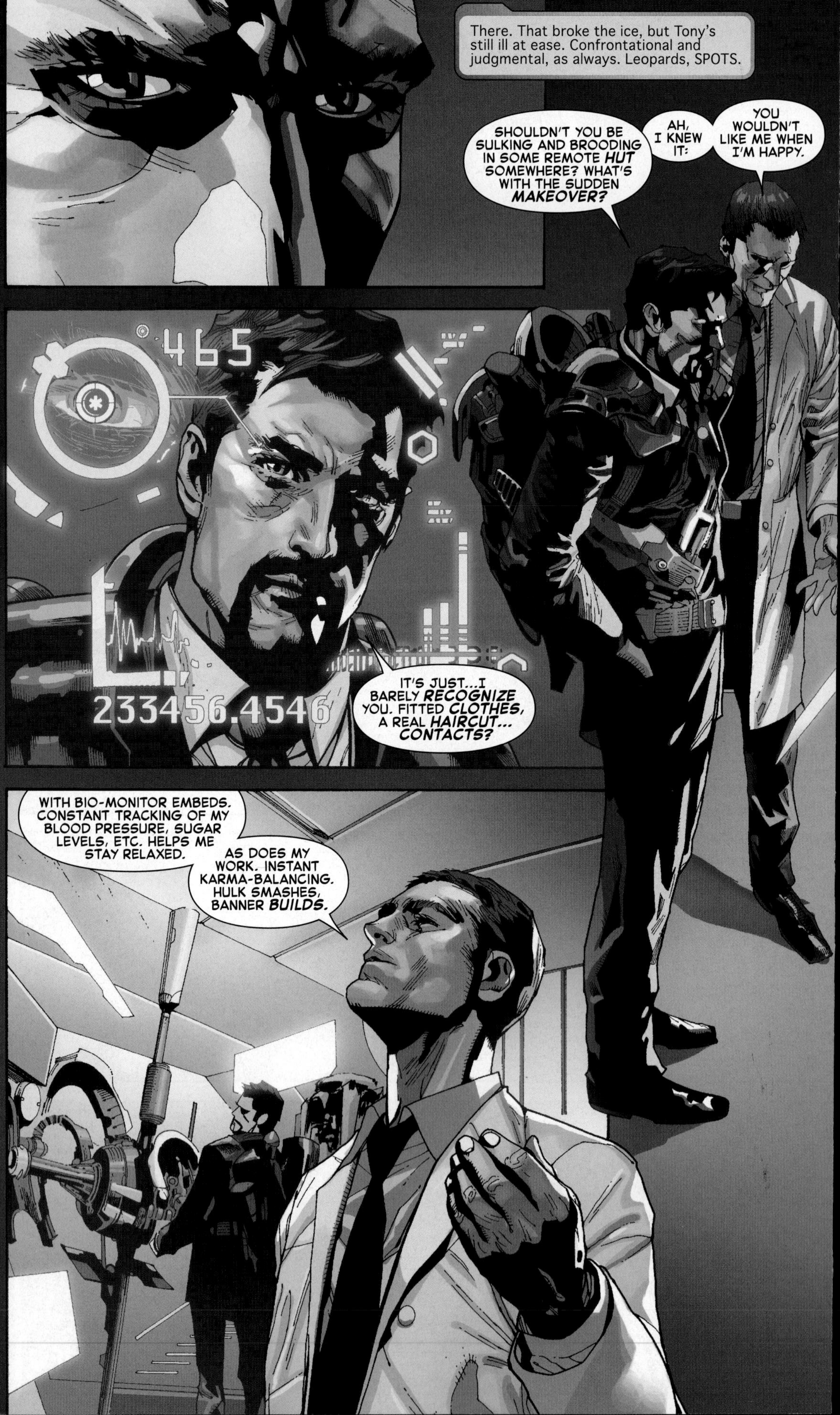
There. That broke the ice, but Tony's still ill at ease. Confrontational and judgmental, as always. Leopards, SPOTS.
SHOULDN'T YOU BE SULKING AND BROODING IN SOME REMOTE HUT SOMEWHERE? WHAT'S WITH THE SUDDEN MAKEOVER?
AH, I KNEW IT:
YOU WOULDN'T LIKE ME WHEN I'M HAPPY.
465
233456.4546
IT'S JUST...I BARELY RECOGNIZE YOU. FITTED CLOTHES, A REAL HAIRCUT... CONTACTS?
WITH BIO-MONITOR EMBEDS. CONSTANT TRACKING OF MY BLOOD PRESSURE, SUGAR LEVELS, ETC. HELPS ME STAY RELAXED.
AS DOES MY WORK. INSTANT KARMA-BALANCING. HULK SMASHES, BANNER BUILDS.

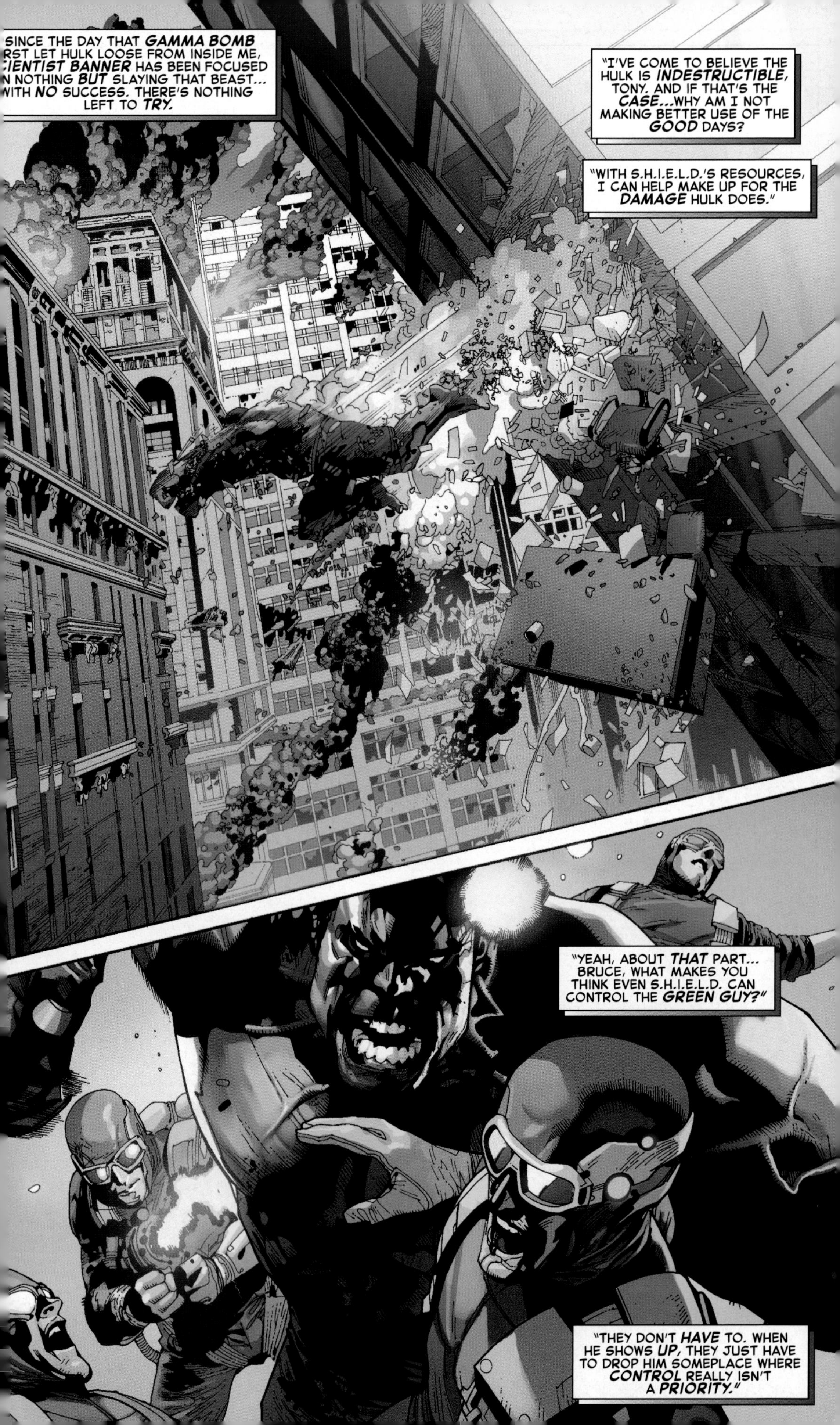
SINCE THE DAY THAT GAMMA BOMB
RST LET HULK LOOSE FROM INSIDE ME,
CIENTIST BANNER HAS BEEN FOCUSED
N NOTHING BUT SLAYING THAT BEAST...
WITH NO SUCCESS. THERE'S NOTHING
LEFT TO TRY.
"I'VE COME TO BELIEVE THE HULK IS INDESTRUCTIBLE, TONY. AND IF THAT'S THE CASE...WHY AM I NOT MAKING BETTER USE OF THE GOOD DAYS?
"WITH S.H.I.E.L.D.'S RESOURCES, I CAN HELP MAKE UP FOR THE DAMAGE HULK DOES."
"YEAH, ABOUT THAT PART... BRUCE, WHAT MAKES YOU THINK EVEN S.H.I.E.L.D. CAN CONTROL THE GREEN GUY?"
"THEY DON'T HAVE TO. WHEN HE SHOWS UP, THEY JUST HAVE TO DROP HIM SOMEPLACE WHERE CONTROL REALLY ISN'T A PRIORITY."

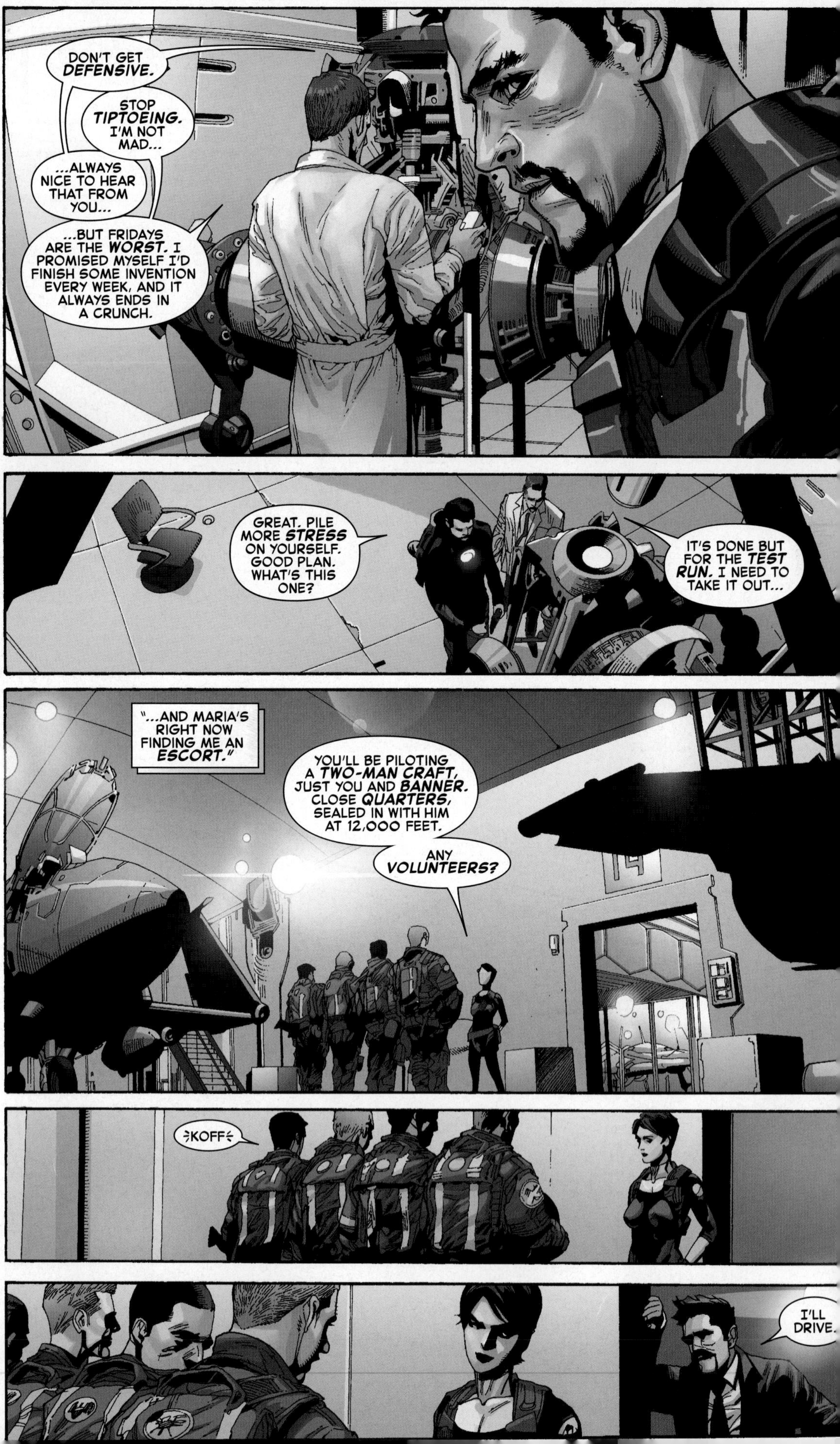
DON'T GET DEFENSIVE.
STOP TIPTOEING. I'M NOT MAD...
...ALWAYS NICE TO HEAR THAT FROM YOU...
...BUT FRIDAYS ARE THE WORST. I PROMISED MYSELF I'D FINISH SOME INVENTION EVERY WEEK, AND IT ALWAYS ENDS IN A CRUNCH.
GREAT. PILE MORE STRESS ON YOURSELF. GOOD PLAN. WHAT'S THIS ONE?
IT'S DONE BUT FOR THE TEST RUN. I NEED TO TAKE IT OUT...
"...AND MARIA'S RIGHT NOW FINDING ME AN ESCORT."
YOU'LL BE PILOTING A TWO-MAN CRAFT, JUST YOU AND BANNER. CLOSE QUARTERS, SEALED IN WITH HIM AT 12,000 FEET.
ANY VOLUNTEERS?
KOFF
I'LL DRIVE.

Twenty minutes ahead of schedule (Tony couldn't resist "tinkering" with the engines), we set down in the HIMALAYAS.

He still doesn't suspect.

Good.

THIS IS WHY I CONDUCT MOST OF *MY* EXPERIMENTS IN *ARUBA.* YOU WARM ENOUGH IN WHATEVER FASHION-ATTACK IT IS *YOU'RE* WEARING?

Good old TONY SNARK. Relax, Bruce. Keep it together...

I ADAPTED A S.H.I.E.L.D. ISSUE BIOSUIT. I'M TOASTY. WE'RE HERE FOR *TWO REASONS.*

FIRST, THIS IS ONE OF THE LARGEST AS-YET-UNDISCOVERED *NATURAL GAS DEPOSITS* ON *EARTH.* AND THIS IS A *PROBE.*

SO YOU'RE POKING AT SOMETHING THAT'S NOT ONLY INCREDIBLY *EXPLOSIVE* BUT INCREDIBLY *VOLATILE.*

OH, THE IRONY. BUT I'M NOT *"POKING."* THIS IS A PROTOTYPE *GAMMA-FRACKER.*

SHLOK

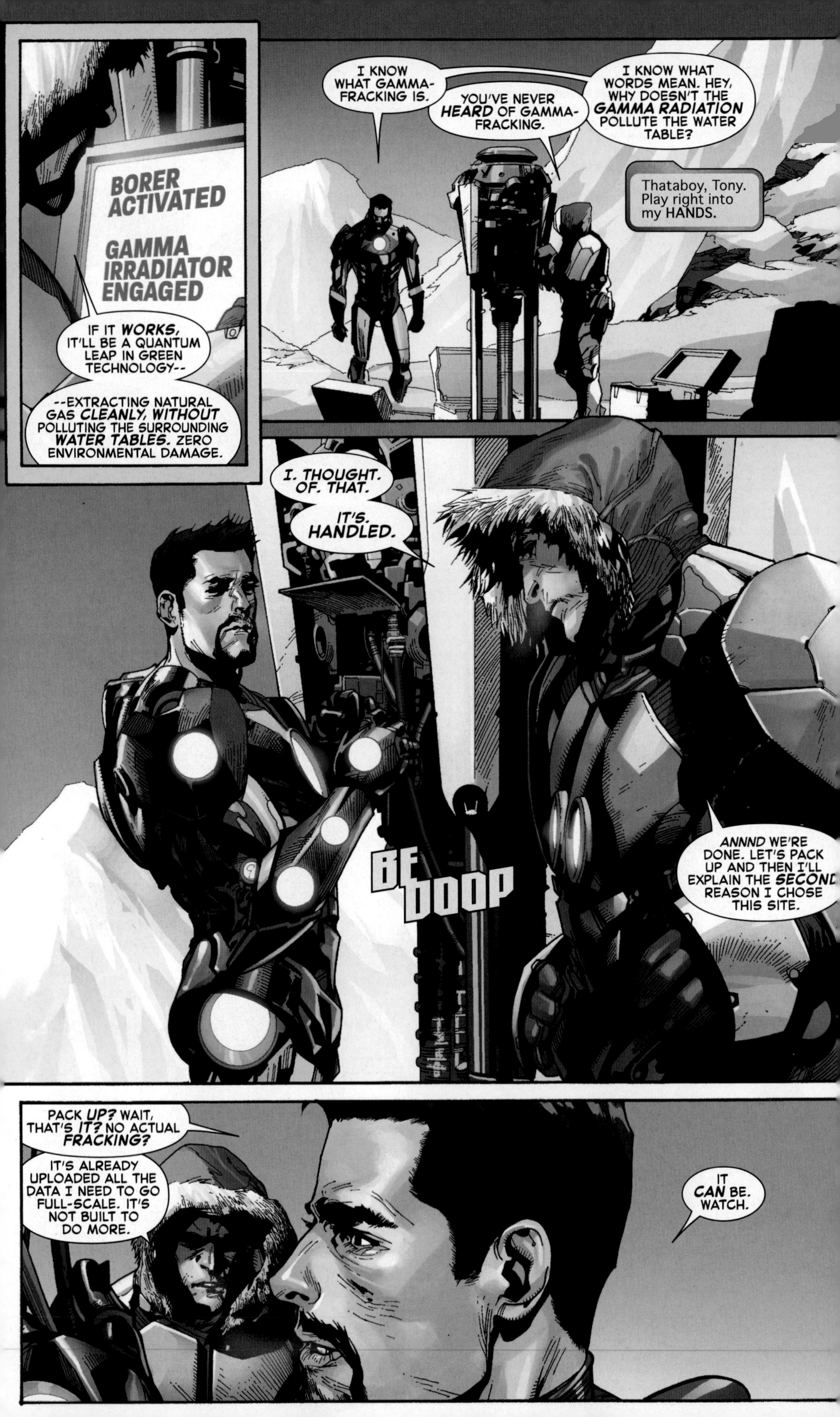
BORER ACTIVATED
GAMMA IRRADIATOR ENGAGED
IF IT WORKS, IT'LL BE A QUANTUM LEAP IN GREEN TECHNOLOGY--
--EXTRACTING NATURAL GAS CLEANLY, WITHOUT POLLUTING THE SURROUNDING WATER TABLES. ZERO ENVIRONMENTAL DAMAGE.
I KNOW WHAT GAMMA-FRACKING IS.
YOU'VE NEVER HEARD OF GAMMA-FRACKING.
I KNOW WHAT WORDS MEAN. HEY, WHY DOESN'T THE GAMMA RADIATION POLLUTE THE WATER TABLE?
Thataboy, Tony. Play right into my HANDS.
I. THOUGHT. OF. THAT.
IT'S. HANDLED.
BE DOOP
ANNND WE'RE DONE. LET'S PACK UP AND THEN I'LL EXPLAIN THE SECOND REASON I CHOSE THIS SITE.
PACK UP? WAIT, THAT'S IT? NO ACTUAL FRACKING?
IT'S ALREADY UPLOADED ALL THE DATA I NEED TO GO FULL-SCALE. IT'S NOT BUILT TO DO MORE.
IT CAN BE. WATCH.

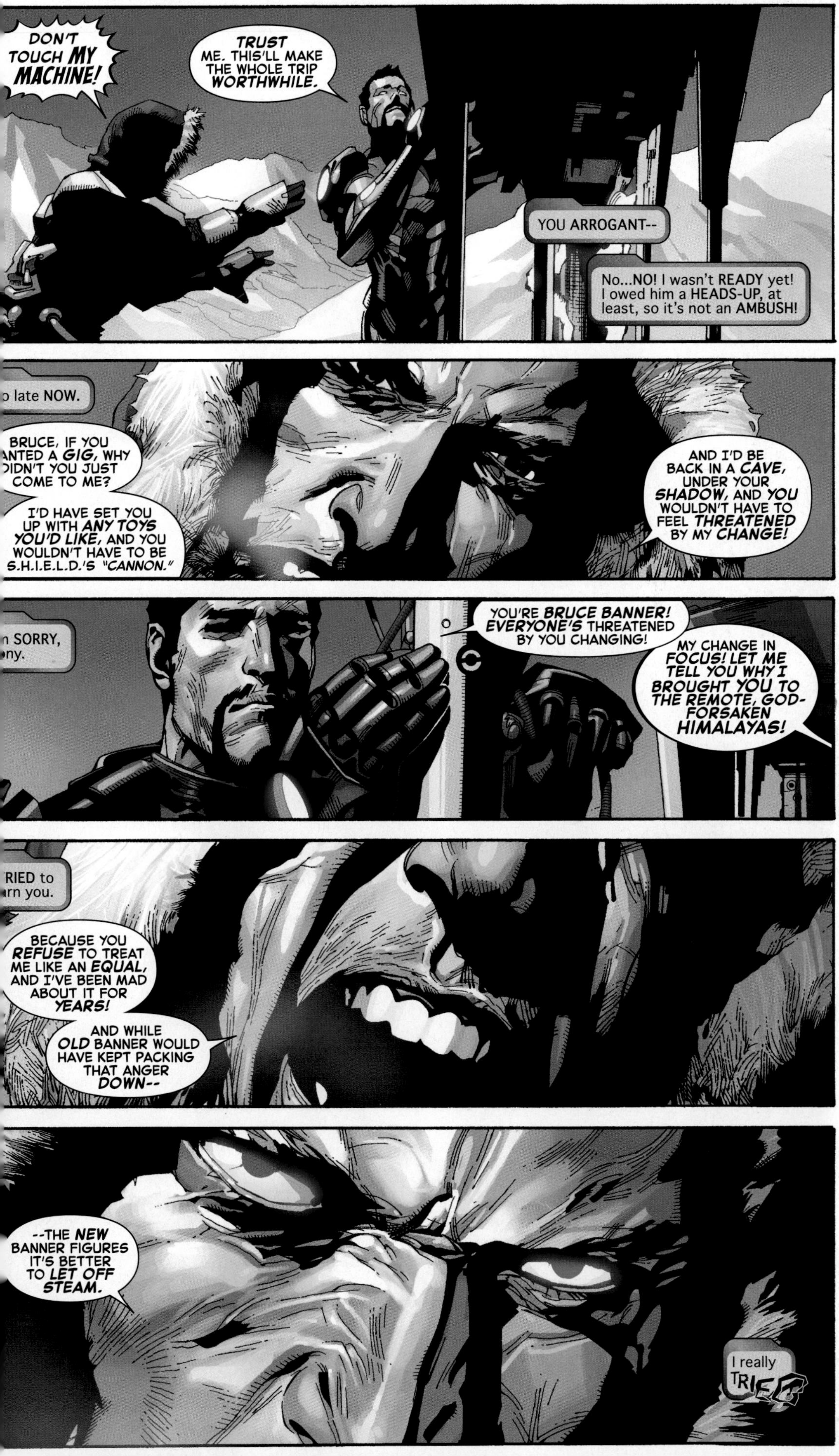
DON'T TOUCH MY MACHINE!
TRUST ME. THIS'LL MAKE THE WHOLE TRIP WORTHWHILE.
YOU ARROGANT--
No...NO! I wasn't READY yet! I owed him a HEADS-UP, at least, so it's not an AMBUSH!
late NOW.
BRUCE, IF YOU ANTED A GIG, WHY IDN'T YOU JUST COME TO ME?
I'D HAVE SET YOU UP WITH ANY TOYS YOU'D LIKE, AND YOU WOULDN'T HAVE TO BE S.H.I.E.L.D.'S "CANNON."
AND I'D BE BACK IN A CAVE, UNDER YOUR SHADOW, AND YOU WOULDN'T HAVE TO FEEL THREATENED BY MY CHANGE!
SORRY, ny.
YOU'RE BRUCE BANNER! EVERYONE'S THREATENED BY YOU CHANGING!
MY CHANGE IN FOCUS! LET ME TELL YOU WHY I BROUGHT YOU TO THE REMOTE, GOD-FORSAKEN HIMALAYAS!
RIED to rn you.
BECAUSE YOU REFUSE TO TREAT ME LIKE AN EQUAL, AND I'VE BEEN MAD ABOUT IT FOR YEARS!
AND WHILE OLD BANNER WOULD HAVE KEPT PACKING THAT ANGER DOWN--
--THE NEW BANNER FIGURES IT'S BETTER TO LET OFF STEAM.
I really TRIED

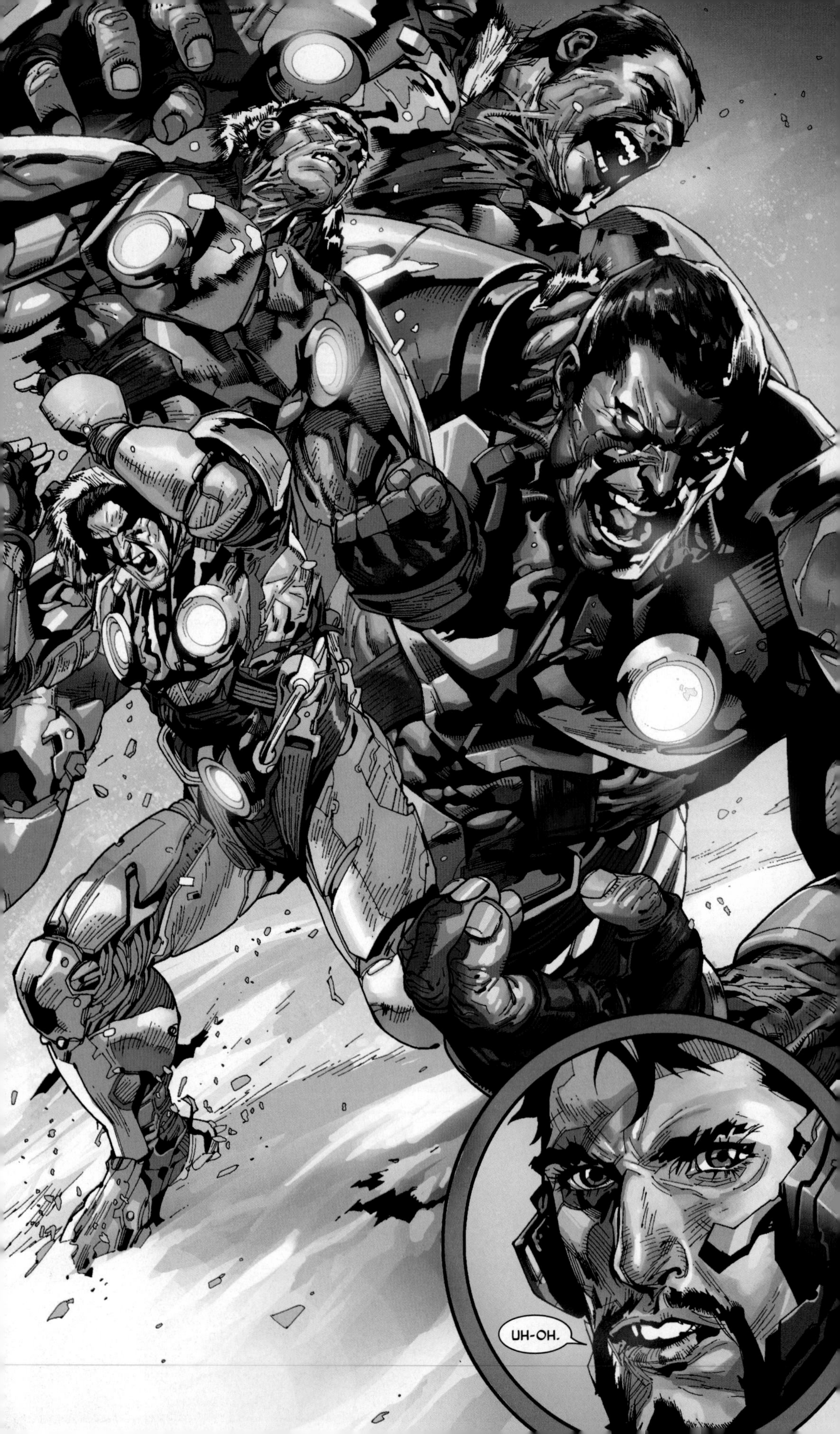
UH-OH.

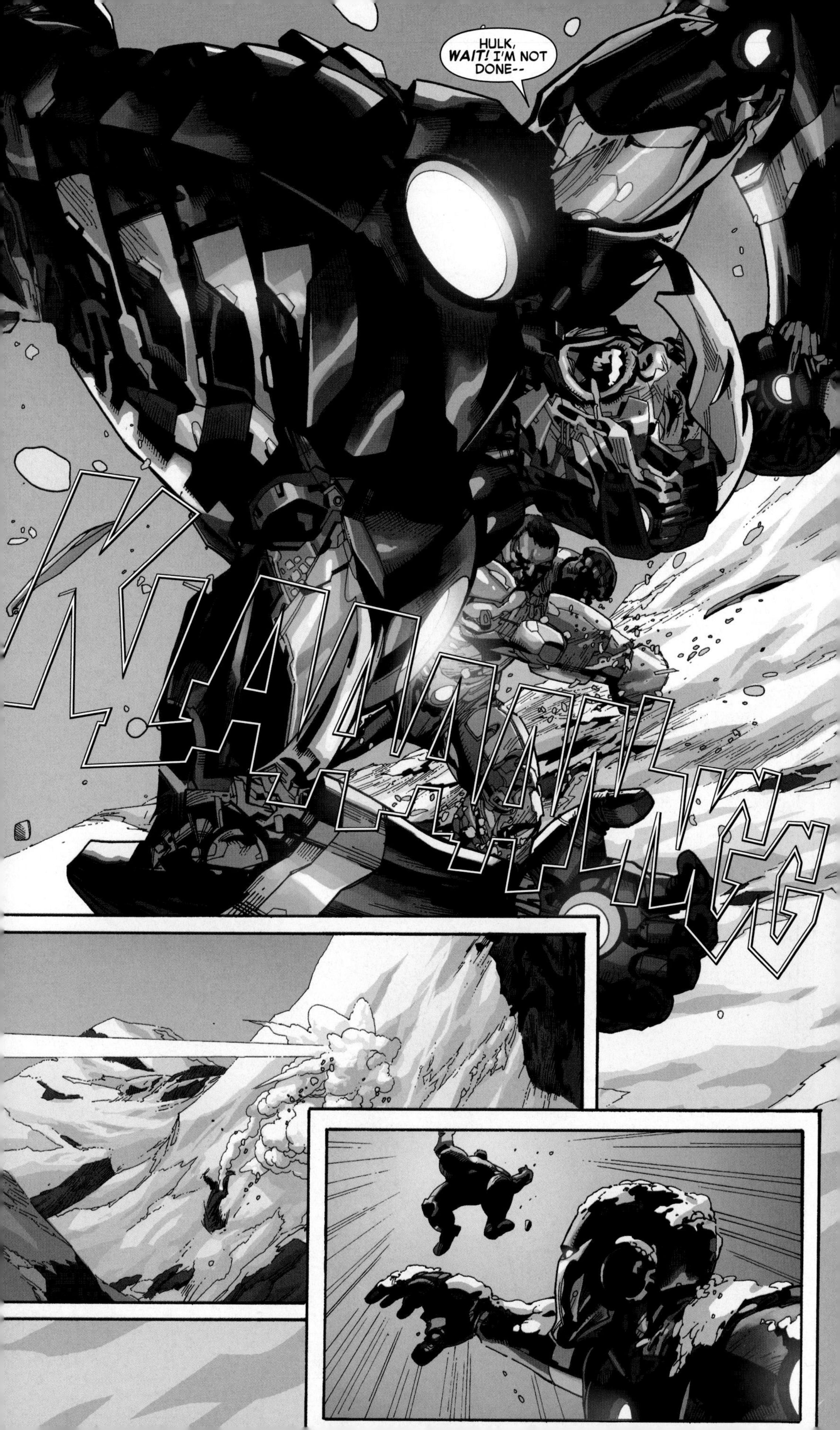
HULK, WAIT! I'M NOT DONE--

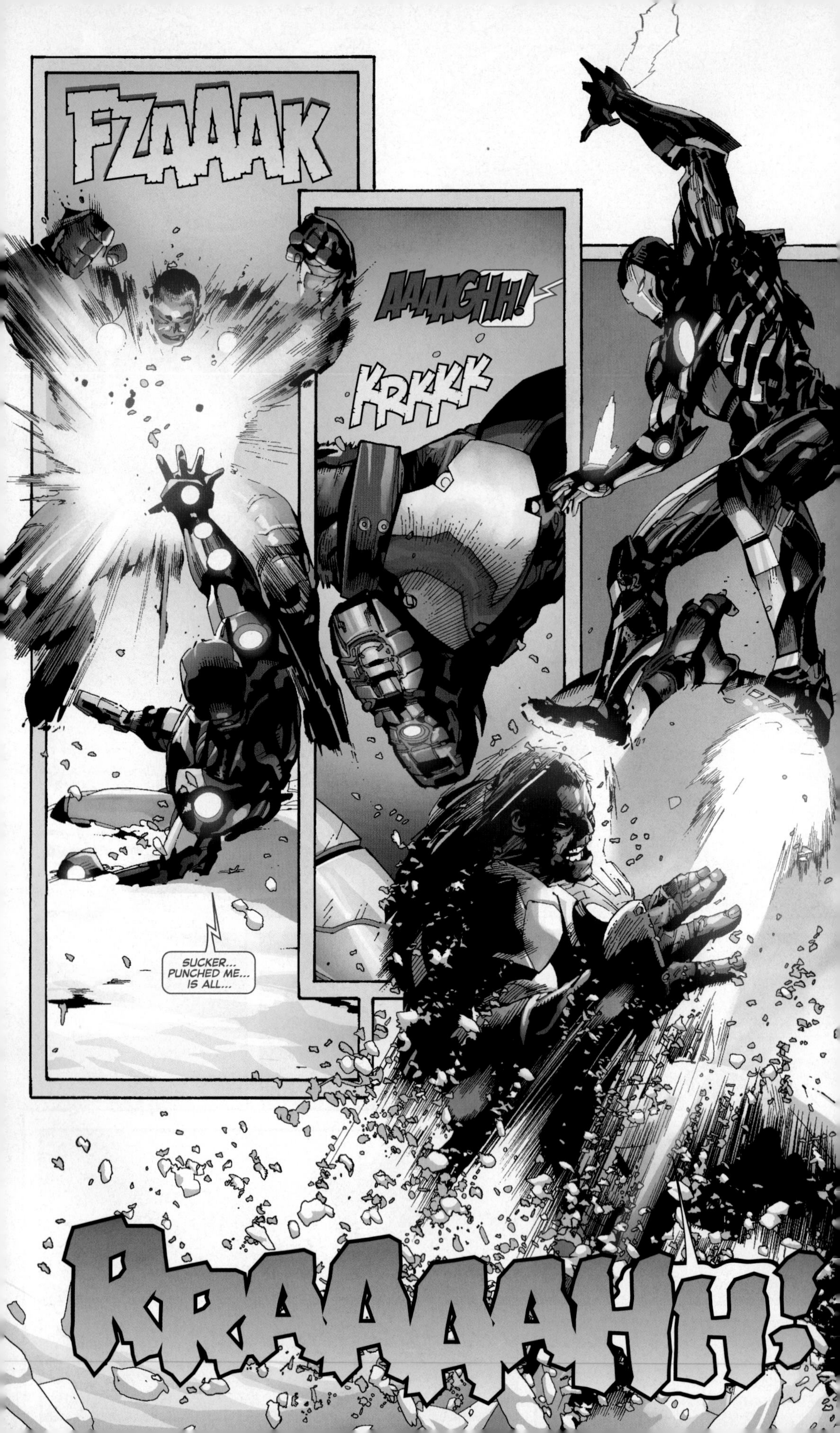
FZAAAK
AAAAGHH!
KRKKK
SUCKER... PUNCHED ME... IS ALL...
RRAAAAHH!

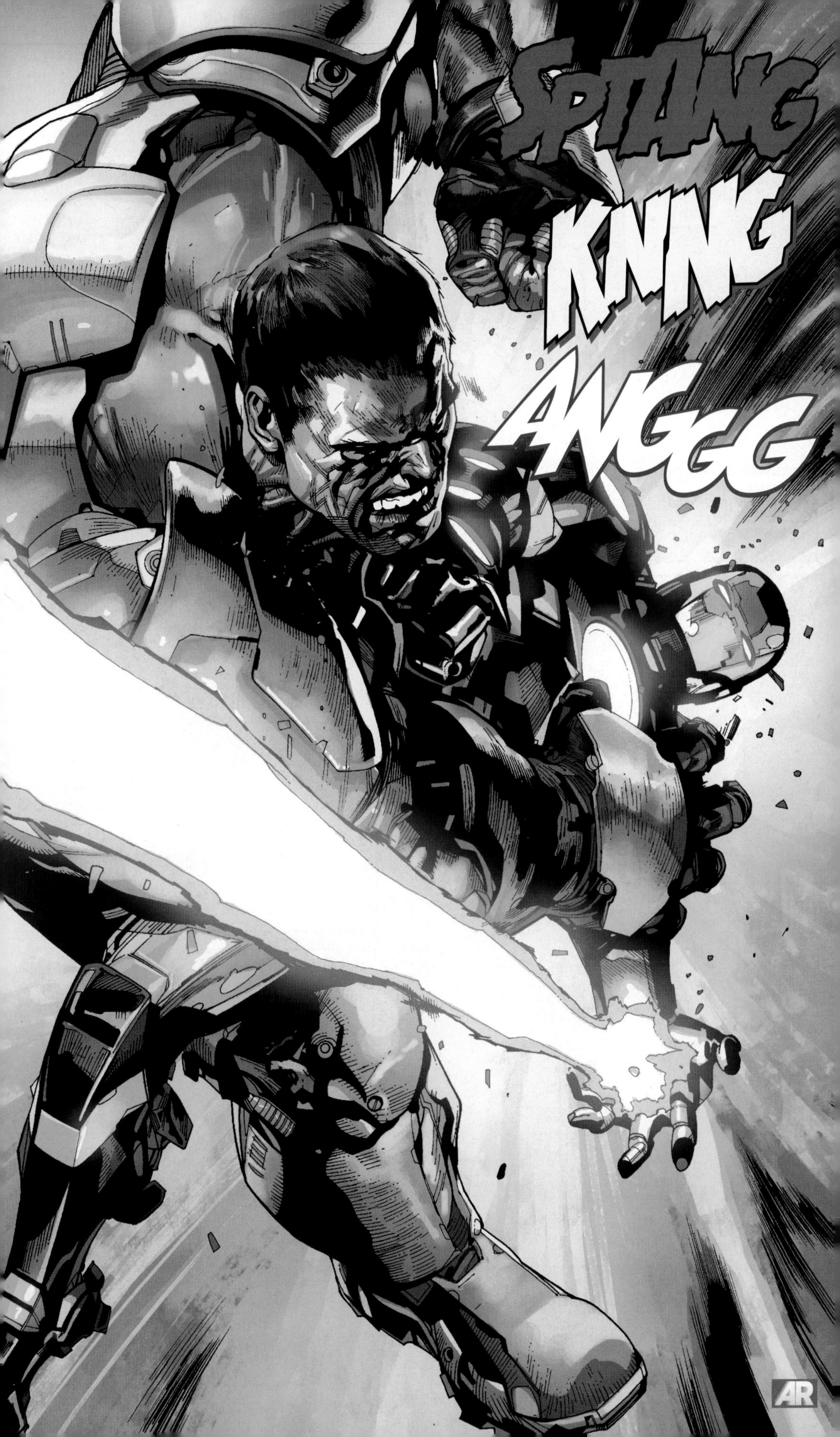
SPTANG
KNNG
ANGGG

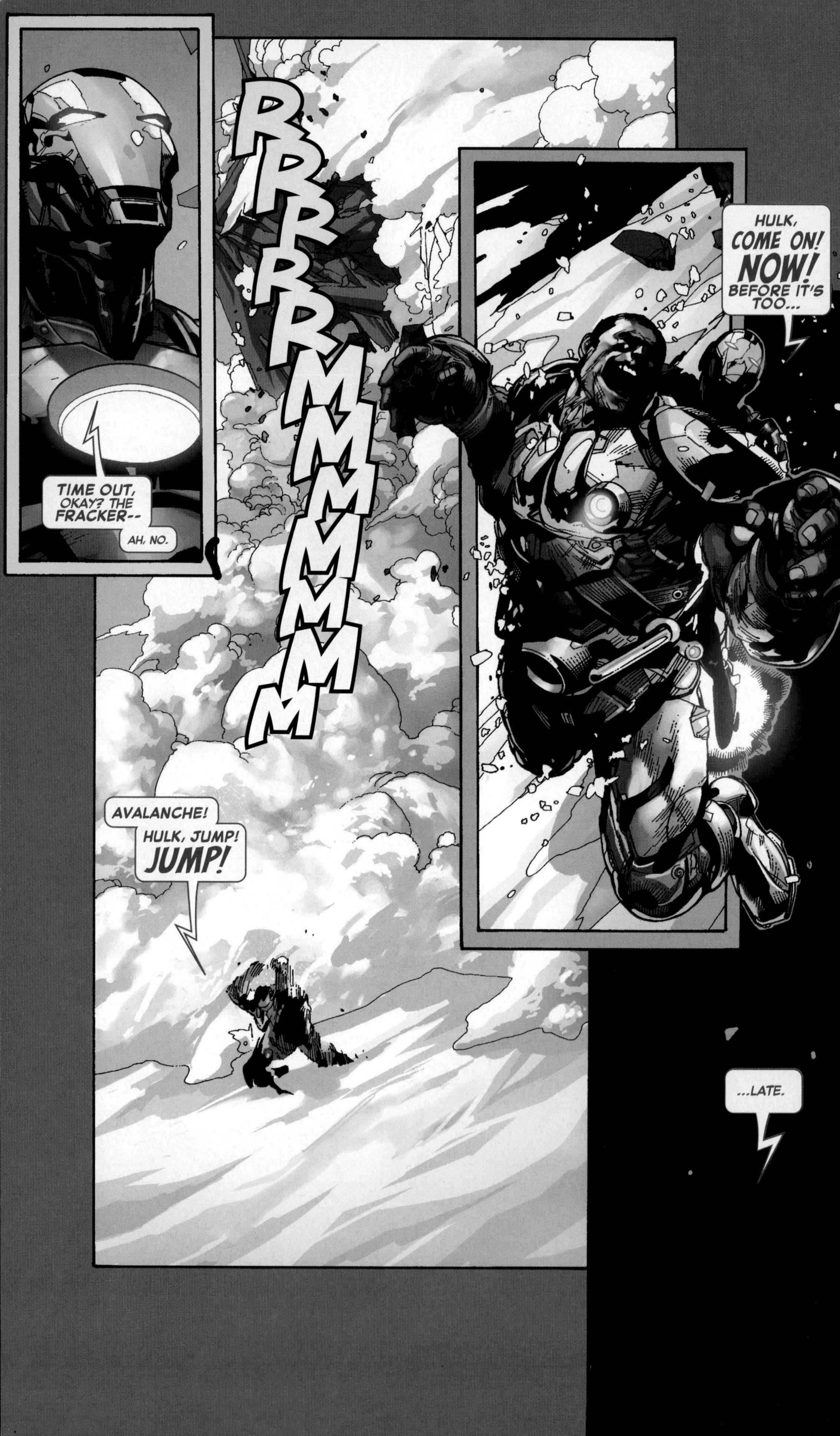
TIME OUT, OKAY? THE FRACKER--
AH, NO.
RRRRRMMMMMMMM
HULK, COME ON! NOW! BEFORE IT'S TOO...
AVALANCHE!
HULK, JUMP! JUMP!
...LATE.

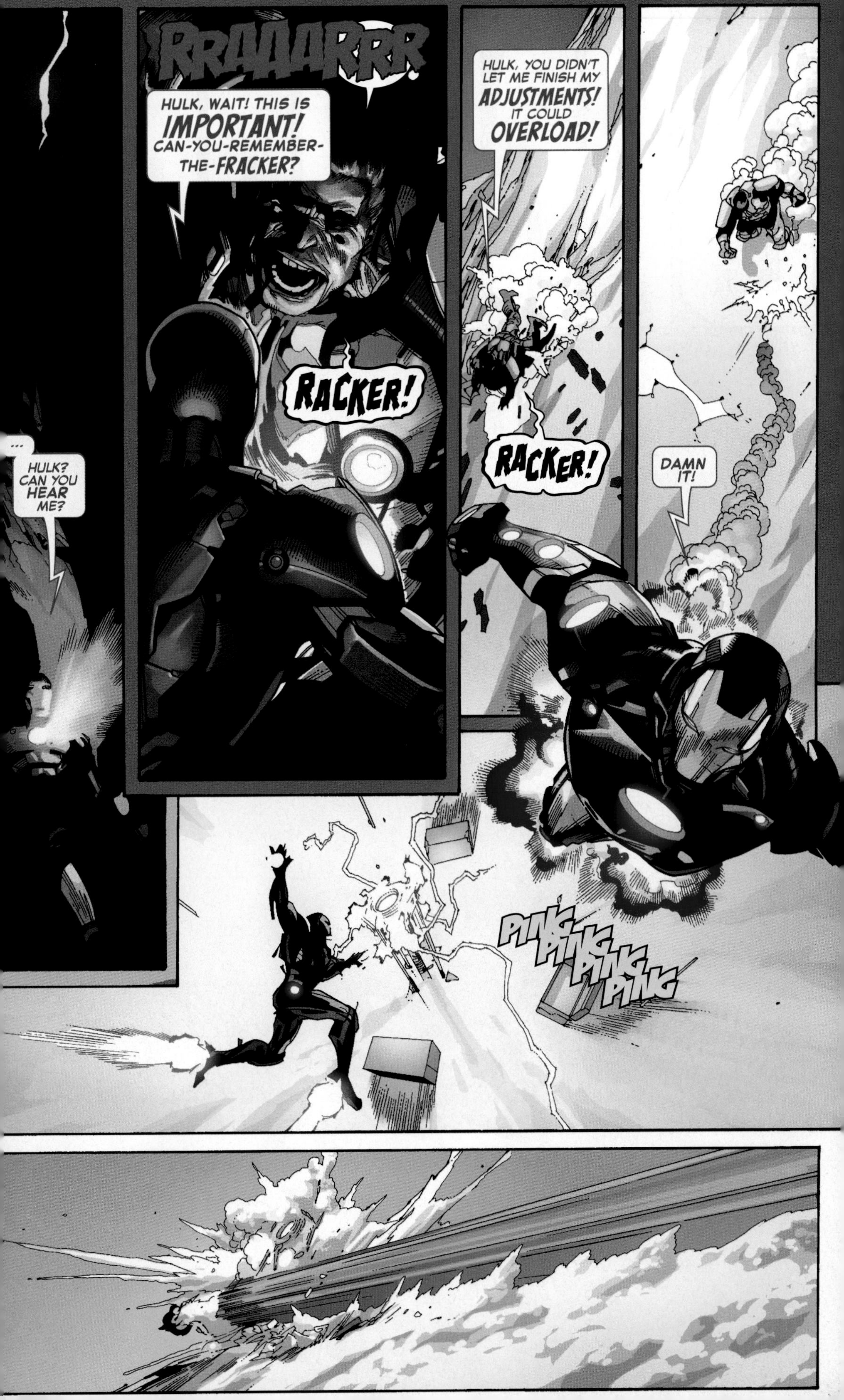
...
HULK? CAN YOU HEAR ME?
RRAAARRR
HULK, WAIT! THIS IS IMPORTANT! CAN-YOU-REMEMBER-THE-FRACKER?
RACKER!
HULK, YOU DIDN'T LET ME FINISH MY ADJUSTMENTS! IT COULD OVERLOAD!
RACKER!
DAMN IT!
PING PING PING PING

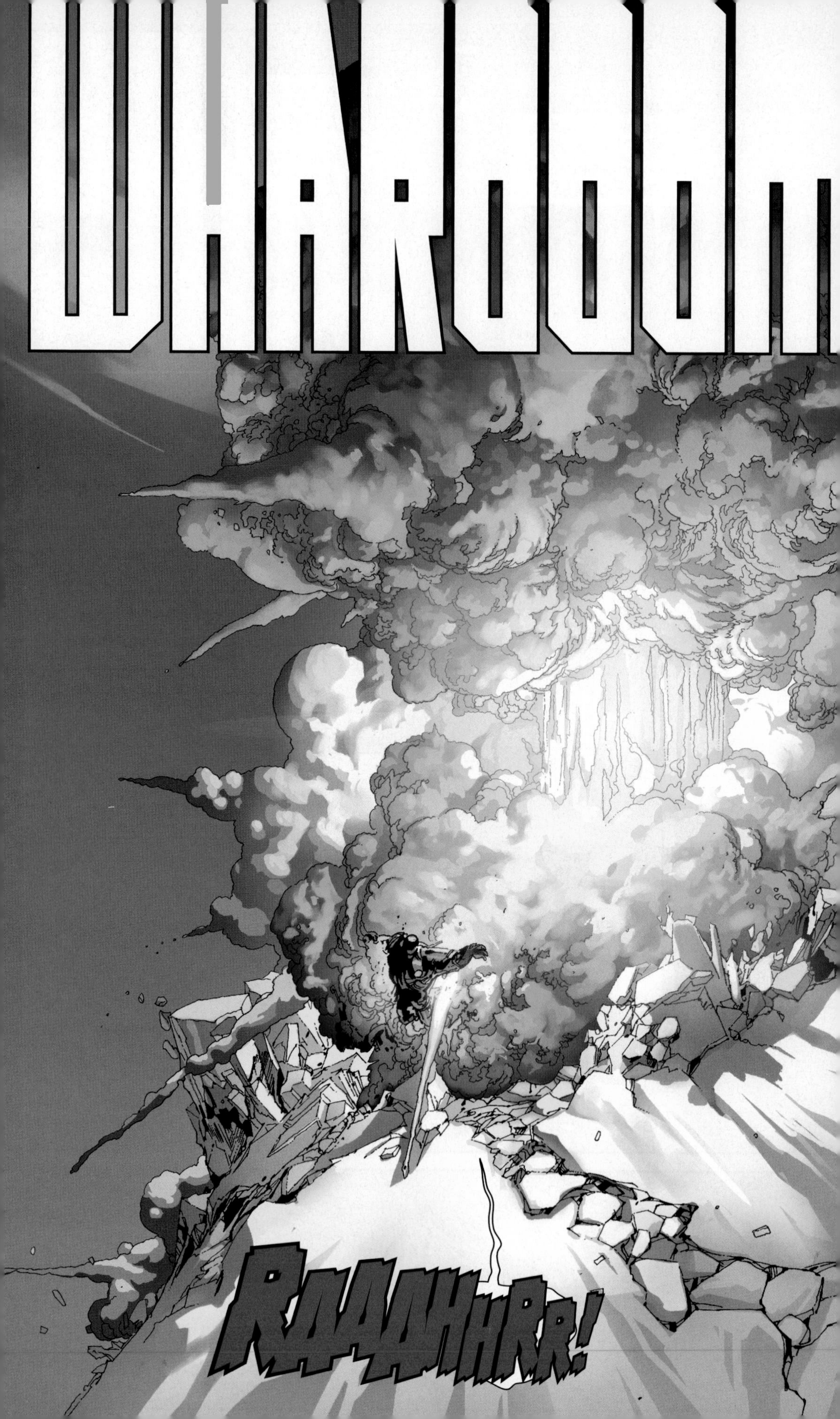
WAROOOM
RAAAHHRR!

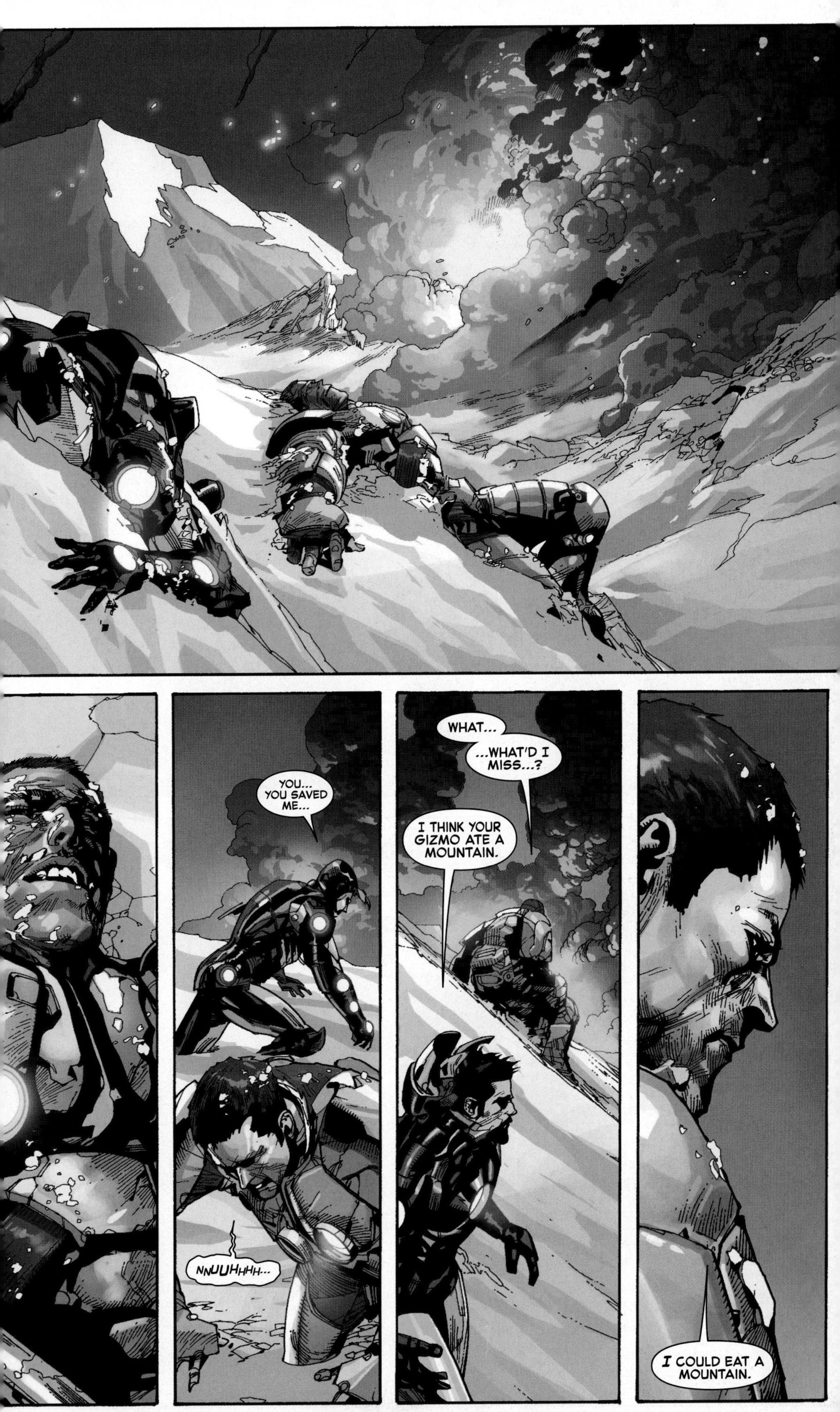
YOU... YOU SAVED ME...
NNUUHHHH...
WHAT...
...WHAT'D I MISS...?
I THINK YOUR GIZMO ATE A MOUNTAIN.
I COULD EAT A MOUNTAIN.

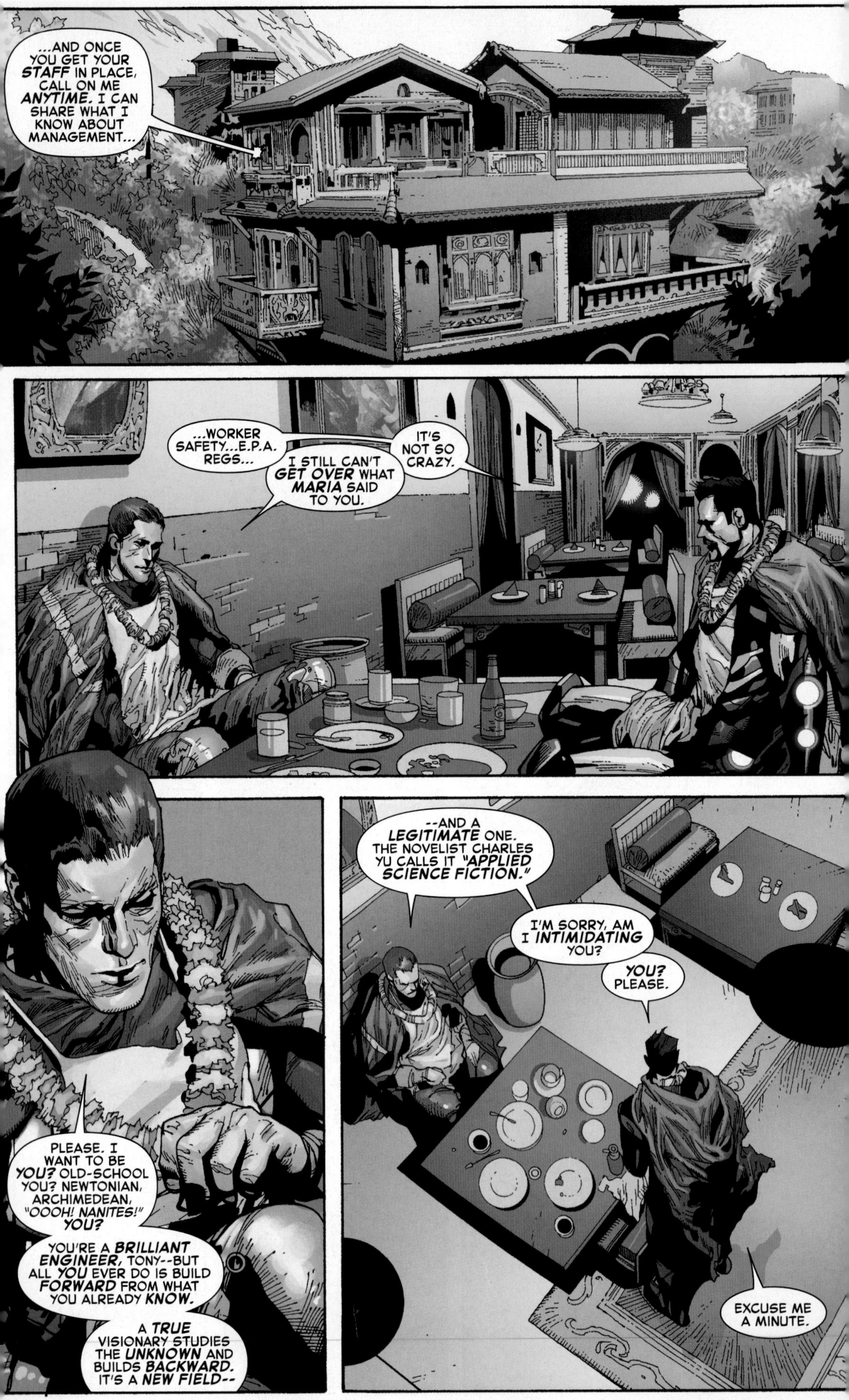
...AND ONCE YOU GET YOUR STAFF IN PLACE, CALL ON ME ANYTIME. I CAN SHARE WHAT I KNOW ABOUT MANAGEMENT...
...WORKER SAFETY...E.P.A. REGS...
IT'S NOT SO CRAZY.
I STILL CAN'T GET OVER WHAT MARIA SAID TO YOU.
PLEASE. I WANT TO BE YOU? OLD-SCHOOL YOU? NEWTONIAN, ARCHIMEDEAN, "OOOH! NANITES!" YOU?
YOU'RE A BRILLIANT ENGINEER, TONY--BUT ALL YOU EVER DO IS BUILD FORWARD FROM WHAT YOU ALREADY KNOW.
A TRUE VISIONARY STUDIES THE UNKNOWN AND BUILDS BACKWARD. IT'S A NEW FIELD--
--AND A LEGITIMATE ONE. THE NOVELIST CHARLES YU CALLS IT "APPLIED SCIENCE FICTION."
I'M SORRY, AM I INTIMIDATING YOU?
YOU? PLEASE.
EXCUSE ME A MINUTE.

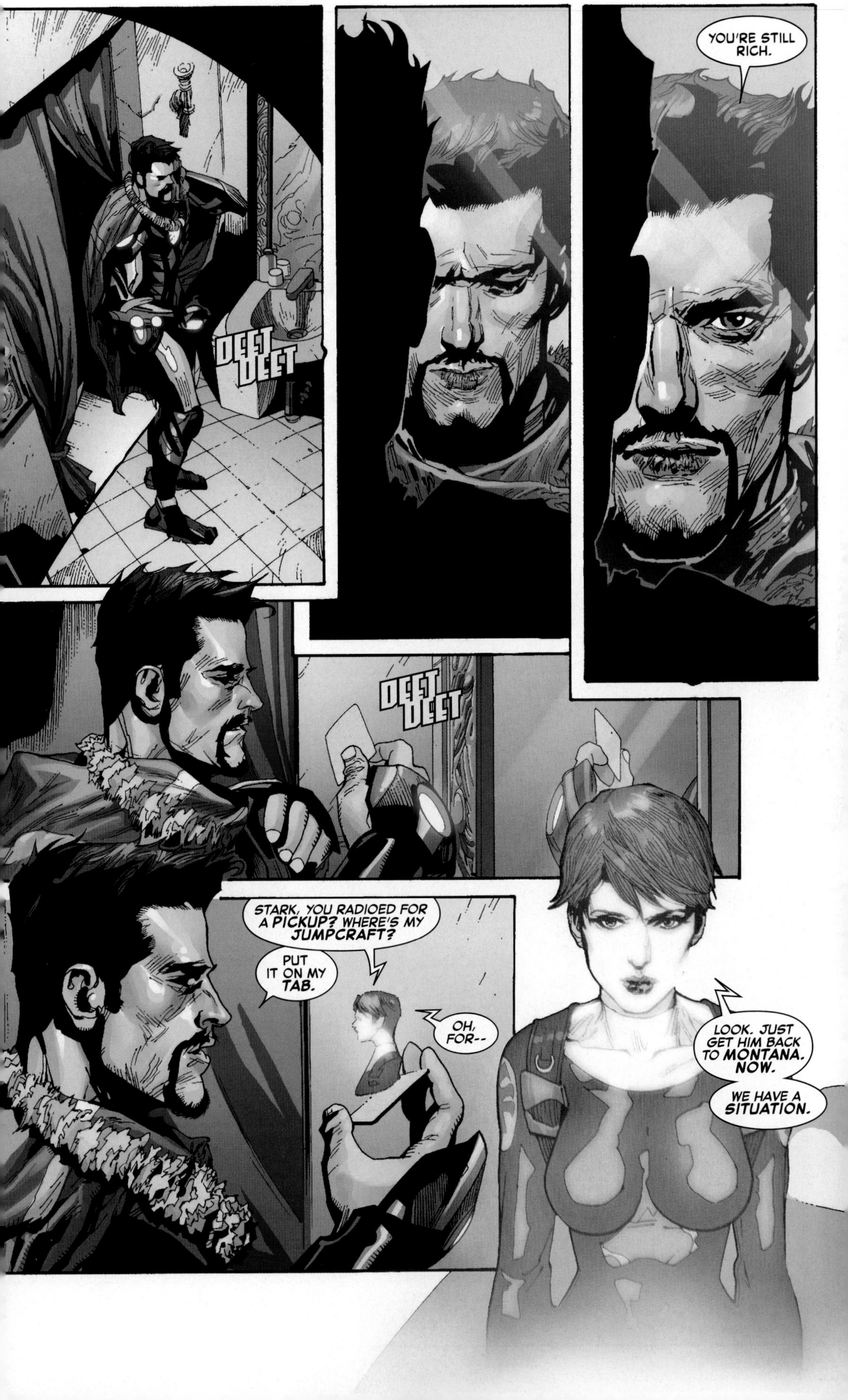
DEET DEET
YOU'RE STILL RICH.
DEET DEET
STARK, YOU RADIOED FOR A PICKUP? WHERE'S MY JUMPCRAFT?
PUT IT ON MY TAB.
OH, FOR--
LOOK. JUST GET HIM BACK TO MONTANA. NOW.
WE HAVE A SITUATION.

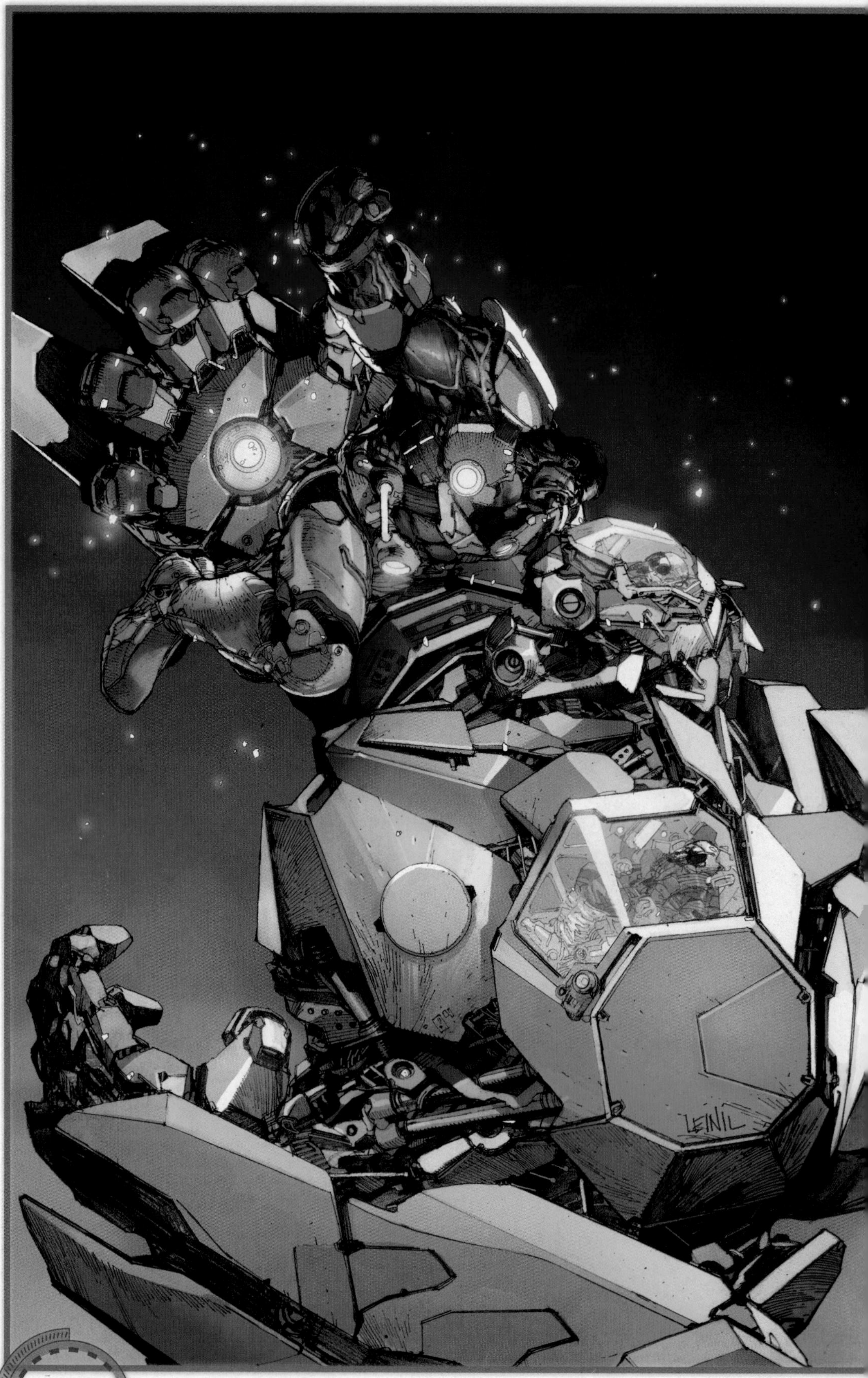
LEINIL

03

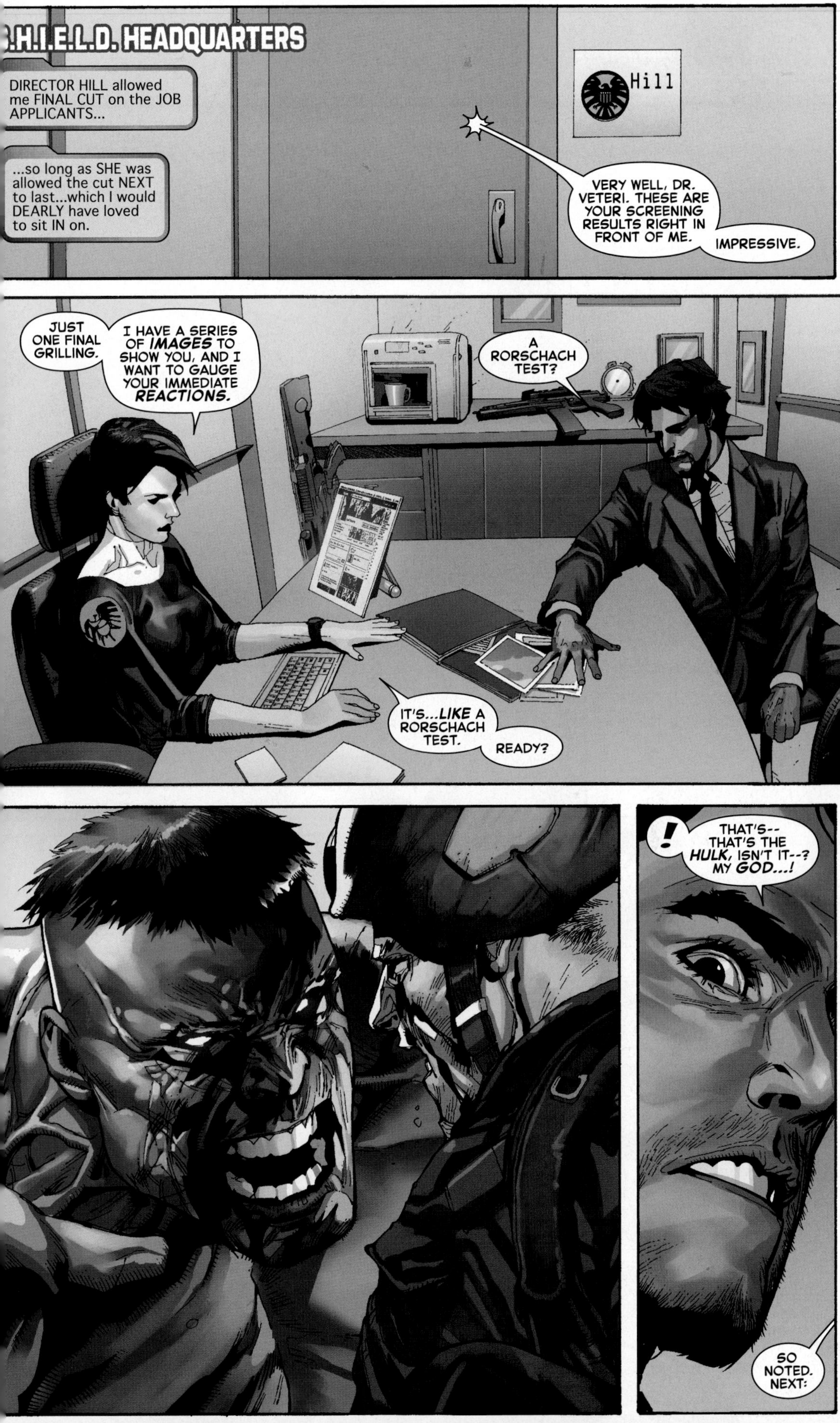

.H.I.E.L.D. HEADQUARTERS
DIRECTOR HILL allowed me FINAL CUT on the JOB APPLICANTS...
...so long as SHE was allowed the cut NEXT to last...which I would DEARLY have loved to sit IN on.
Hill
VERY WELL, DR. VETERI. THESE ARE YOUR SCREENING RESULTS RIGHT IN FRONT OF ME.
IMPRESSIVE.
JUST ONE FINAL GRILLING.
I HAVE A SERIES OF IMAGES TO SHOW YOU, AND I WANT TO GAUGE YOUR IMMEDIATE REACTIONS.
A RORSCHACH TEST?
IT'S...LIKE A RORSCHACH TEST.
READY?
!
THAT'S-- THAT'S THE HULK, ISN'T IT--? MY GOD...!
SO NOTED. NEXT:

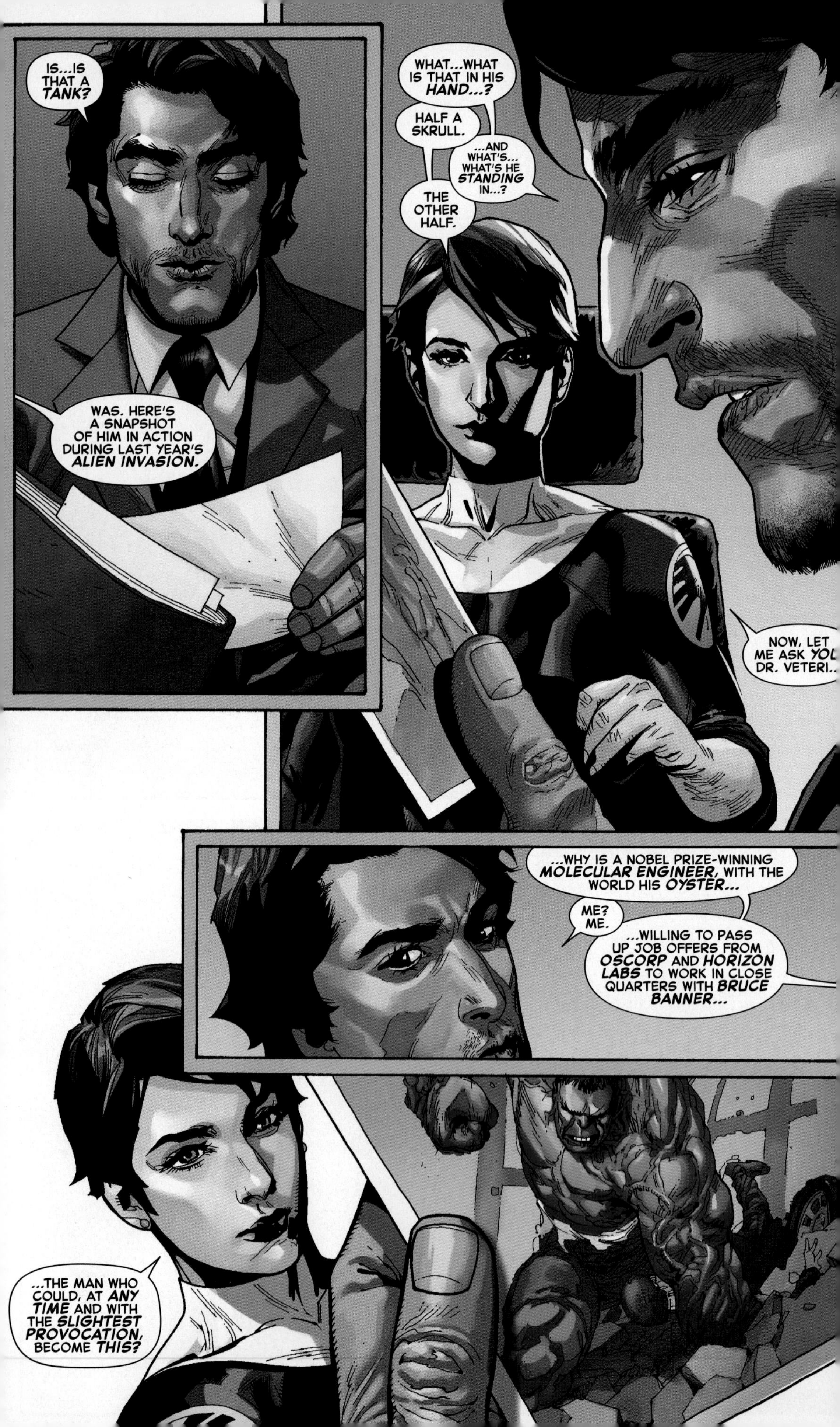
IS...IS THAT A TANK?
WAS. HERE'S A SNAPSHOT OF HIM IN ACTION DURING LAST YEAR'S ALIEN INVASION.
WHAT...WHAT IS THAT IN HIS HAND...?
HALF A SKRULL.
...AND WHAT'S... WHAT'S HE STANDING IN...?
THE OTHER HALF.
NOW, LET ME ASK YOU DR. VETERI...
...WHY IS A NOBEL PRIZE-WINNING MOLECULAR ENGINEER, WITH THE WORLD HIS OYSTER...
ME? ME.
...WILLING TO PASS UP JOB OFFERS FROM OSCORP AND HORIZON LABS TO WORK IN CLOSE QUARTERS WITH BRUCE BANNER...
...THE MAN WHO COULD, AT ANY TIME AND WITH THE SLIGHTEST PROVOCATION, BECOME THIS?

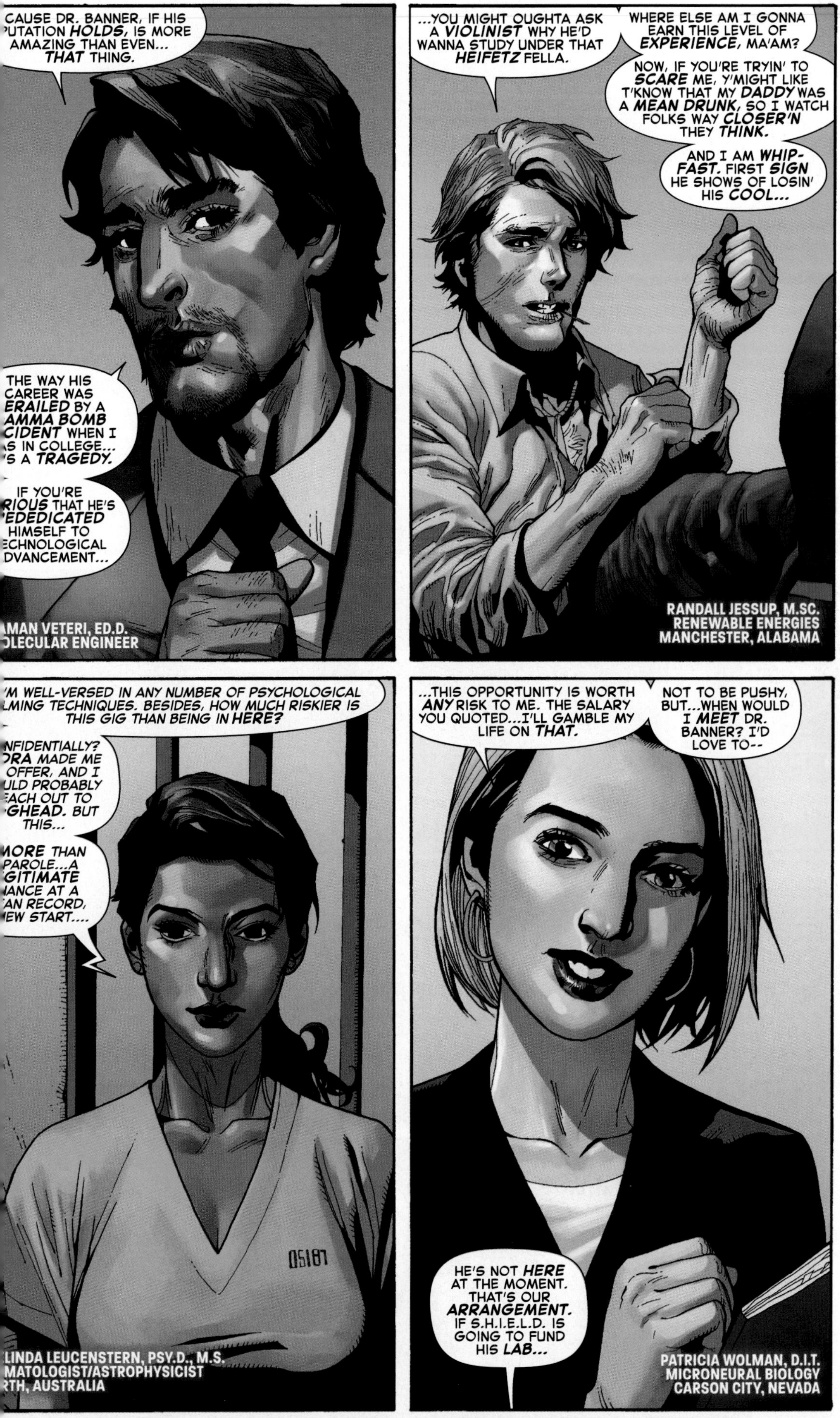
CAUSE DR. BANNER, IF HIS
PUTATION HOLDS, IS MORE AMAZING THAN EVEN... THAT THING.
THE WAY HIS CAREER WAS ERAILED BY A AMMA BOMB CIDENT WHEN I S IN COLLEGE... 'S A TRAGEDY.
IF YOU'RE RIOUS THAT HE'S EDEDICATED HIMSELF TO ECHNOLOGICAL DVANCEMENT...
AMAN VETERI, ED.D.
OLECULAR ENGINEER
...YOU MIGHT OUGHTA ASK A VIOLINIST WHY HE'D WANNA STUDY UNDER THAT HEIFETZ FELLA.
WHERE ELSE AM I GONNA EARN THIS LEVEL OF EXPERIENCE, MA'AM?
NOW, IF YOU'RE TRYIN' TO SCARE ME, Y'MIGHT LIKE T'KNOW THAT MY DADDY WAS A MEAN DRUNK, SO I WATCH FOLKS WAY CLOSER'N THEY THINK.
AND I AM WHIP-FAST. FIRST SIGN HE SHOWS OF LOSIN' HIS COOL...
RANDALL JESSUP, M.SC.
RENEWABLE ENERGIES
MANCHESTER, ALABAMA
'M WELL-VERSED IN ANY NUMBER OF PSYCHOLOGICAL LMING TECHNIQUES. BESIDES, HOW MUCH RISKIER IS THIS GIG THAN BEING IN HERE?
NFIDENTIALLY? DRA MADE ME OFFER, AND I ULD PROBABLY EACH OUT TO GHEAD. BUT THIS...
MORE THAN PAROLE...A GITIMATE ANCE AT A AN RECORD, EW START....
05187
LINDA LEUCENSTERN, PSY.D., M.S.
MATOLOGIST/ASTROPHYSICIST
RTH, AUSTRALIA
...THIS OPPORTUNITY IS WORTH ANY RISK TO ME. THE SALARY YOU QUOTED...I'LL GAMBLE MY LIFE ON THAT.
NOT TO BE PUSHY, BUT...WHEN WOULD I MEET DR. BANNER? I'D LOVE TO--
HE'S NOT HERE AT THE MOMENT. THAT'S OUR ARRANGEMENT. IF S.H.I.E.L.D. IS GOING TO FUND HIS LAB...
PATRICIA WOLMAN, D.I.T.
MICRONEURAL BIOLOGY
CARSON CITY, NEVADA

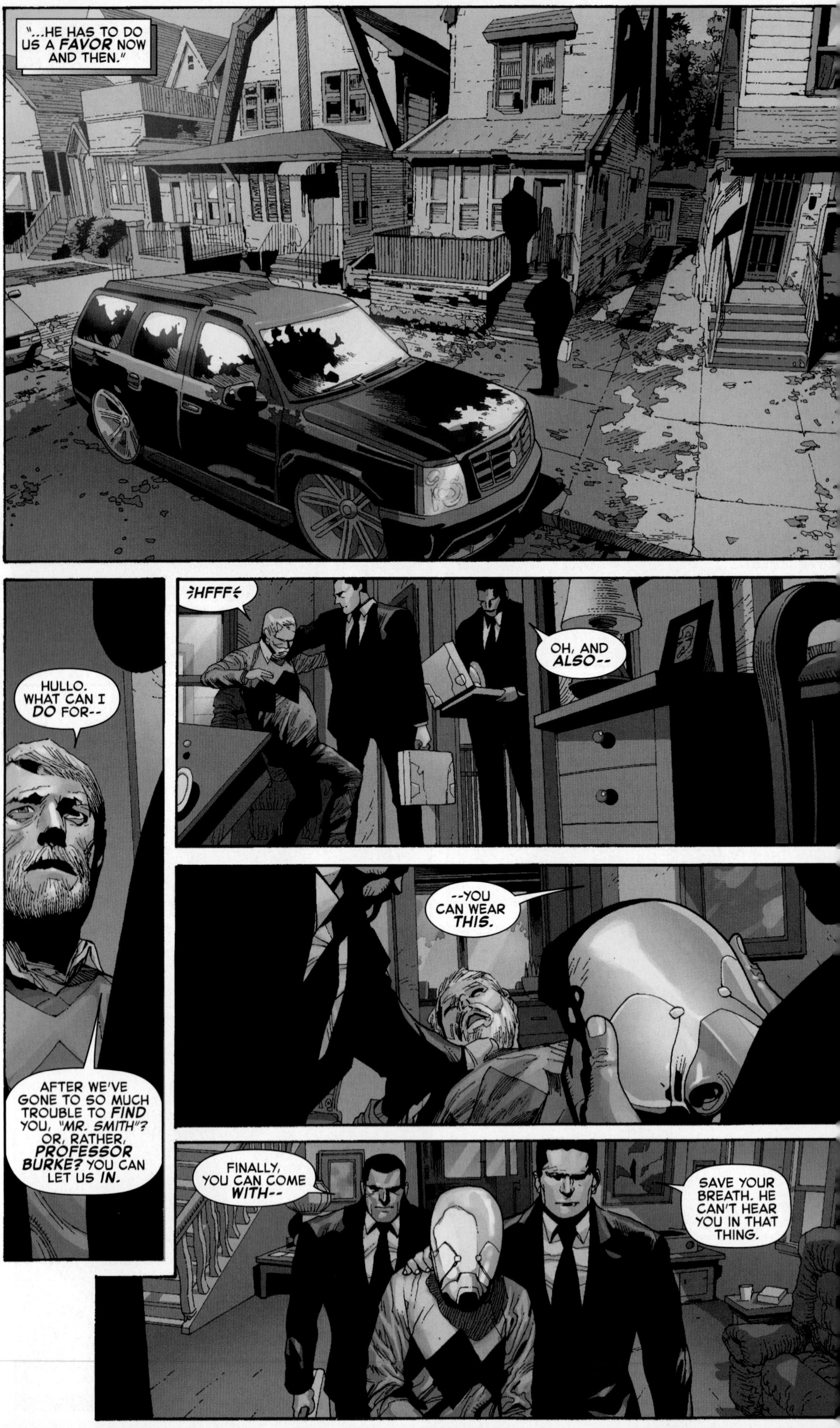
"...HE HAS TO DO US A FAVOR NOW AND THEN."
HULLO. WHAT CAN I DO FOR--
AFTER WE'VE GONE TO SO MUCH TROUBLE TO FIND YOU, "MR. SMITH"? OR, RATHER, PROFESSOR BURKE? YOU CAN LET US IN.
HFFF
OH, AND ALSO--
--YOU CAN WEAR THIS.
FINALLY, YOU CAN COME WITH--
SAVE YOUR BREATH. HE CAN'T HEAR YOU IN THAT THING.

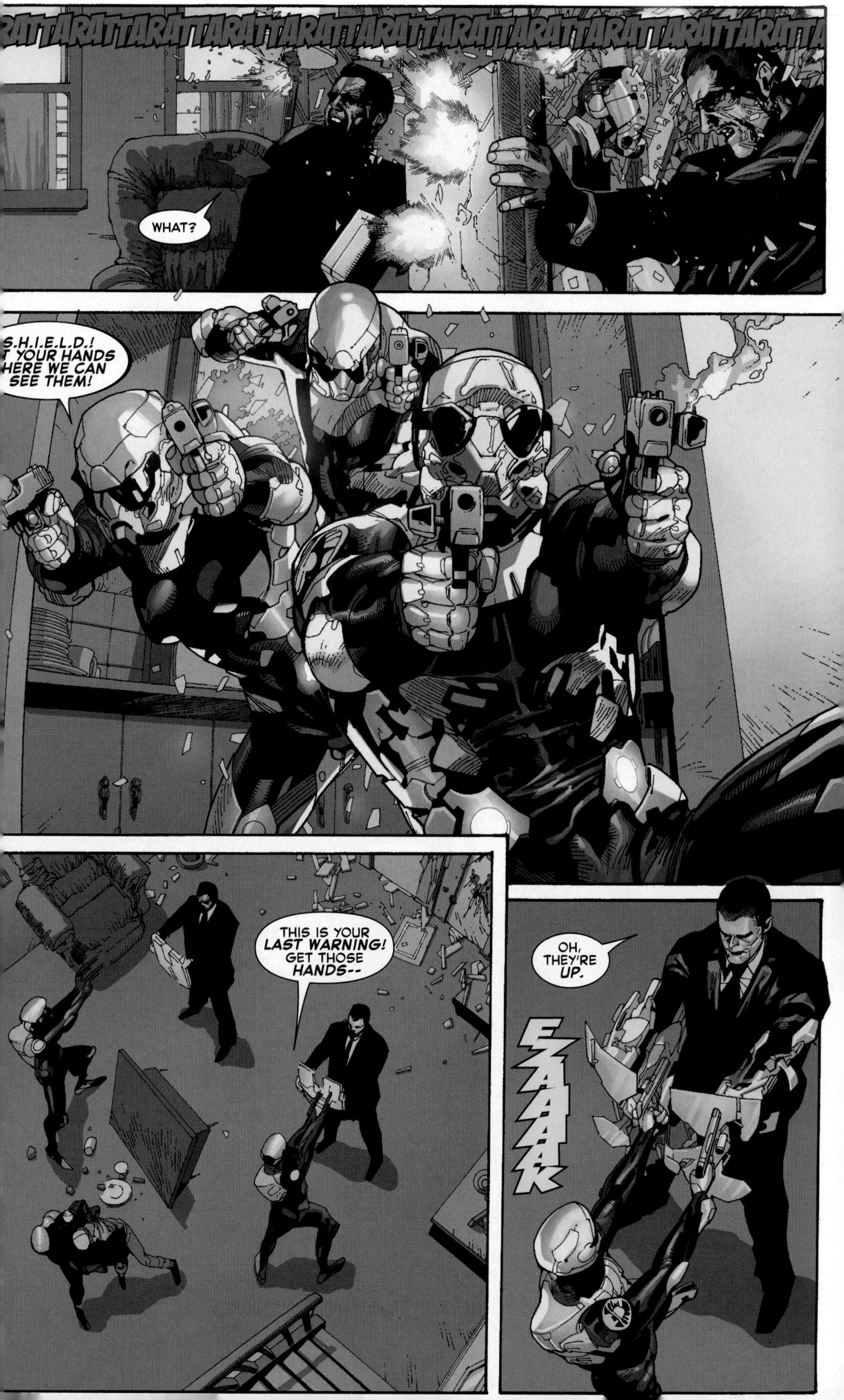
RATTTARATTTARATTTARATTTARATTTARATTTARATTTARATTTARATTTARATTTARATT
WHAT?
S.H.I.E.L.D.! T YOUR HANDS HERE WE CAN SEE THEM!
THIS IS YOUR LAST WARNING! GET THOSE HANDS--
OH, THEY'RE UP.
EZAAAAK

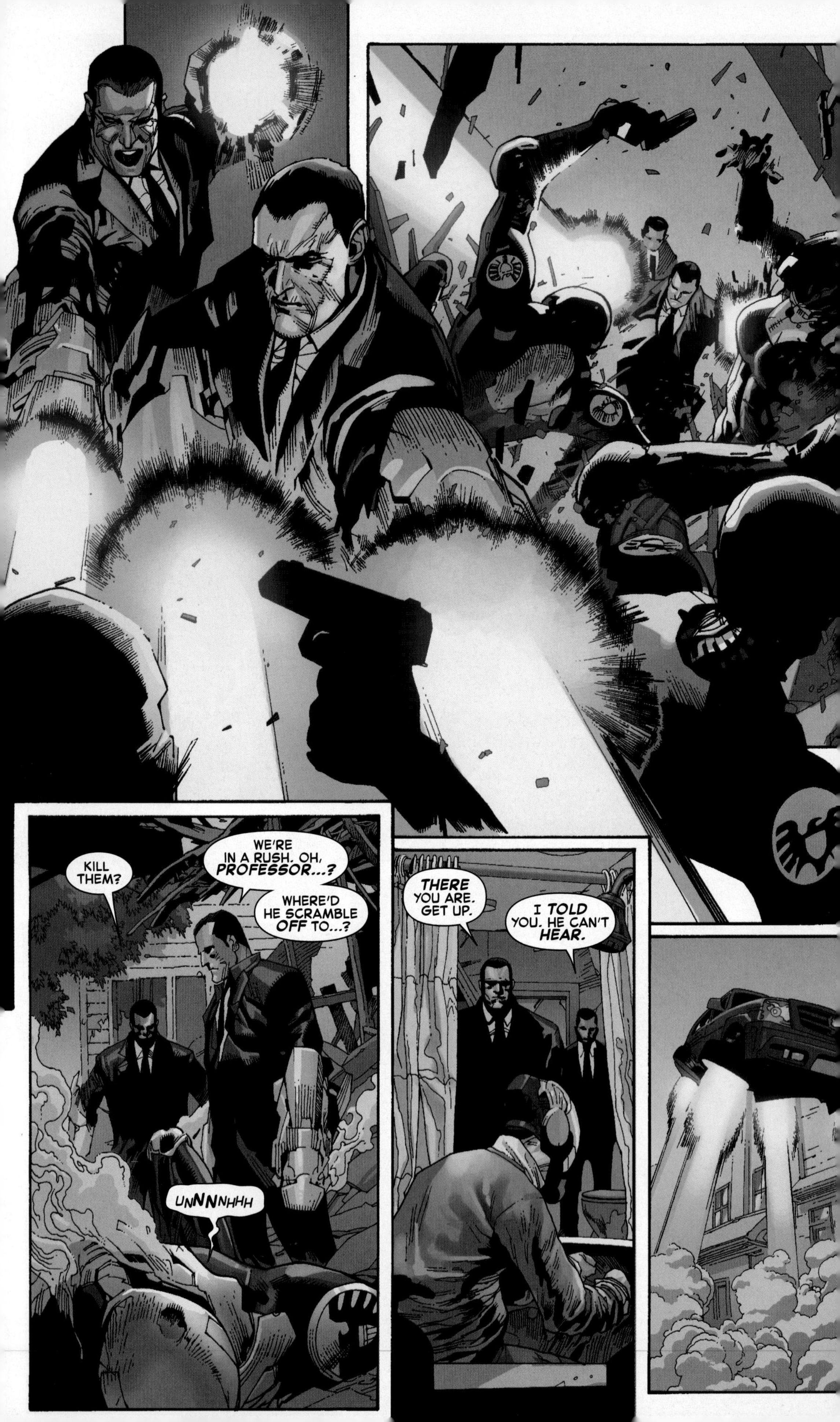
KILL THEM?
WE'RE IN A RUSH. OH, PROFESSOR...?
WHERE'D HE SCRAMBLE OFF TO...?
UNNNNHHH
THERE YOU ARE. GET UP.
I TOLD YOU. HE CAN'T HEAR.

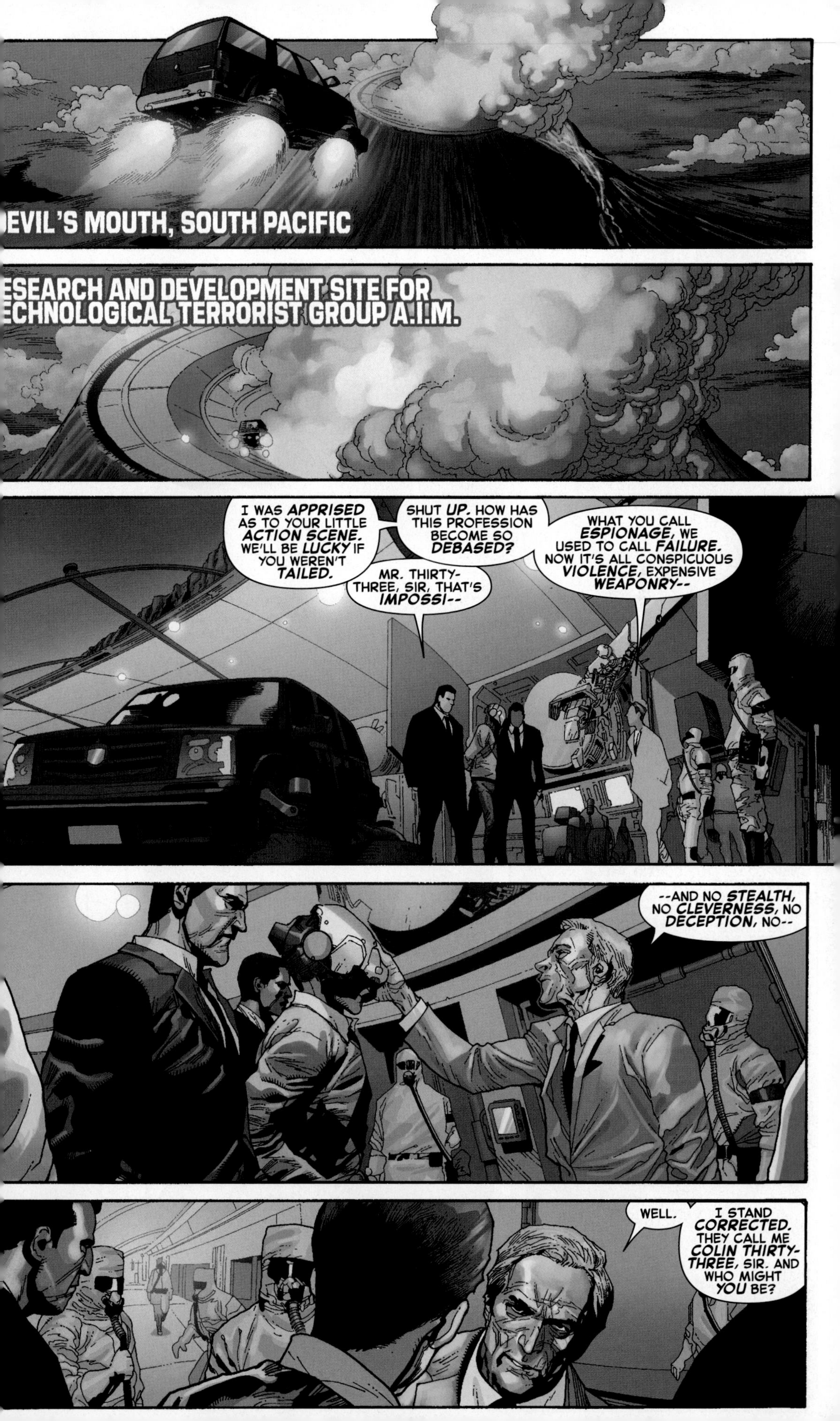
EVIL'S MOUTH, SOUTH PACIFIC
ESEARCH AND DEVELOPMENT SITE FOR
ECHNOLOGICAL TERRORIST GROUP A.I.M.
I WAS APPRISED AS TO YOUR LITTLE ACTION SCENE. WE'LL BE LUCKY IF YOU WEREN'T TAILED.
MR. THIRTY-THREE, SIR, THAT'S IMPOSSI--
SHUT UP. HOW HAS THIS PROFESSION BECOME SO DEBASED?
WHAT YOU CALL ESPIONAGE, WE USED TO CALL FAILURE. NOW IT'S ALL CONSPICUOUS VIOLENCE, EXPENSIVE WEAPONRY--
--AND NO STEALTH, NO CLEVERNESS, NO DECEPTION, NO--
WELL.
I STAND CORRECTED. THEY CALL ME COLIN THIRTY-THREE, SIR. AND WHO MIGHT YOU BE?

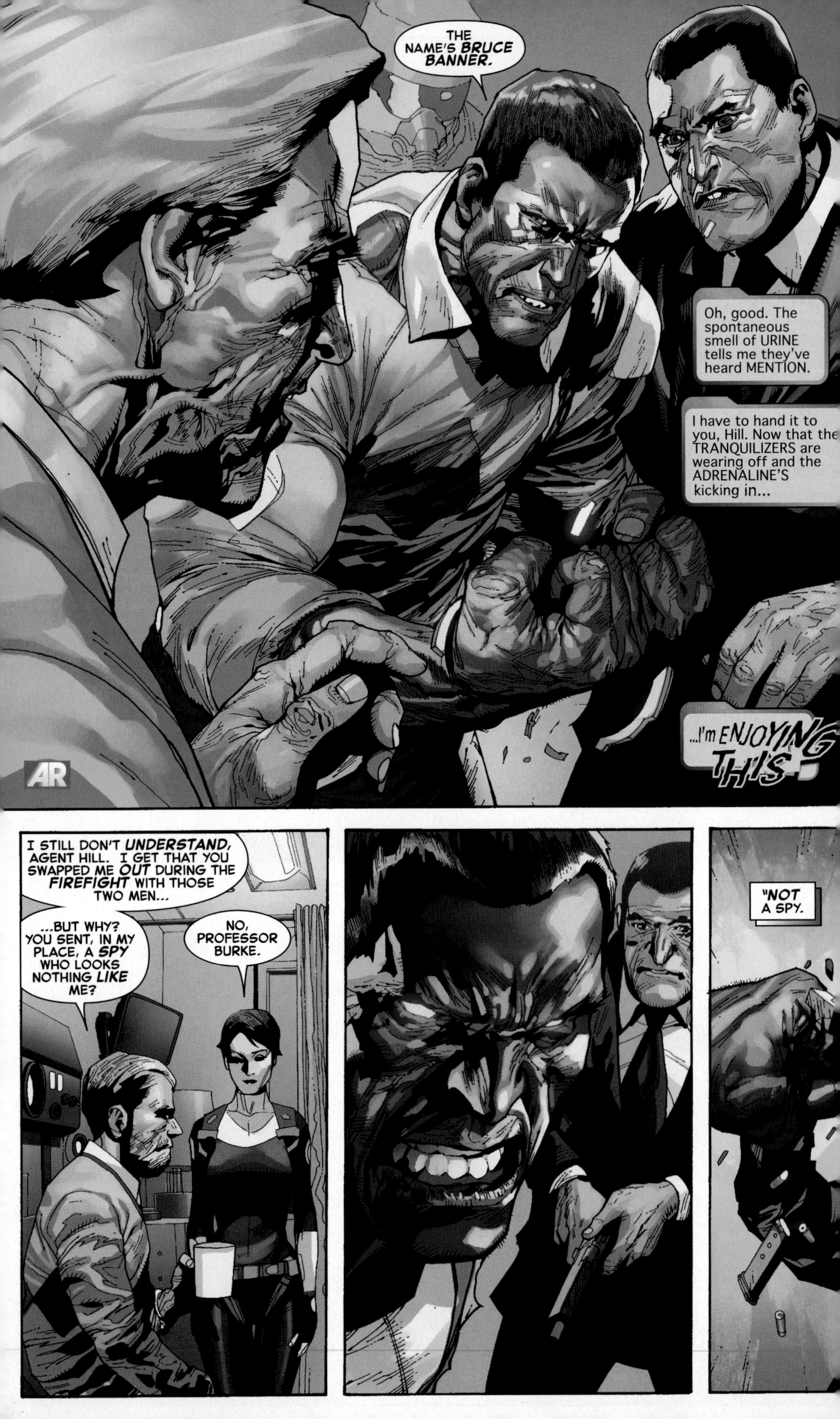
THE NAME'S BRUCE BANNER.
Oh, good. The spontaneous smell of URINE tells me they've heard MENTION.
I have to hand it to you, Hill. Now that the TRANQUILIZERS are wearing off and the ADRENALINE'S kicking in...
...I'm ENJOYING THIS!
I STILL DON'T UNDERSTAND, AGENT HILL. I GET THAT YOU SWAPPED ME OUT DURING THE FIREFIGHT WITH THOSE TWO MEN...
...BUT WHY? YOU SENT, IN MY PLACE, A SPY WHO LOOKS NOTHING LIKE ME?
NO, PROFESSOR BURKE.
"NOT A SPY.

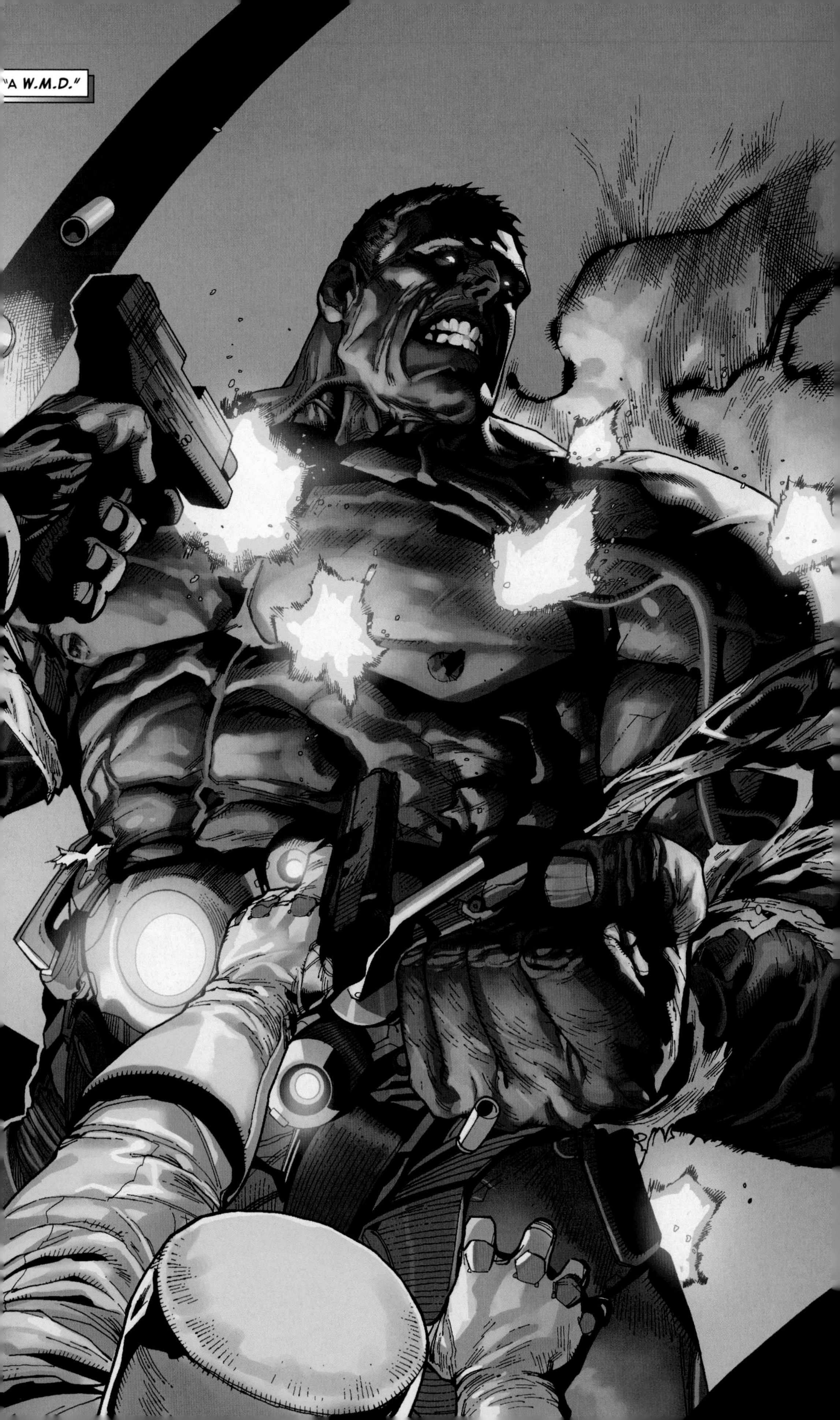
"A W.M.D."

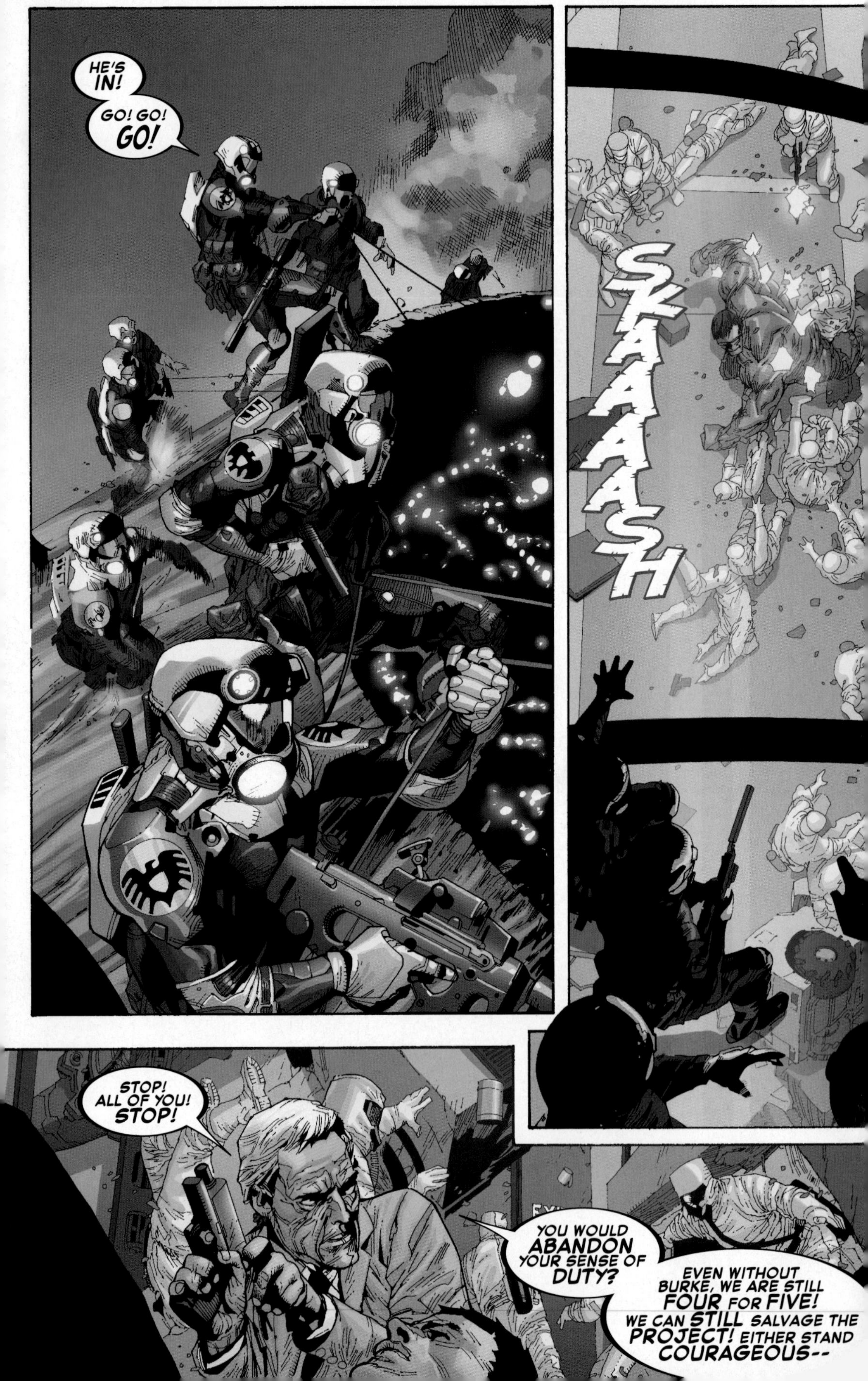
HE'S IN!
GO! GO! GO!
SKAAAASH
STOP! ALL OF YOU! STOP!
YOU WOULD ABANDON YOUR SENSE OF DUTY?
EVEN WITHOUT BURKE, WE ARE STILL FOUR FOR FIVE! WE CAN STILL SALVAGE THE PROJECT! EITHER STAND COURAGEOUS--

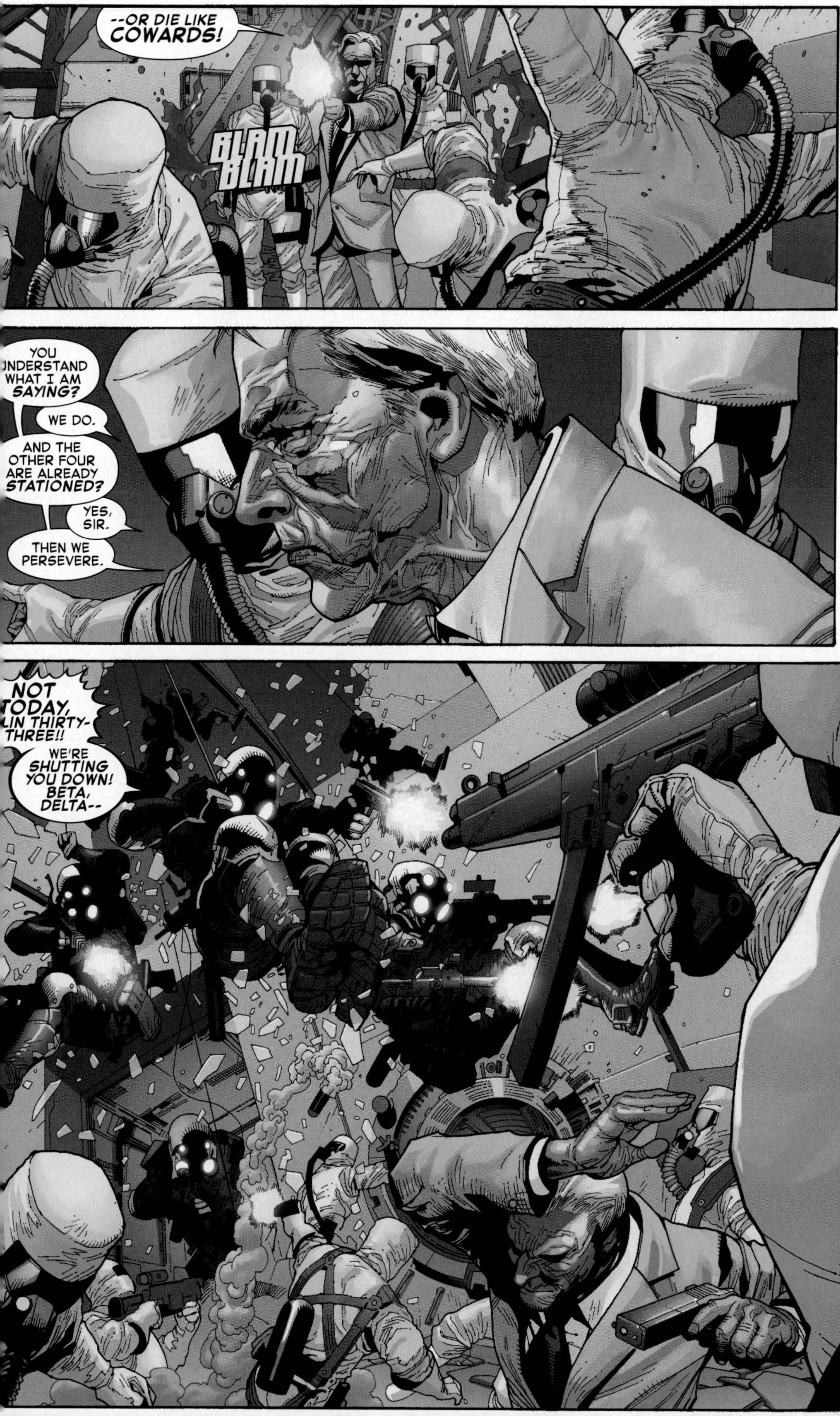
--OR DIE LIKE COWARDS!
BLAM BLAM
YOU UNDERSTAND WHAT I AM SAYING?
WE DO.
AND THE OTHER FOUR ARE ALREADY STATIONED?
YES, SIR.
THEN WE PERSEVERE.
NOT TODAY, LIN THIRTY-THREE!!
WE'RE SHUTTING YOU DOWN! BETA, DELTA--

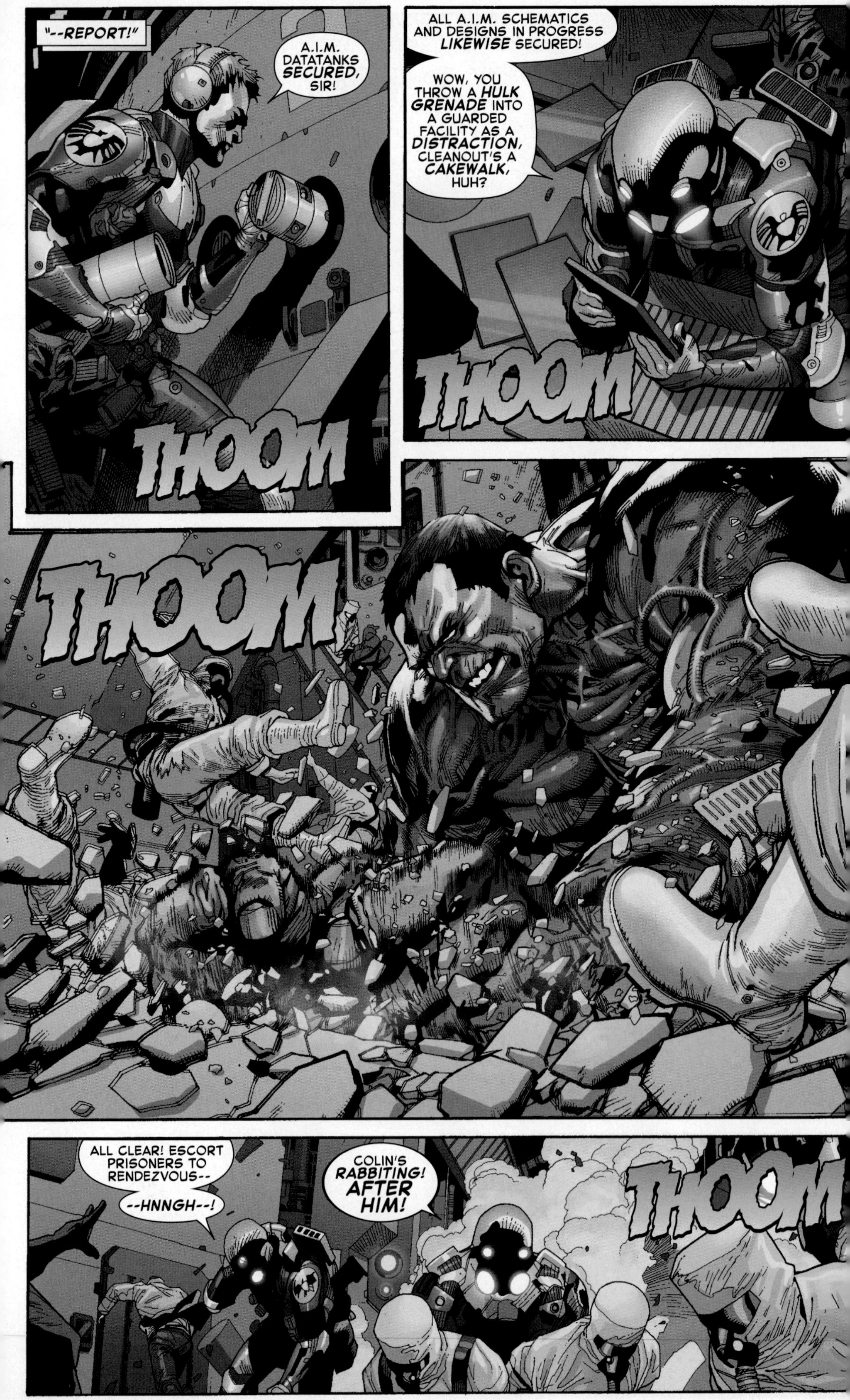
"--REPORT!"
A.I.M. DATATANKS SECURED, SIR!
THOOM
ALL A.I.M. SCHEMATICS AND DESIGNS IN PROGRESS LIKEWISE SECURED!
WOW, YOU THROW A HULK GRENADE INTO A GUARDED FACILITY AS A DISTRACTION, CLEANOUT'S A CAKEWALK, HUH?
THOOM
THOOM
ALL CLEAR! ESCORT PRISONERS TO RENDEZVOUS--
--HNNGH--!
COLIN'S RABBITING! AFTER HIM!
THOOM

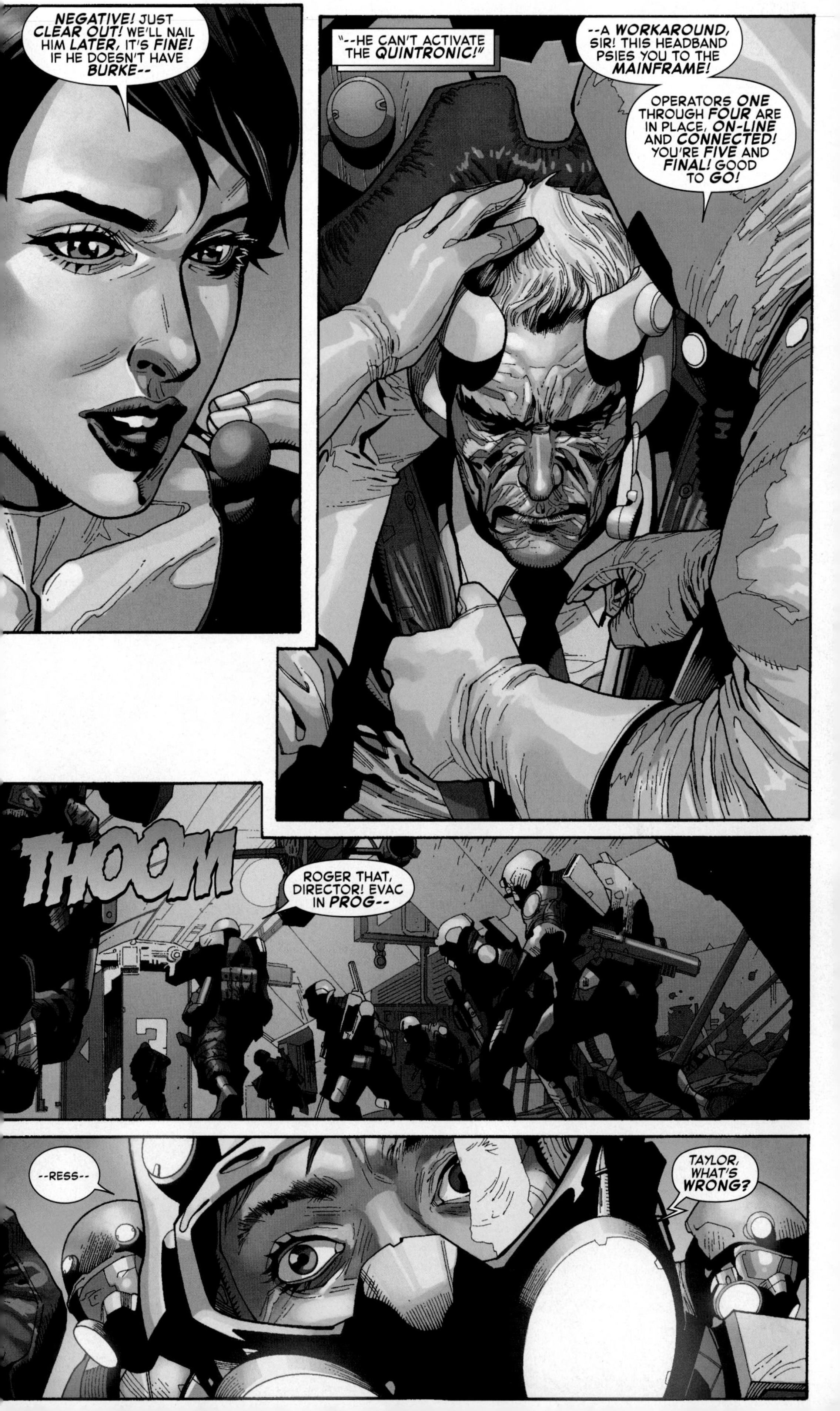
NEGATIVE! JUST CLEAR OUT! WE'LL NAIL HIM LATER, IT'S FINE! IF HE DOESN'T HAVE BURKE--
"--HE CAN'T ACTIVATE THE QUINTRONIC!"
--A WORKAROUND, SIR! THIS HEADBAND PSIES YOU TO THE MAINFRAME!
OPERATORS ONE THROUGH FOUR ARE IN PLACE, ON-LINE AND CONNECTED! YOU'RE FIVE AND FINAL! GOOD TO GO!
THOOM
ROGER THAT, DIRECTOR! EVAC IN PROG--
--RESS--
TAYLOR, WHAT'S WRONG?

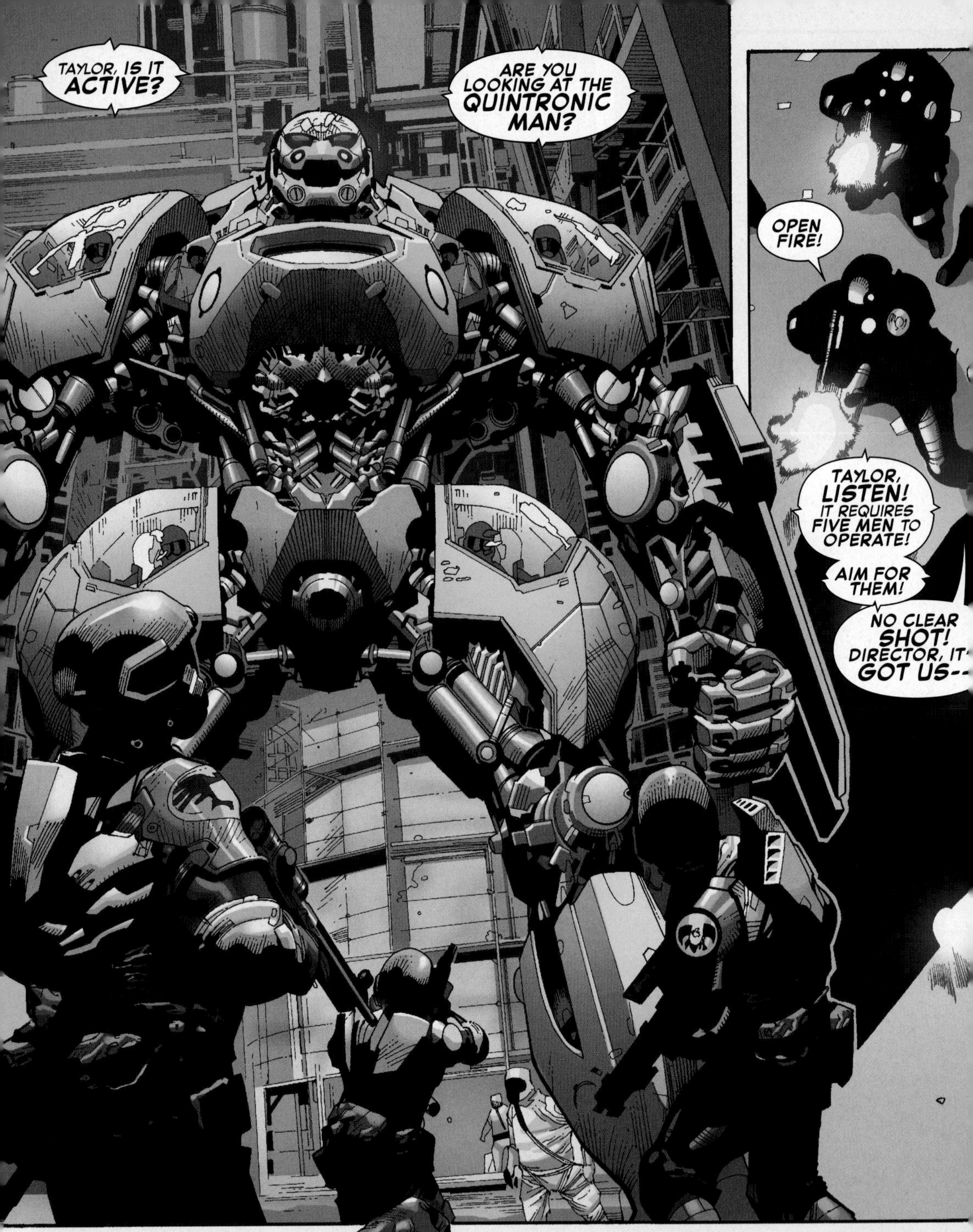
TAYLOR, IS IT ACTIVE?
ARE YOU LOOKING AT THE QUINTRONIC MAN?
OPEN FIRE!
TAYLOR, LISTEN! IT REQUIRES FIVE MEN TO OPERATE!
AIM FOR THEM!
NO CLEAR SHOT! DIRECTOR, IT GOT US--

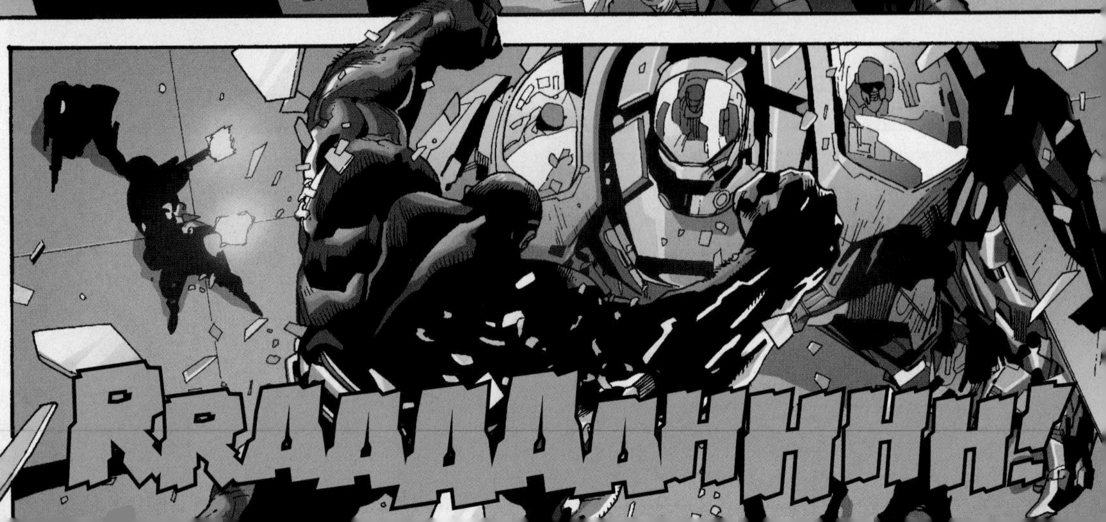
RRAAAAAHHHHH!

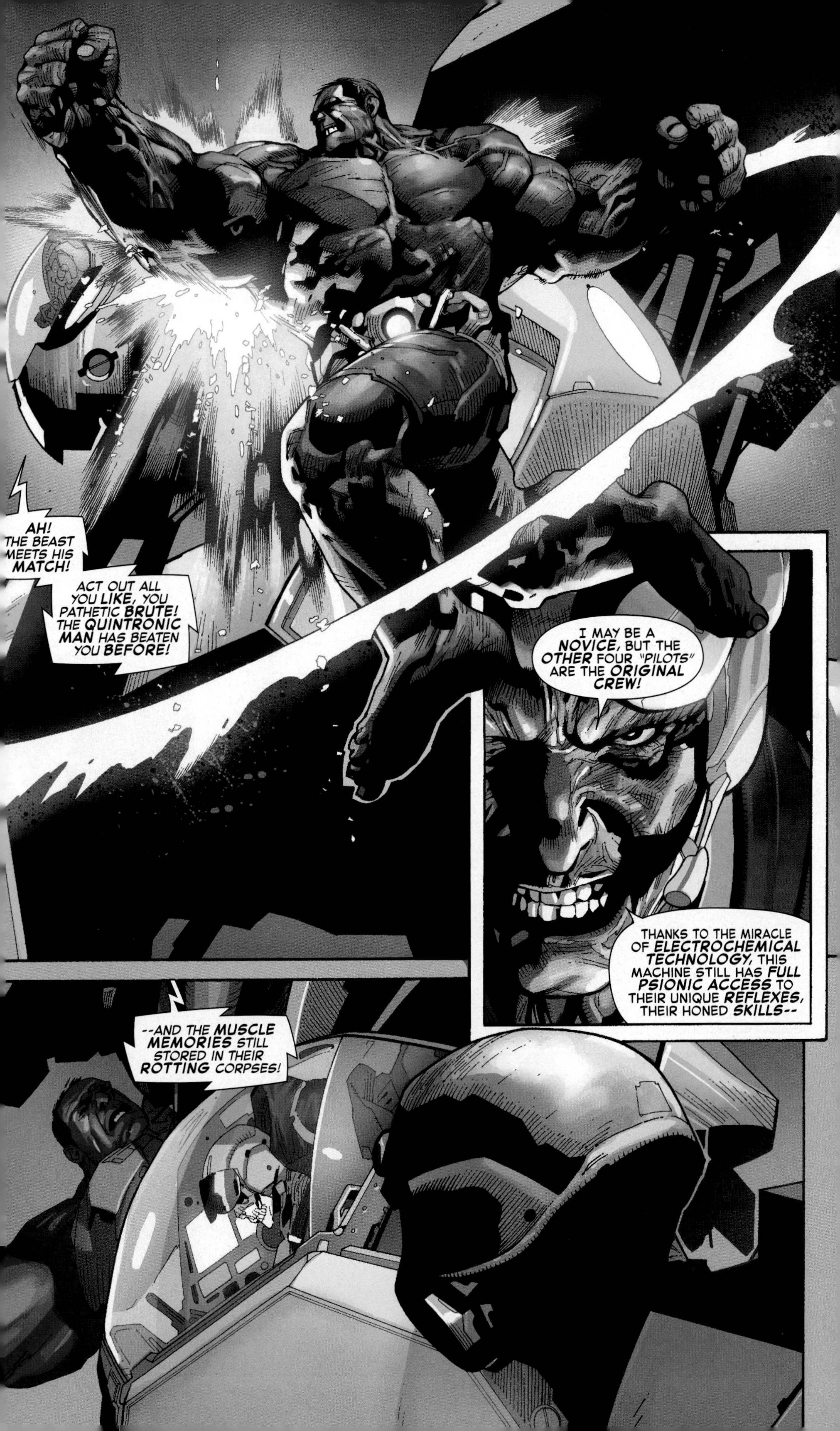

AH! THE BEAST MEETS HIS MATCH!
ACT OUT ALL YOU LIKE, YOU PATHETIC BRUTE! THE QUINTRONIC MAN HAS BEATEN YOU BEFORE!
I MAY BE A NOVICE, BUT THE OTHER FOUR "PILOTS" ARE THE ORIGINAL CREW!
THANKS TO THE MIRACLE OF ELECTROCHEMICAL TECHNOLOGY, THIS MACHINE STILL HAS FULL PSIONIC ACCESS TO THEIR UNIQUE REFLEXES, THEIR HONED SKILLS--
--AND THE MUSCLE MEMORIES STILL STORED IN THEIR ROTTING CORPSES!

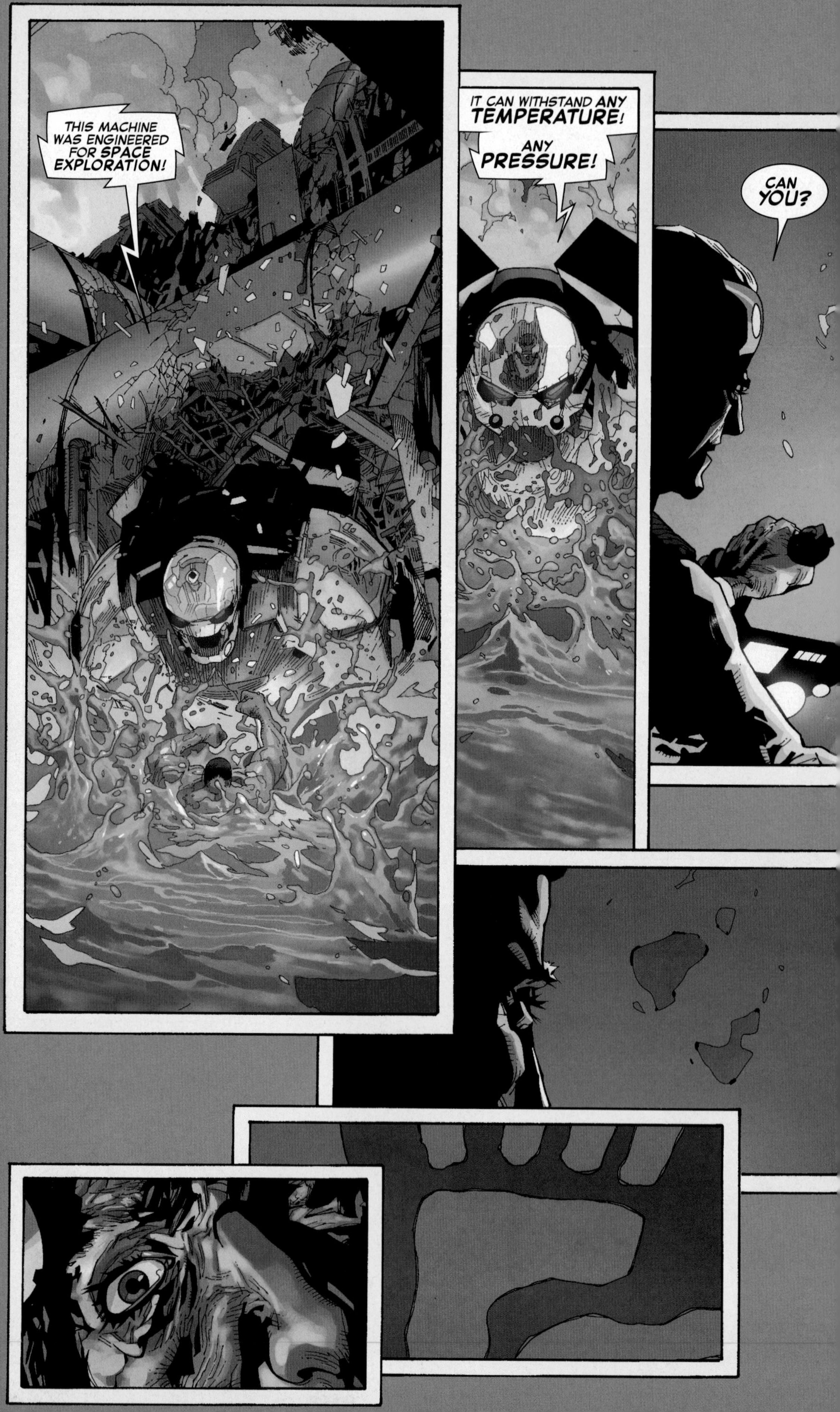
THIS MACHINE WAS ENGINEERED FOR SPACE EXPLORATION!
IT CAN WITHSTAND ANY TEMPERATURE!
ANY PRESSURE!
CAN YOU?

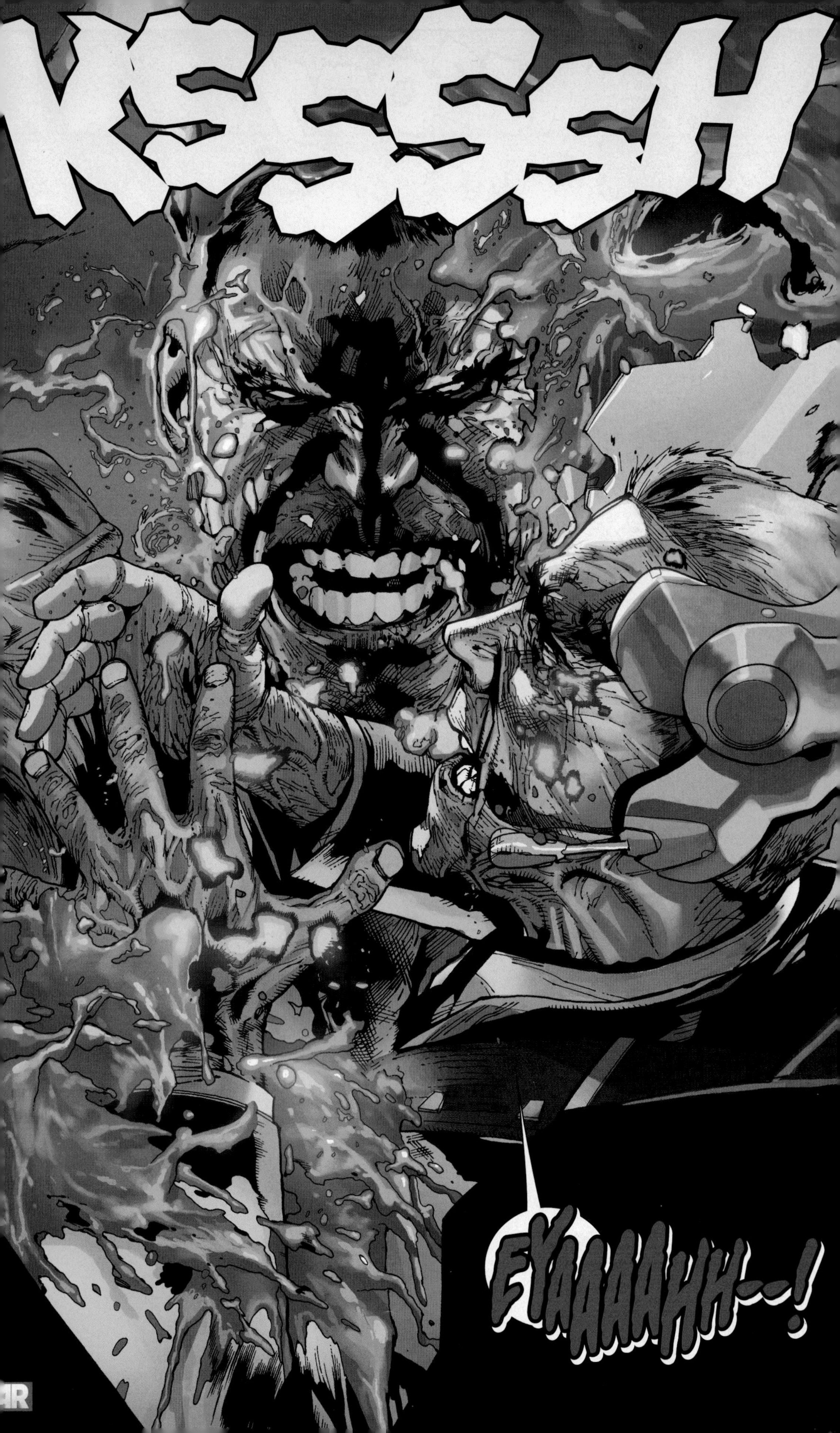
KSSSH
EYAAAAHH--!

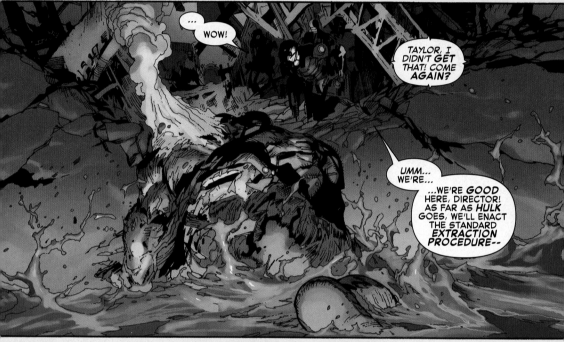

... WOW!

TAYLOR, I DIDN'T *GET* THAT! COME *AGAIN*?

UMM... WE'RE...

...WE'RE *GOOD* HERE, DIRECTOR! AS FAR AS *HULK* GOES, WE'LL ENACT THE STANDARD *EXTRACTION PROCEDURE*--

"--AS SOON AS HE'S COOL TO THE *TOUCH*!"

MEDILAB

...SO THAT'S WHY THEY CAME AFTER *BURKE.*

TWENTY-FOUR HOURS LATER.

HE WAS THE *LAST* OF THE ORIGINAL QUINTRONIC CREW. THE ONLY ONES EVER FULLY TRAINED IN ITS *OPERATION.* EVEN WITH THE OTHER FOUR *LONG-DEAD...*

...A.I.M. PLANNED TO WETWORK THEIR NEURAL PATTERNS AND MEMORIES *THROUGH* HIM TO REUNITE THE *BAND,* SO TO SPEAK.

YOU'LL PROBABLY HAVE TO REPEAT ALL THAT WHEN THE *PAINKILLERS* WEAR OFF.

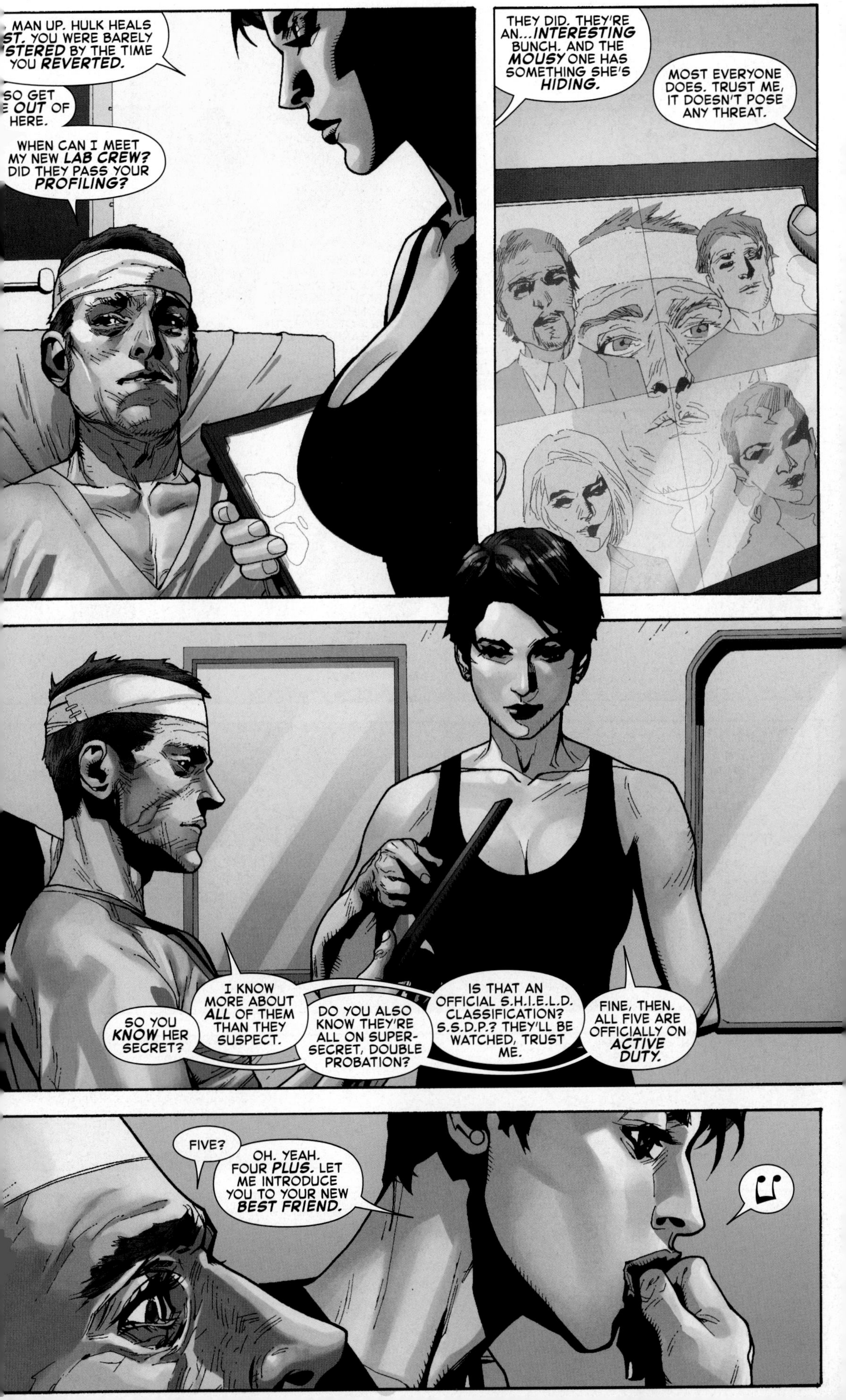
MAN UP. HULK HEALS ST. YOU WERE BARELY STERED BY THE TIME YOU REVERTED.
SO GET OUT OF HERE.
WHEN CAN I MEET MY NEW LAB CREW? DID THEY PASS YOUR PROFILING?
THEY DID. THEY'RE AN... INTERESTING BUNCH. AND THE MOUSY ONE HAS SOMETHING SHE'S HIDING.
MOST EVERYONE DOES. TRUST ME, IT DOESN'T POSE ANY THREAT.
SO YOU KNOW HER SECRET?
I KNOW MORE ABOUT ALL OF THEM THAN THEY SUSPECT.
DO YOU ALSO KNOW THEY'RE ALL ON SUPER-SECRET, DOUBLE PROBATION?
IS THAT AN OFFICIAL S.H.I.E.L.D. CLASSIFICATION? S.S.D.P.? THEY'LL BE WATCHED, TRUST ME.
FINE, THEN. ALL FIVE ARE OFFICIALLY ON ACTIVE DUTY.
FIVE?
OH. YEAH. FOUR PLUS. LET ME INTRODUCE YOU TO YOUR NEW BEST FRIEND.

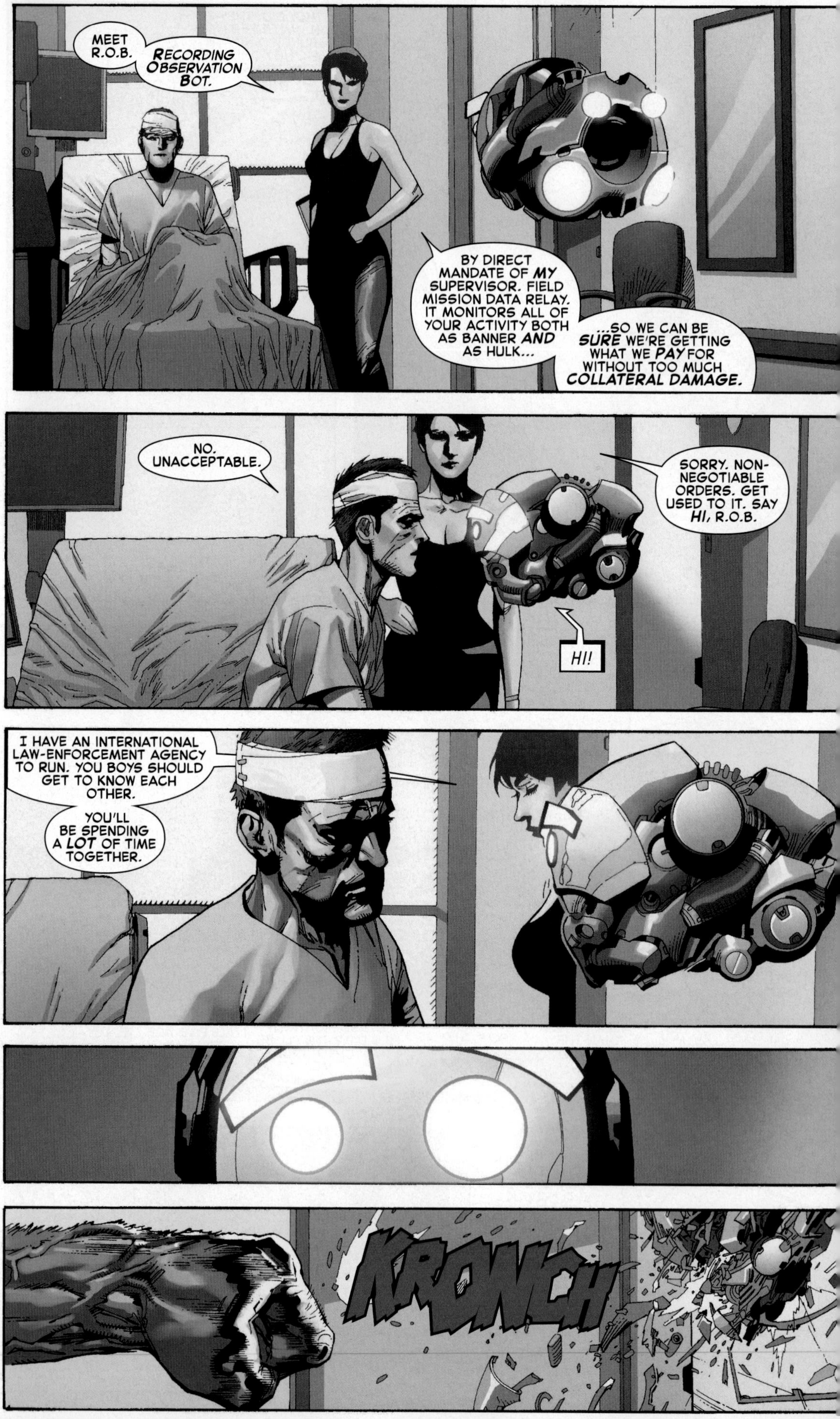
MEET R.O.B.
RECORDING OBSERVATION BOT.
BY DIRECT MANDATE OF MY SUPERVISOR. FIELD MISSION DATA RELAY. IT MONITORS ALL OF YOUR ACTIVITY BOTH AS BANNER AND AS HULK...
...SO WE CAN BE SURE WE'RE GETTING WHAT WE PAY FOR WITHOUT TOO MUCH COLLATERAL DAMAGE.
NO. UNACCEPTABLE.
SORRY. NON-NEGOTIABLE ORDERS. GET USED TO IT. SAY HI, R.O.B.
HI!
I HAVE AN INTERNATIONAL LAW-ENFORCEMENT AGENCY TO RUN. YOU BOYS SHOULD GET TO KNOW EACH OTHER.
YOU'LL BE SPENDING A LOT OF TIME TOGETHER.
KRONCH

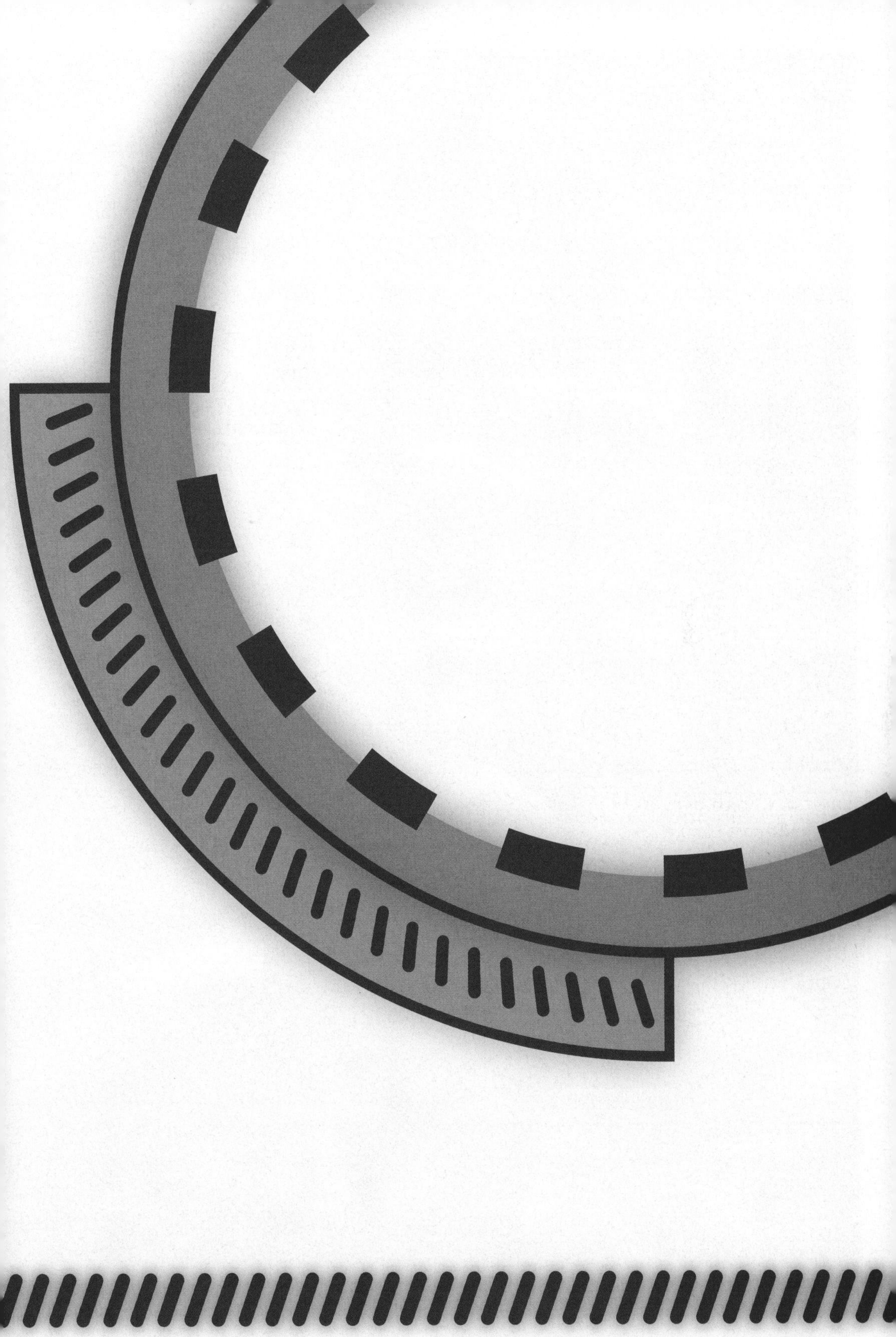

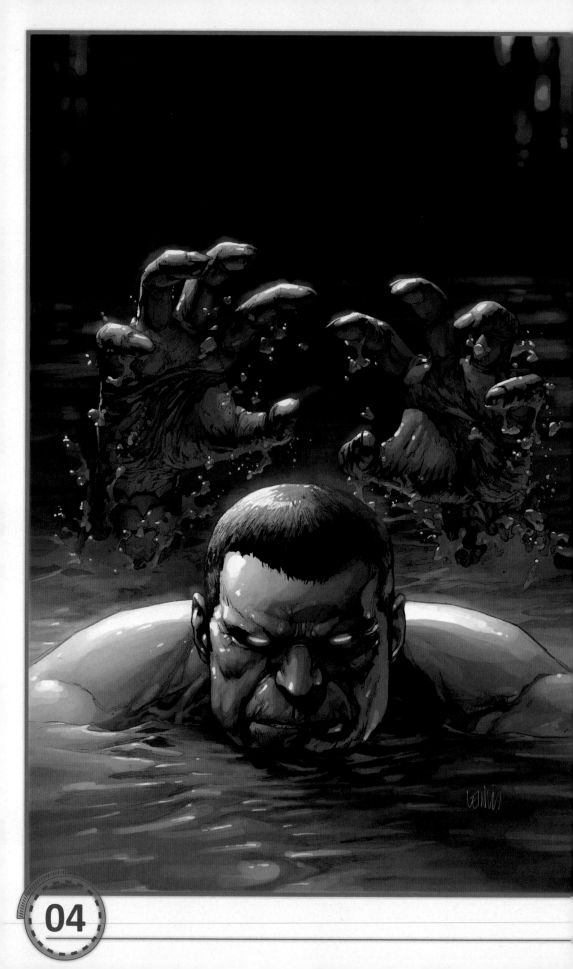

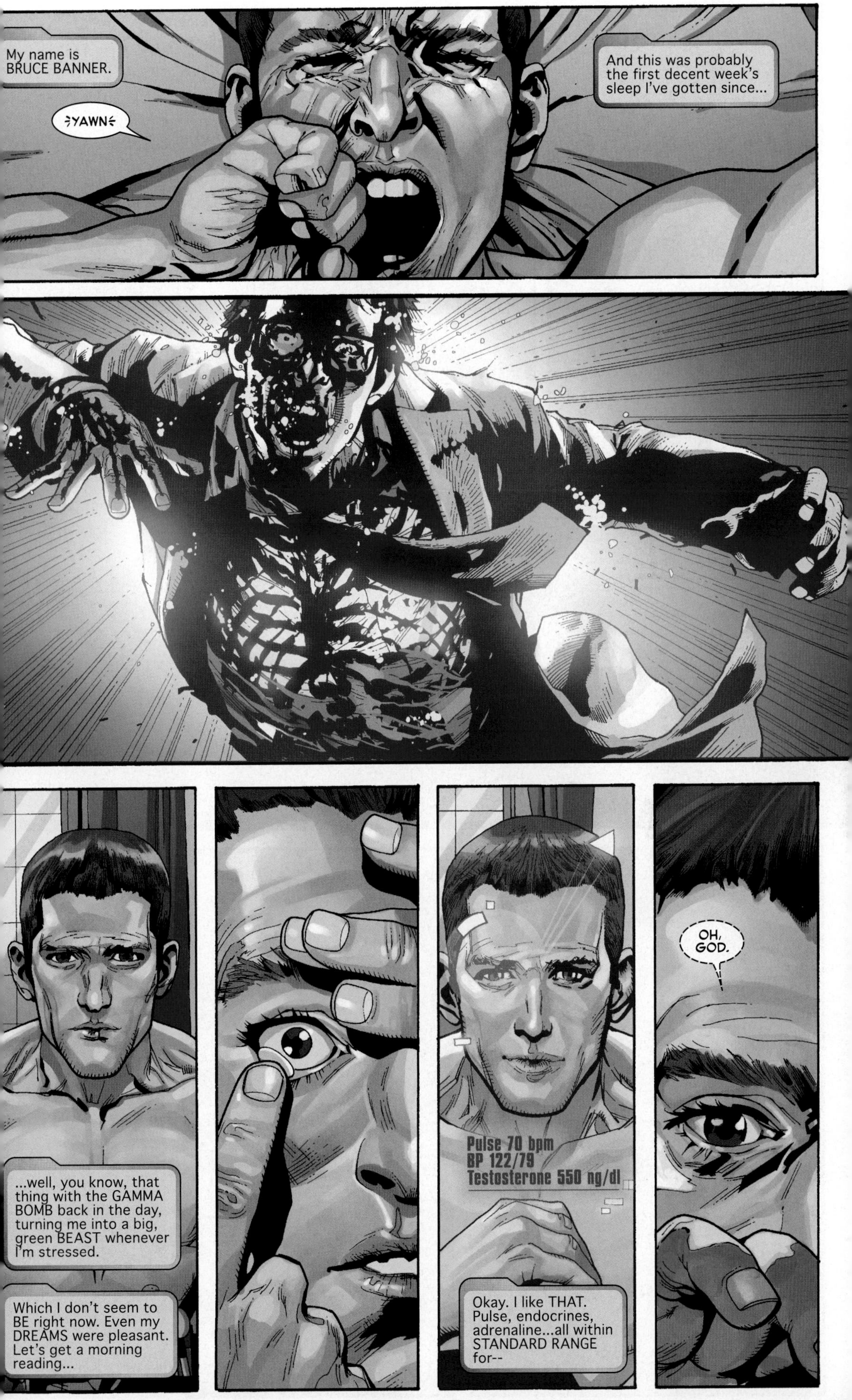
My name is BRUCE BANNER.
YAWN
And this was probably the first decent week's sleep I've gotten since...
...well, you know, that thing with the GAMMA BOMB back in the day, turning me into a big, green BEAST whenever I'm stressed.
Which I don't seem to BE right now. Even my DREAMS were pleasant. Let's get a morning reading...
Pulse 70 bpm
BP 122/79
Testosterone 550 ng/dl
Okay. I like THAT. Pulse, endocrines, adrenaline...all within STANDARD RANGE for--
OH, GOD.

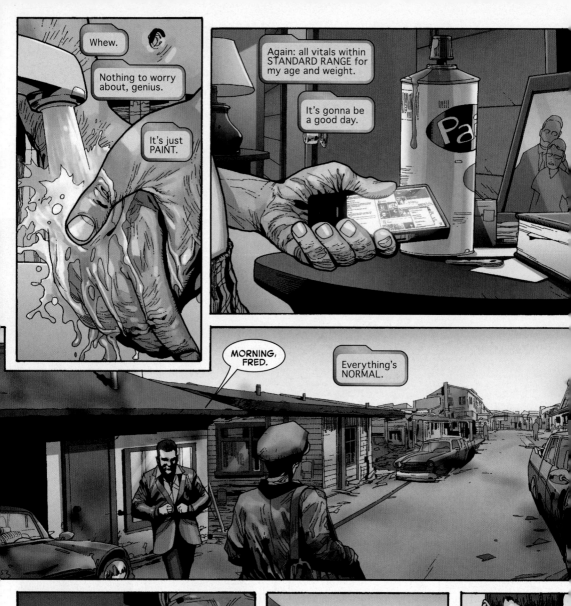

Whew.

Nothing to worry about, genius.

It's just PAINT.

Again: all vitals within STANDARD RANGE for my age and weight.

It's gonna be a good day.

MORNING, FRED.

Everything's NORMAL.

₴TCH₴

THERE YOU GO, BOY.

THAT'S BETTER.

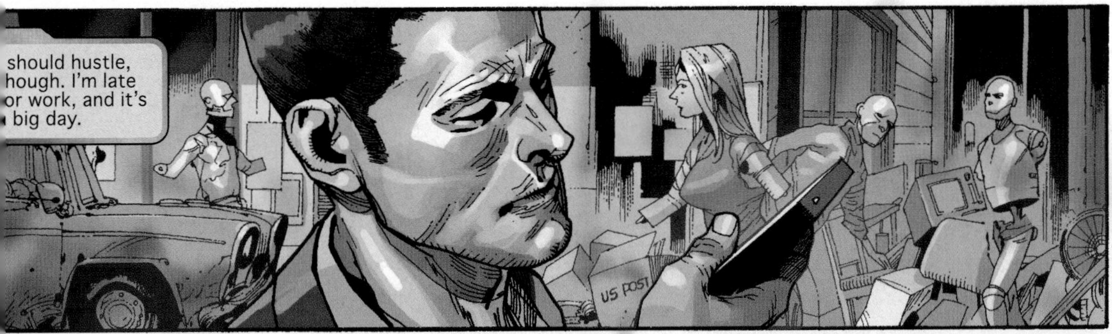
should hustle,
hough. I'm late
or work, and it's
big day.
US POST

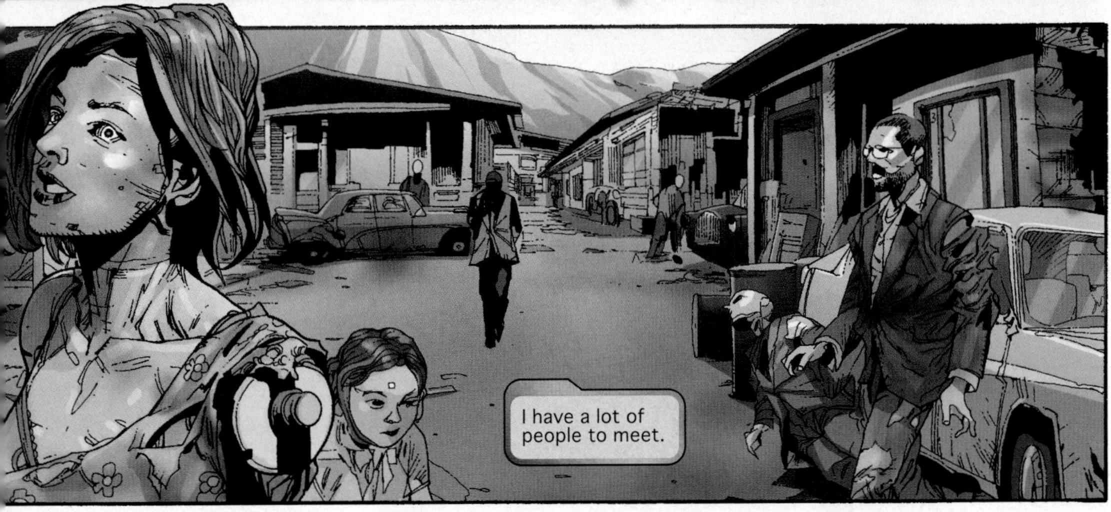
I have a lot of
people to meet.

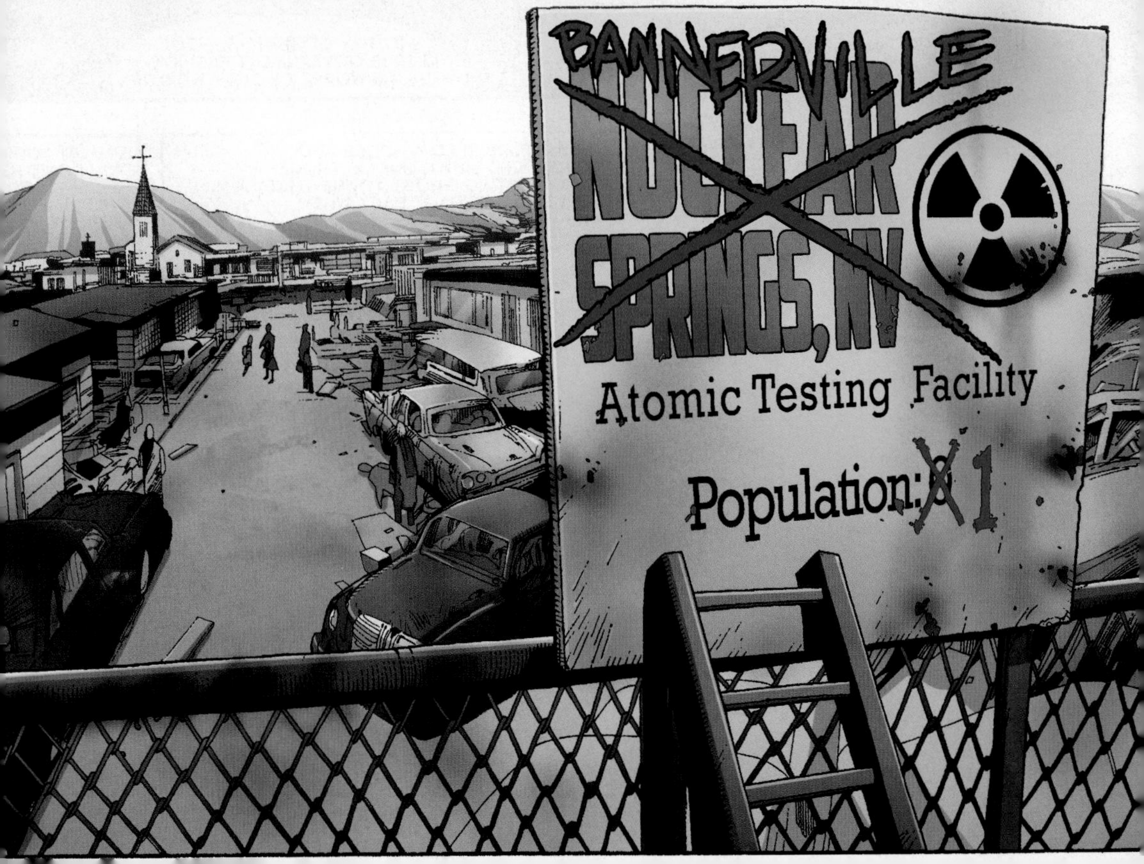
BANNERVILLE
NUCLEAR SPRINGS, NV
Atomic Testing Facility
Population: X 1

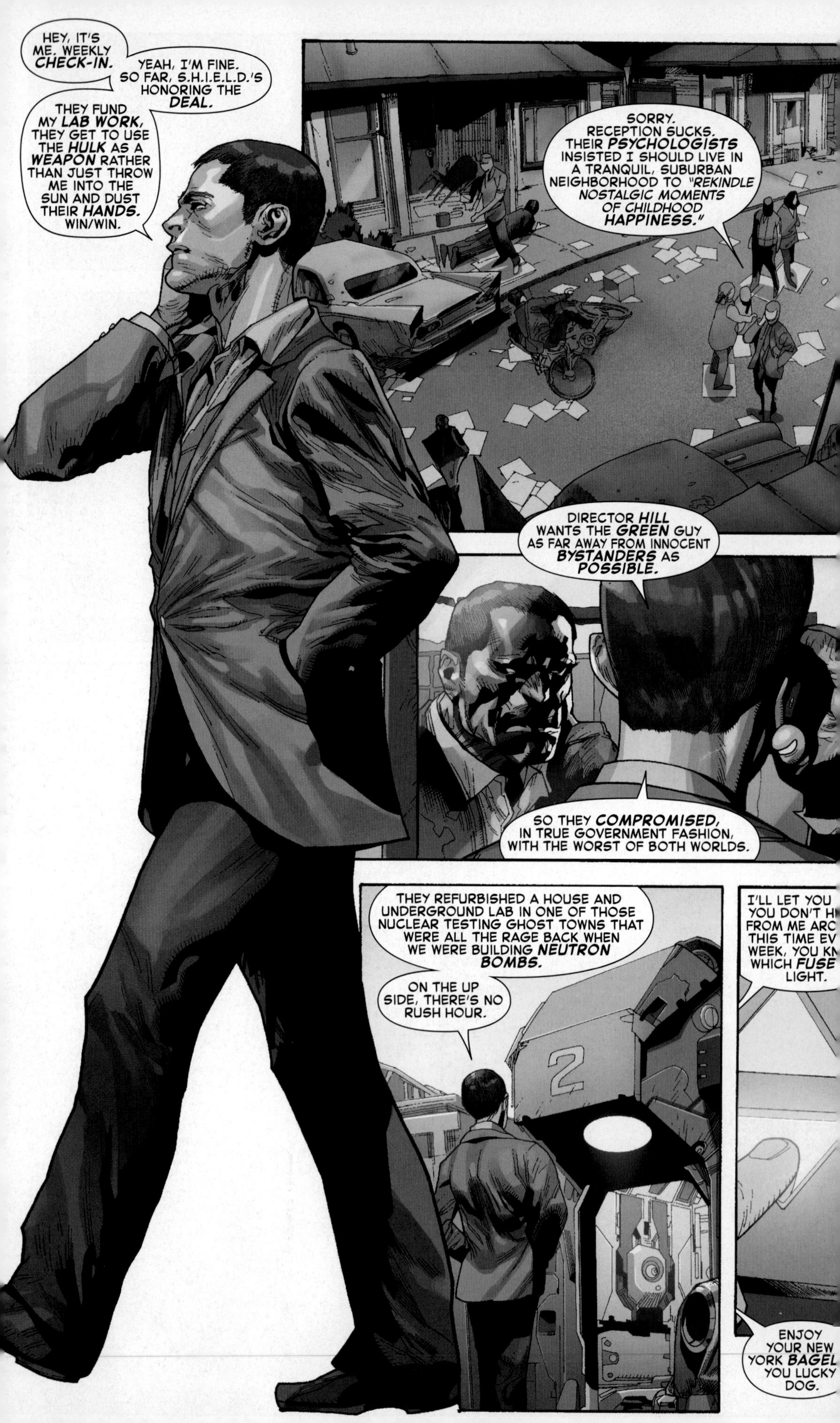
HEY, IT'S ME. WEEKLY CHECK-IN.
YEAH, I'M FINE. SO FAR, S.H.I.E.L.D.'S HONORING THE DEAL.
THEY FUND MY LAB WORK, THEY GET TO USE THE HULK AS A WEAPON RATHER THAN JUST THROW ME INTO THE SUN AND DUST THEIR HANDS. WIN/WIN.
SORRY. RECEPTION SUCKS. THEIR PSYCHOLOGISTS INSISTED I SHOULD LIVE IN A TRANQUIL, SUBURBAN NEIGHBORHOOD TO "REKINDLE NOSTALGIC MOMENTS OF CHILDHOOD HAPPINESS."
DIRECTOR HILL WANTS THE GREEN GUY AS FAR AWAY FROM INNOCENT BYSTANDERS AS POSSIBLE.
SO THEY COMPROMISED, IN TRUE GOVERNMENT FASHION, WITH THE WORST OF BOTH WORLDS.
THEY REFURBISHED A HOUSE AND UNDERGROUND LAB IN ONE OF THOSE NUCLEAR TESTING GHOST TOWNS THAT WERE ALL THE RAGE BACK WHEN WE WERE BUILDING NEUTRON BOMBS.
ON THE UP SIDE, THERE'S NO RUSH HOUR.
2
ENJOY YOUR NEW YORK BAGEL YOU LUCKY DOG.

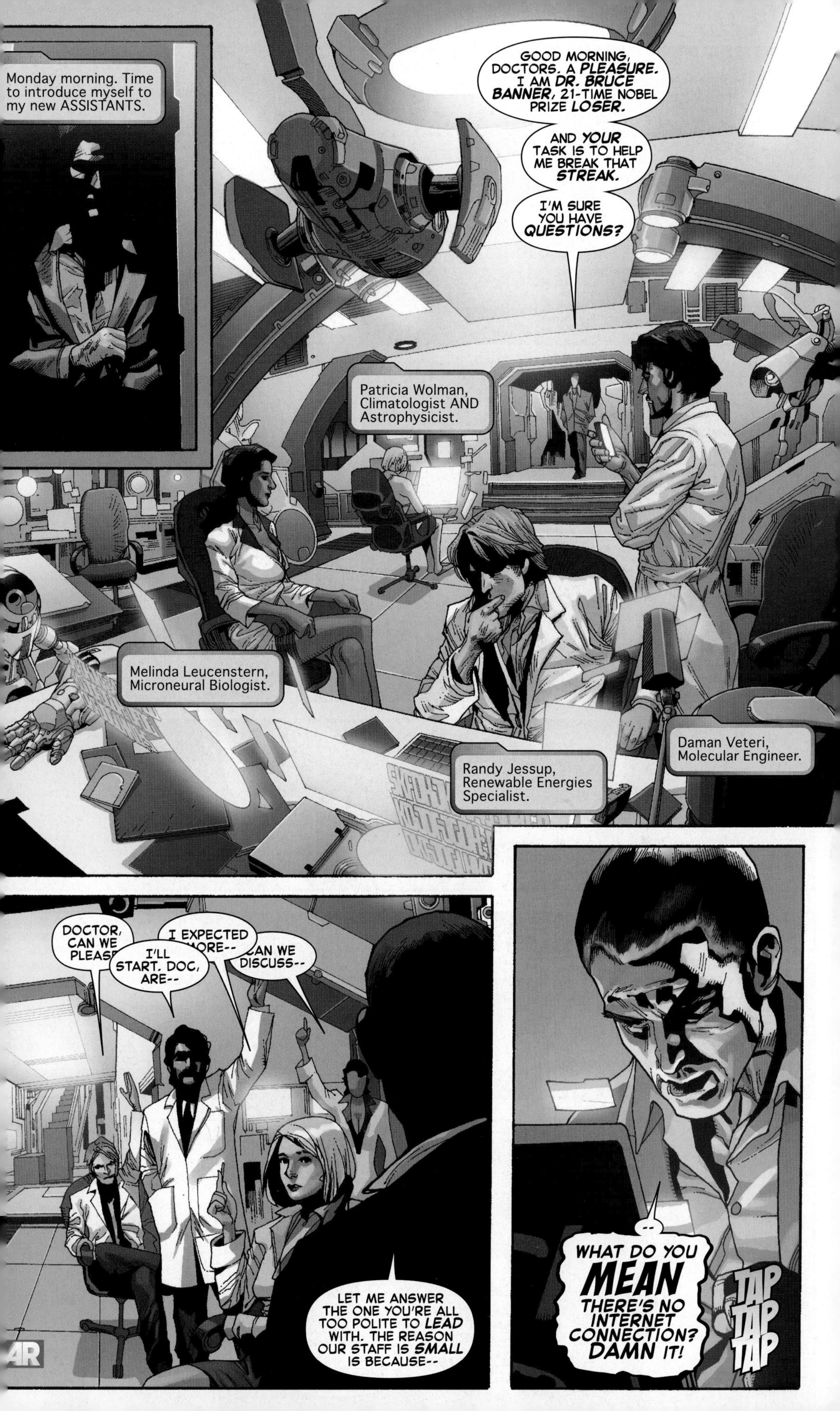

Monday morning. Time to introduce myself to my new ASSISTANTS.
GOOD MORNING, DOCTORS. A PLEASURE. I AM DR. BRUCE BANNER, 21-TIME NOBEL PRIZE LOSER.
AND YOUR TASK IS TO HELP ME BREAK THAT STREAK.
I'M SURE YOU HAVE QUESTIONS?
Patricia Wolman, Climatologist AND Astrophysicist.
Melinda Leucenstern, Microneural Biologist.
Randy Jessup, Renewable Energies Specialist.
Daman Veteri, Molecular Engineer.
DOCTOR, CAN WE PLEAS
I'LL START. DOC, ARE--
I EXPECTED MORE--
CAN WE DISCUSS--
LET ME ANSWER THE ONE YOU'RE ALL TOO POLITE TO LEAD WITH. THE REASON OUR STAFF IS SMALL IS BECAUSE--
--
WHAT DO YOU MEAN THERE'S NO INTERNET CONNECTION? DAMN IT!
TAP TAP TAP

--BECAUSE IT'S REALLY HARD TO FIND QUALIFIED TECHNICIANS WHOSE *PANTS* WOULDN'T HAVE EXPLODED JUST NOW.

YOU JUST PASSED YOUR *FINAL EXAM.* TRUST ME, *HULK HAPPENS.* BUT WHEN IT *DOES,* FOR *REAL,* YOU *CAN* GET TO *SAFETY.*

IF YOU RUN.

NOW, LET'S TALK *MISSI STATEMENT.* FOUR WOR VERY SIMPLE.

"HULK BREAKS, BANNER BUILDS."

WITH YOUR *HELP* WE'RE GOING TO E RESTORING MY GO SCIENTIFIC NAME CREATING DEVICES THE BETTERMENT ALL *MANKIND.*

CLEAN ENERGIES. ENVIRONMENT PURIFIERS. DISEASE BARRIERS. THE LIKE. AND, OH, THE *TOYS* AT OUR *DISPOSAL....!*

WHO KNOWS WHAT *THIS* IS? VETERI?

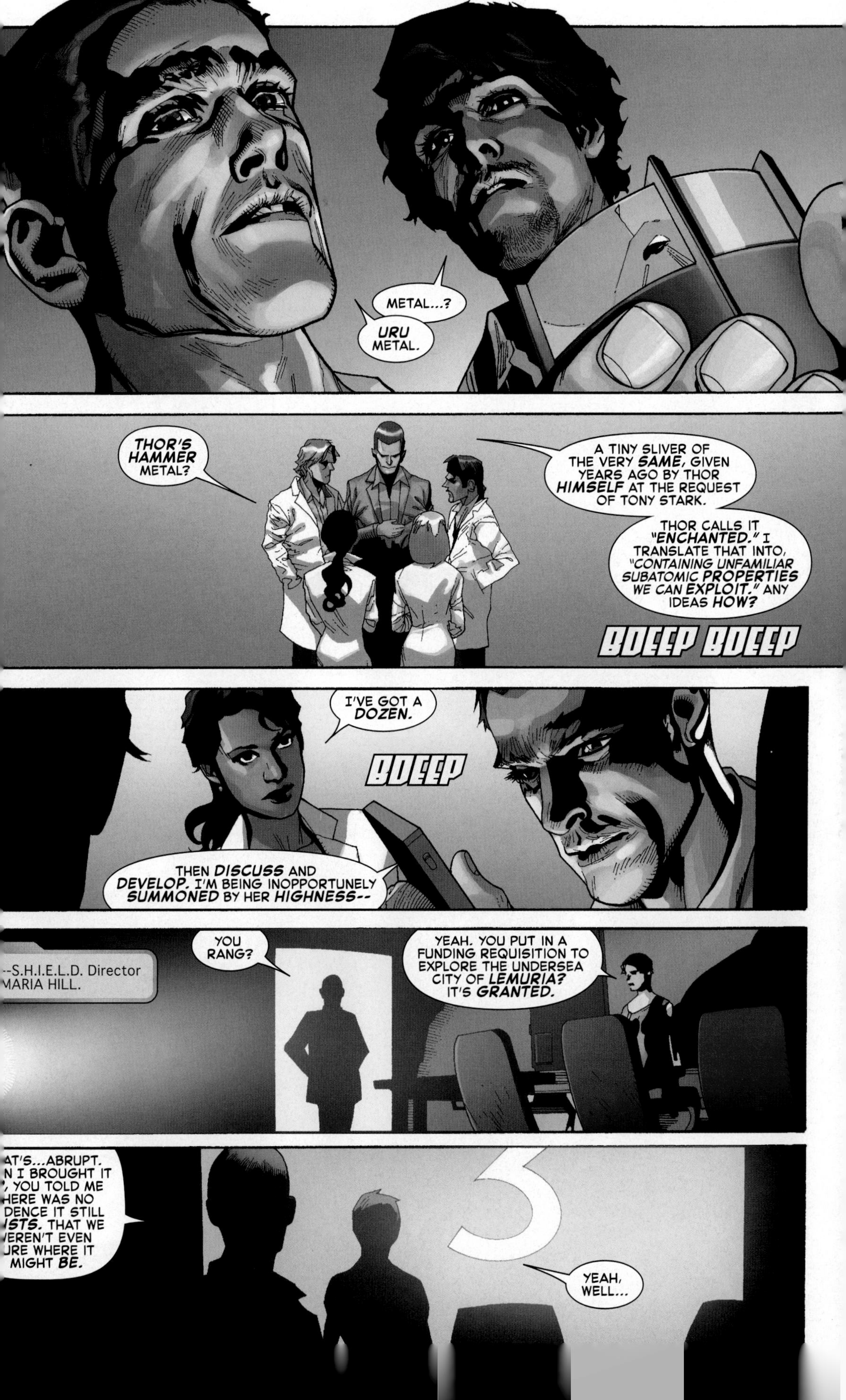
METAL...?
URU METAL.
THOR'S HAMMER METAL?
A TINY SLIVER OF THE VERY SAME, GIVEN YEARS AGO BY THOR HIMSELF AT THE REQUEST OF TONY STARK.
THOR CALLS IT "ENCHANTED." I TRANSLATE THAT INTO, "CONTAINING UNFAMILIAR SUBATOMIC PROPERTIES WE CAN EXPLOIT." ANY IDEAS HOW?
BDEEP BDEEP
I'VE GOT A DOZEN.
BDEEP
THEN DISCUSS AND DEVELOP. I'M BEING INOPPORTUNELY SUMMONED BY HER HIGHNESS--
--S.H.I.E.L.D. Director
MARIA HILL.
YOU RANG?
YEAH. YOU PUT IN A FUNDING REQUISITION TO EXPLORE THE UNDERSEA CITY OF LEMURIA? IT'S GRANTED.
AT'S...ABRUPT. N I BROUGHT IT , YOU TOLD ME HERE WAS NO DENCE IT STILL ISTS. THAT WE VEREN'T EVEN URE WHERE IT MIGHT BE.
YEAH, WELL...

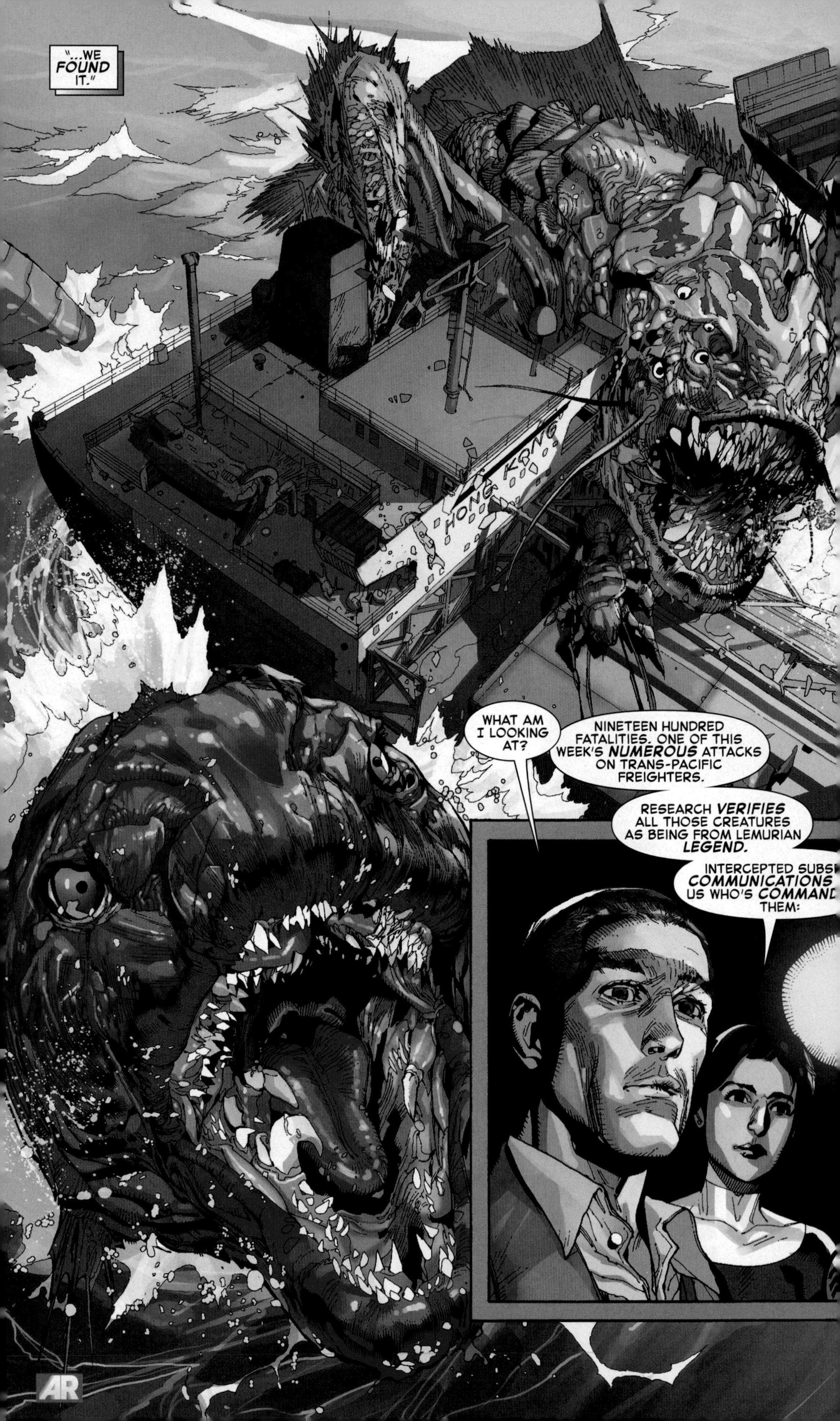
"...WE FOUND IT."
HONG KONG
WHAT AM I LOOKING AT?
NINETEEN HUNDRED FATALITIES. ONE OF THIS WEEK'S NUMEROUS ATTACKS ON TRANS-PACIFIC FREIGHTERS.
RESEARCH VERIFIES ALL THOSE CREATURES AS BEING FROM LEMURIAN LEGEND.
INTERCEPTED SUBS COMMUNICATIONS US WHO'S COMMAND THEM:

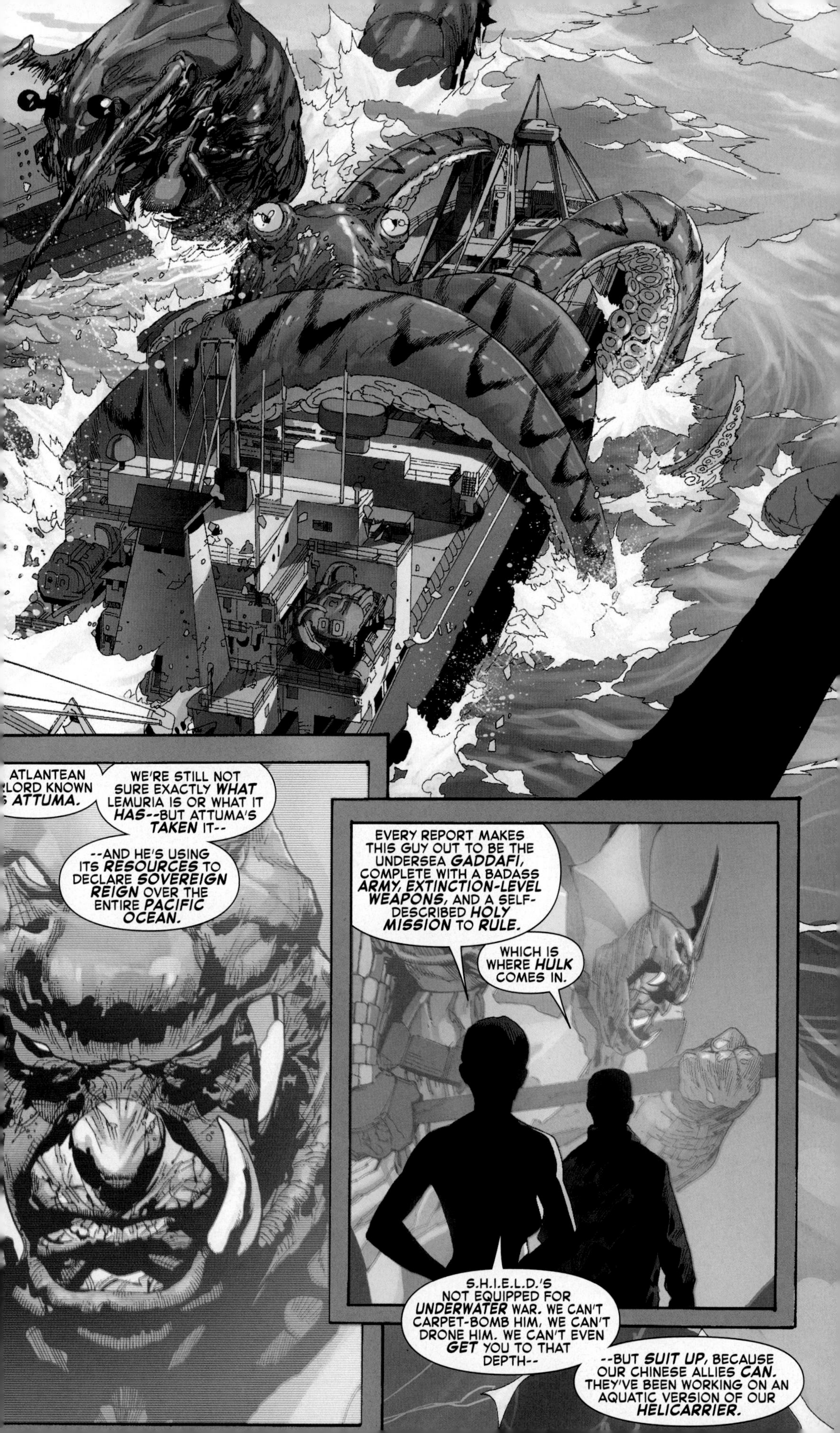
ATLANTEAN RLORD KNOWN ATTUMA.
WE'RE STILL NOT SURE EXACTLY WHAT LEMURIA IS OR WHAT IT HAS--BUT ATTUMA'S TAKEN IT--
--AND HE'S USING ITS RESOURCES TO DECLARE SOVEREIGN REIGN OVER THE ENTIRE PACIFIC OCEAN.
EVERY REPORT MAKES THIS GUY OUT TO BE THE UNDERSEA GADDAFI, COMPLETE WITH A BADASS ARMY, EXTINCTION-LEVEL WEAPONS, AND A SELF-DESCRIBED HOLY MISSION TO RULE.
WHICH IS WHERE HULK COMES IN.
S.H.I.E.L.D.'S NOT EQUIPPED FOR UNDERWATER WAR. WE CAN'T CARPET-BOMB HIM, WE CAN'T DRONE HIM. WE CAN'T EVEN GET YOU TO THAT DEPTH--
--BUT SUIT UP, BECAUSE OUR CHINESE ALLIES CAN. THEY'VE BEEN WORKING ON AN AQUATIC VERSION OF OUR HELICARRIER.

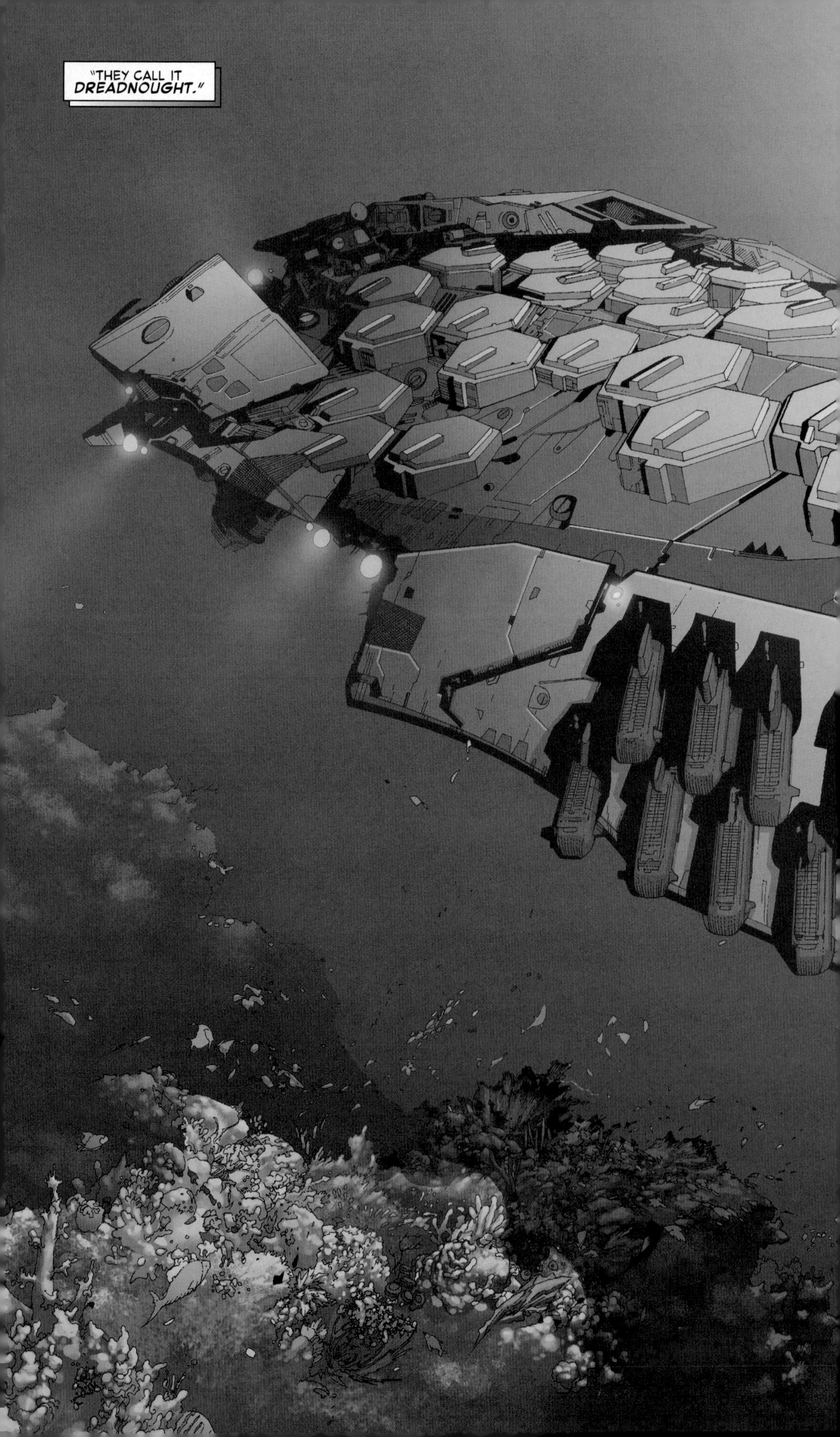
"THEY CALL IT DREADNOUGHT."

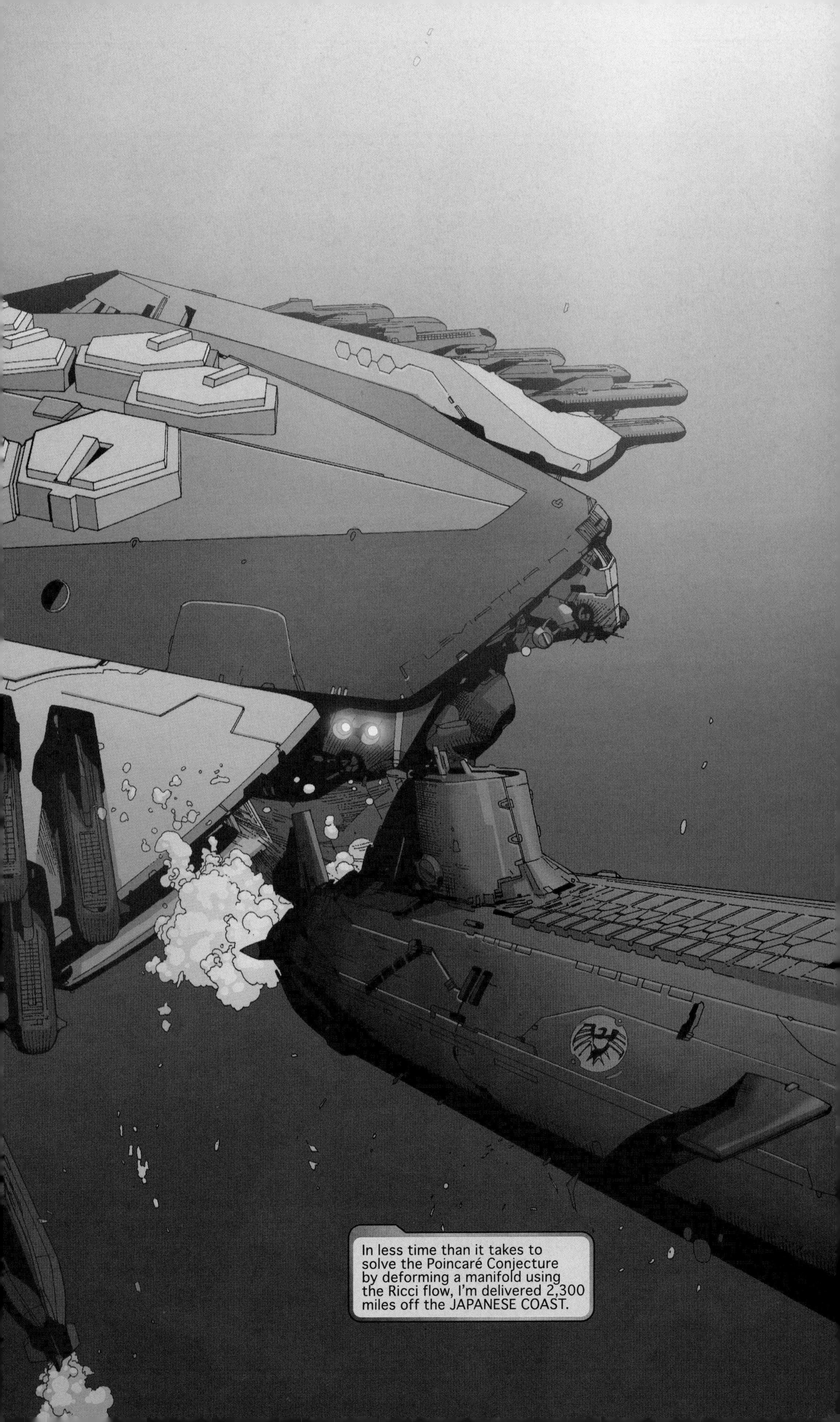
In less time than it takes to solve the Poincaré Conjecture by deforming a manifold using the Ricci flow, I'm delivered 2,300 miles off the JAPANESE COAST.

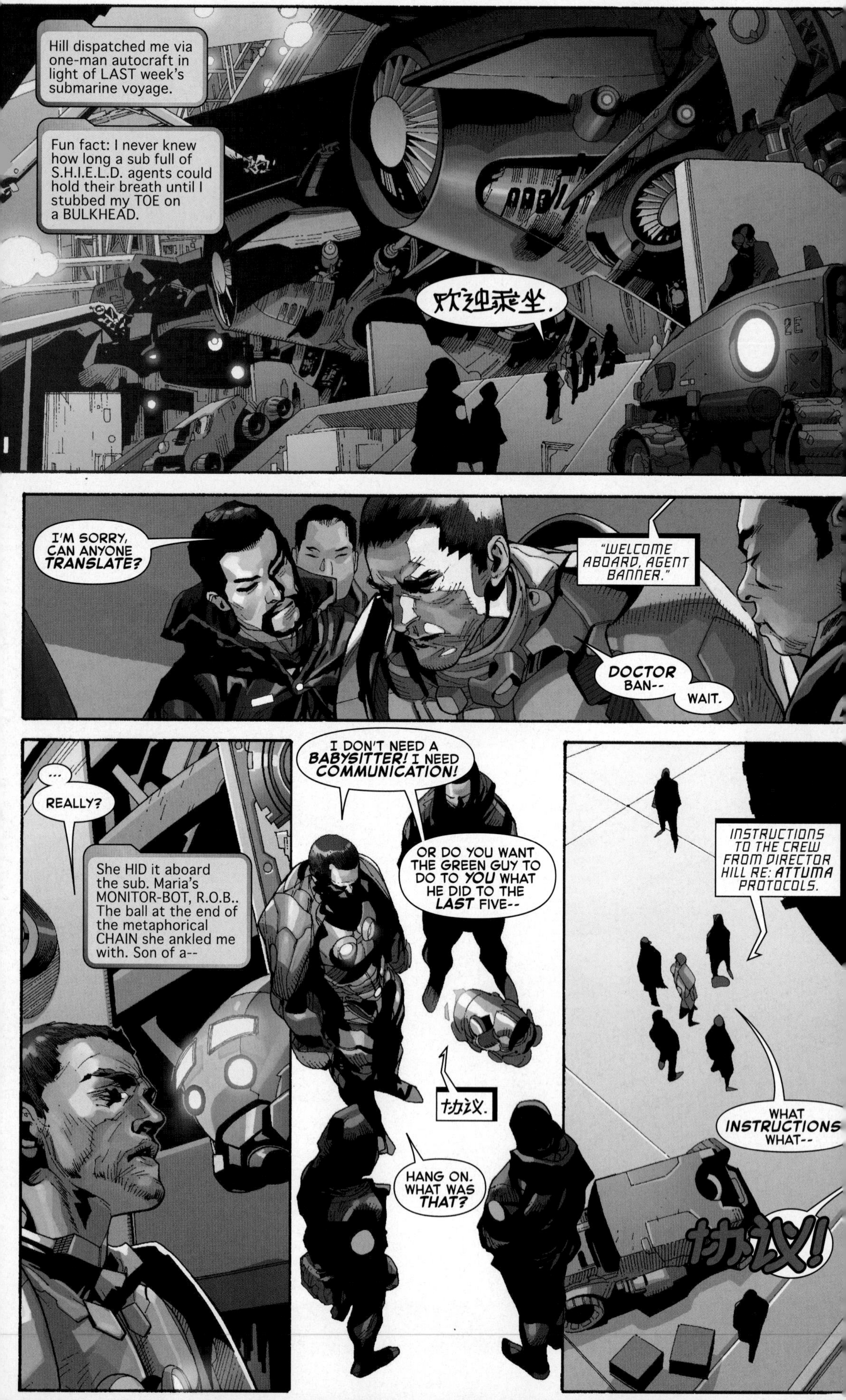
Hill dispatched me via one-man autocraft in light of LAST week's submarine voyage.
Fun fact: I never knew how long a sub full of S.H.I.E.L.D. agents could hold their breath until I stubbed my TOE on a BULKHEAD.
欢迎乘坐.
I'M SORRY, CAN ANYONE *TRANSLATE?*
"WELCOME ABOARD, AGENT BANNER."
DOCTOR BAN--
WAIT.
...
REALLY?
She HID it aboard the sub. Maria's MONITOR-BOT, R.O.B.. The ball at the end of the metaphorical CHAIN she ankled me with. Son of a--
I DON'T NEED A *BABYSITTER!* I NEED *COMMUNICATION!*
OR DO YOU WANT THE GREEN GUY TO DO TO *YOU* WHAT HE DID TO THE *LAST* FIVE--
协议.
HANG ON. WHAT WAS *THAT?*
INSTRUCTIONS TO THE CREW FROM DIRECTOR HILL RE: *ATTUMA* PROTOCOLS.
WHAT *INSTRUCTIONS* WHAT--
协议!

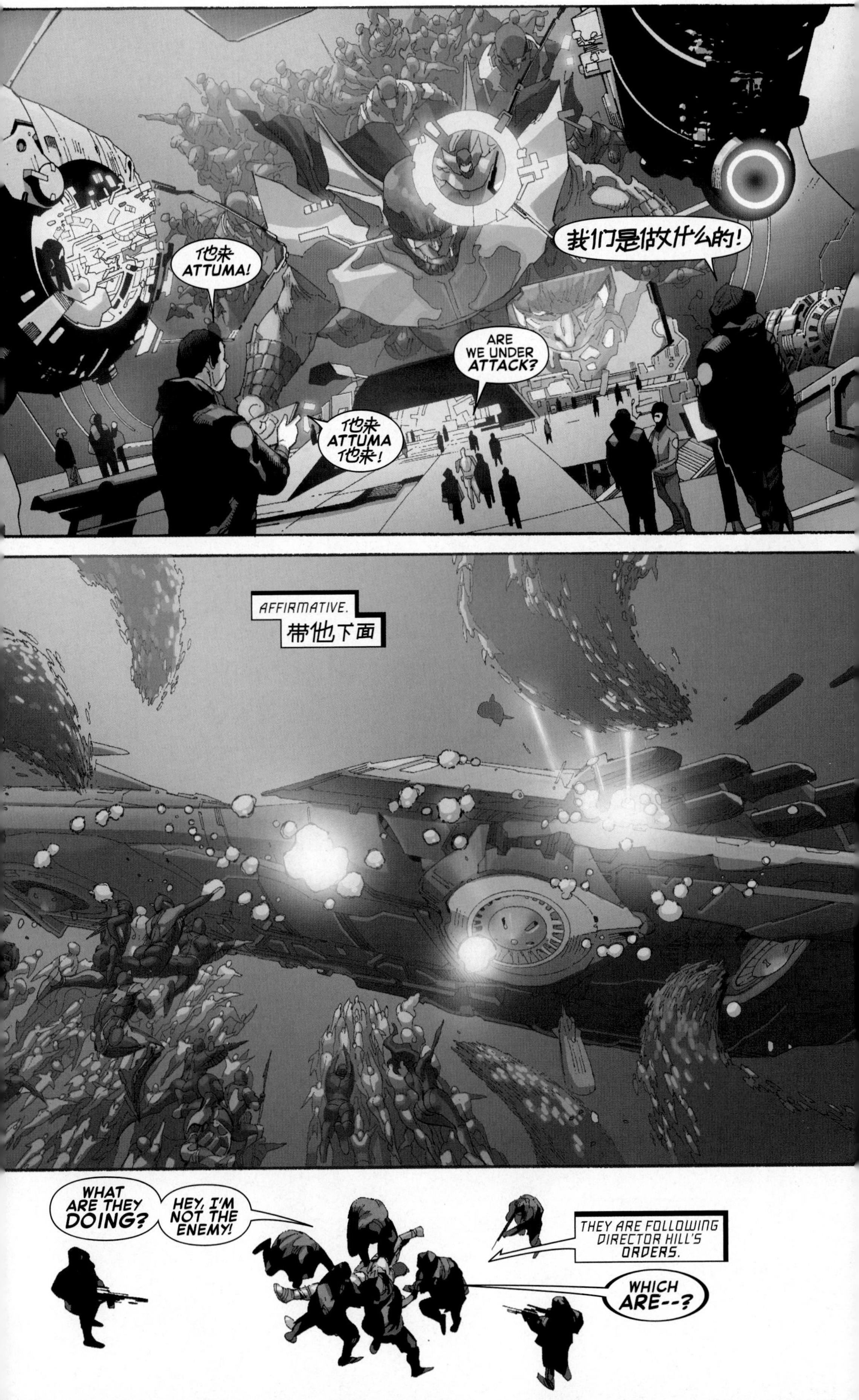
他来 ATTUMA!
我们是做什么的!
ARE WE UNDER ATTACK?
他来 ATTUMA 他来!
AFFIRMATIVE. 带他下面
WHAT ARE THEY DOING?
HEY, I'M NOT THE ENEMY!
THEY ARE FOLLOWING DIRECTOR HILL'S ORDERS.
WHICH ARE--?

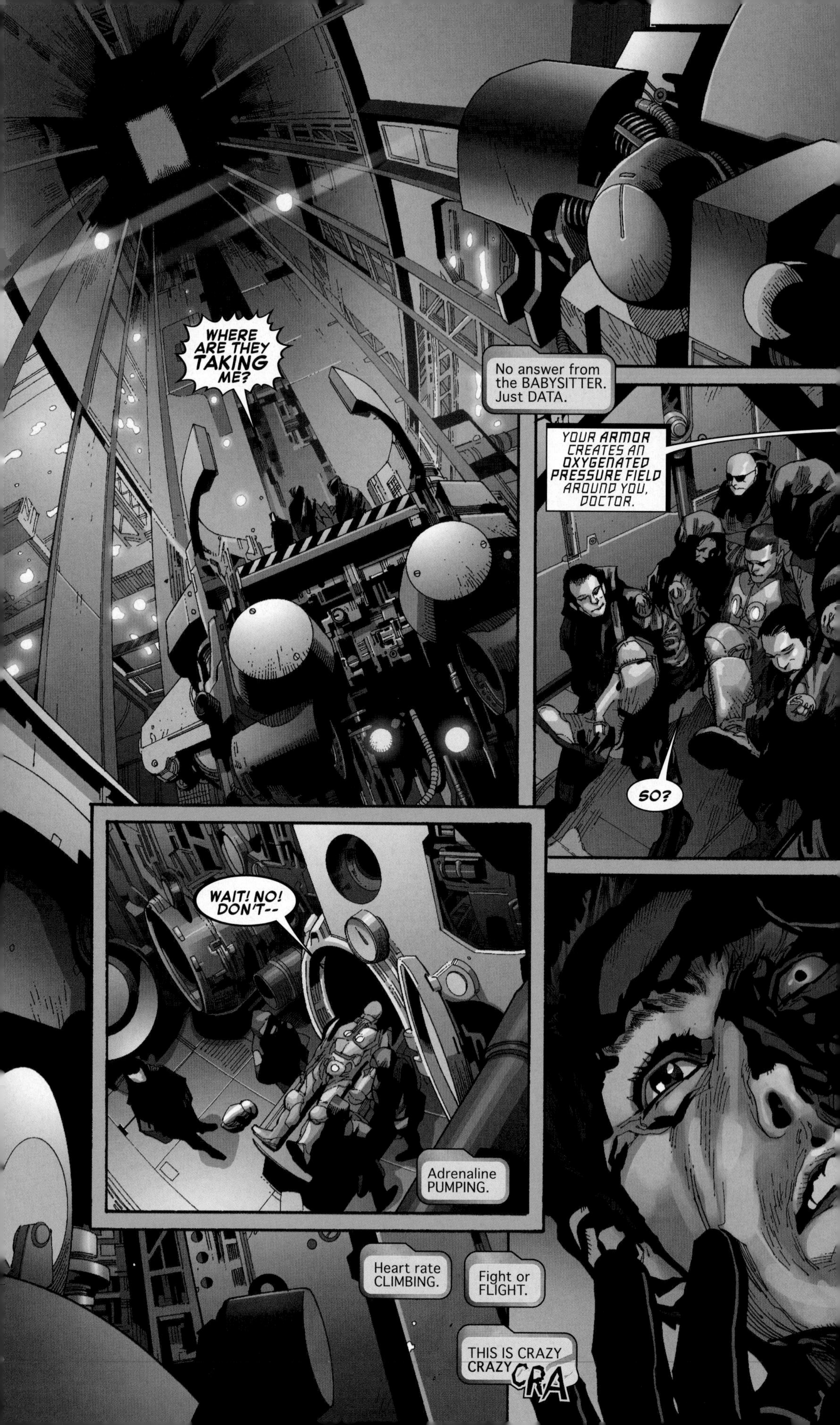

WHERE ARE THEY TAKING ME?
No answer from the BABYSITTER. Just DATA.
YOUR ARMOR CREATES AN OXYGENATED PRESSURE FIELD AROUND YOU, DOCTOR.
SO?
WAIT! NO! DON'T--
Adrenaline PUMPING.
Heart rate CLIMBING.
Fight or FLIGHT.
THIS IS CRAZY CRAZY
CRA

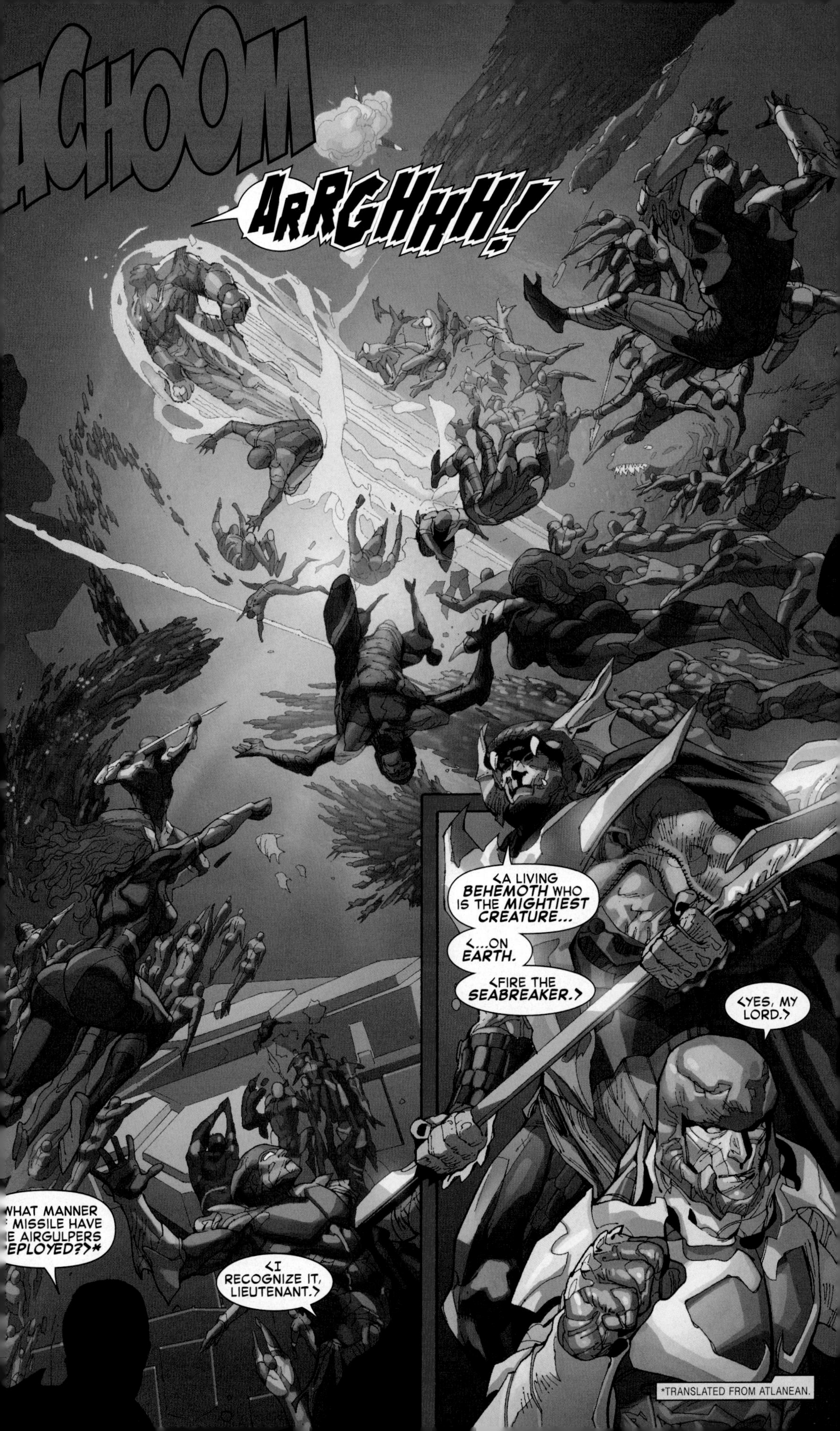

CHOOM
ARRGHHH!
<A LIVING BEHEMOTH WHO IS THE MIGHTIEST CREATURE...
<...ON EARTH.
<FIRE THE SEABREAKER.>
<YES, MY LORD.>
WHAT MANNER MISSILE HAVE AIRGULPERS EPLOYED?>*
<I RECOGNIZE IT, LIEUTENANT.>
*TRANSLATED FROM ATLANEAN.

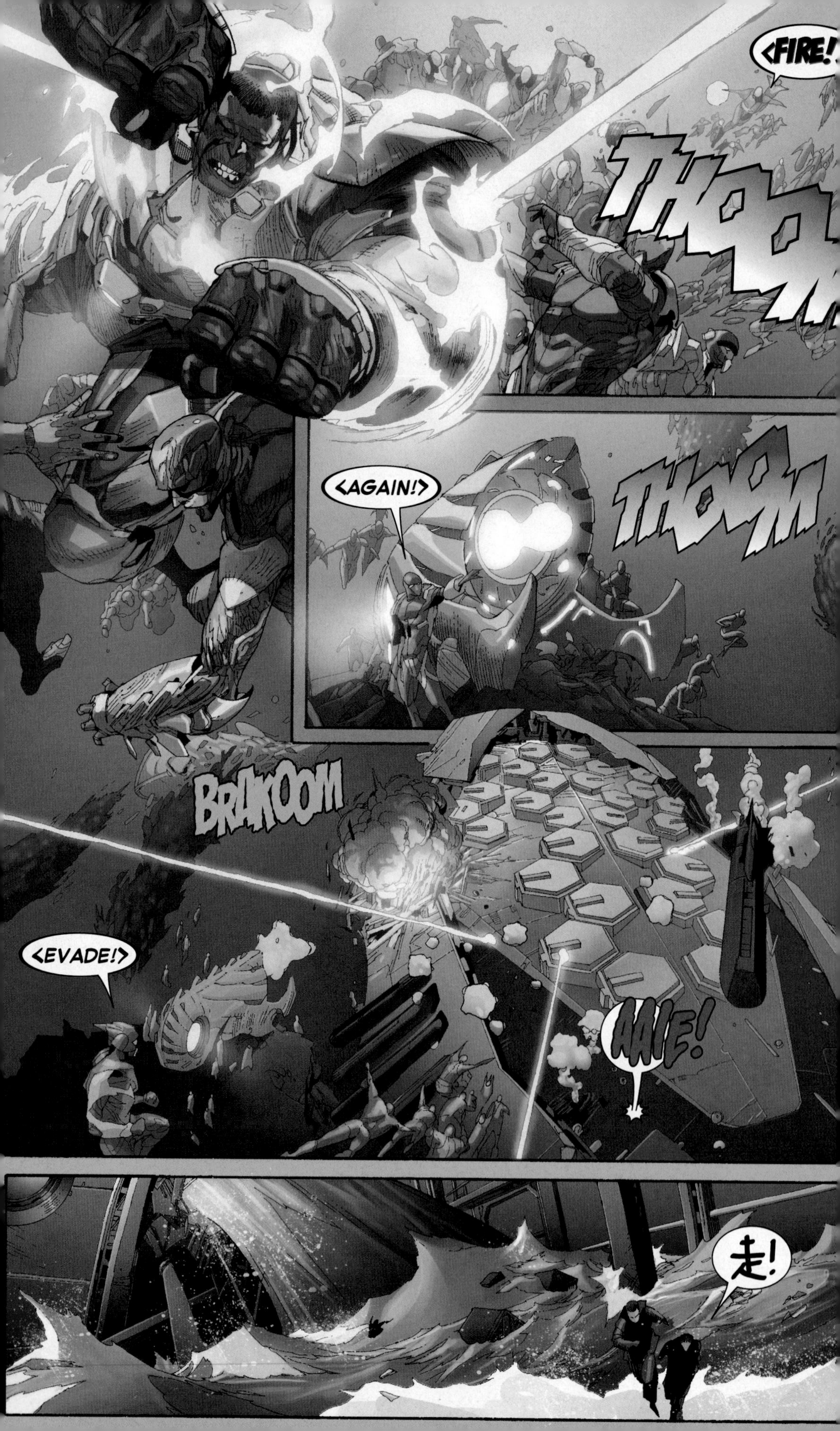
<FIRE!
THOO
<AGAIN!>
THOOM
BRAKOOM
<EVADE!>
AAIE!
走!

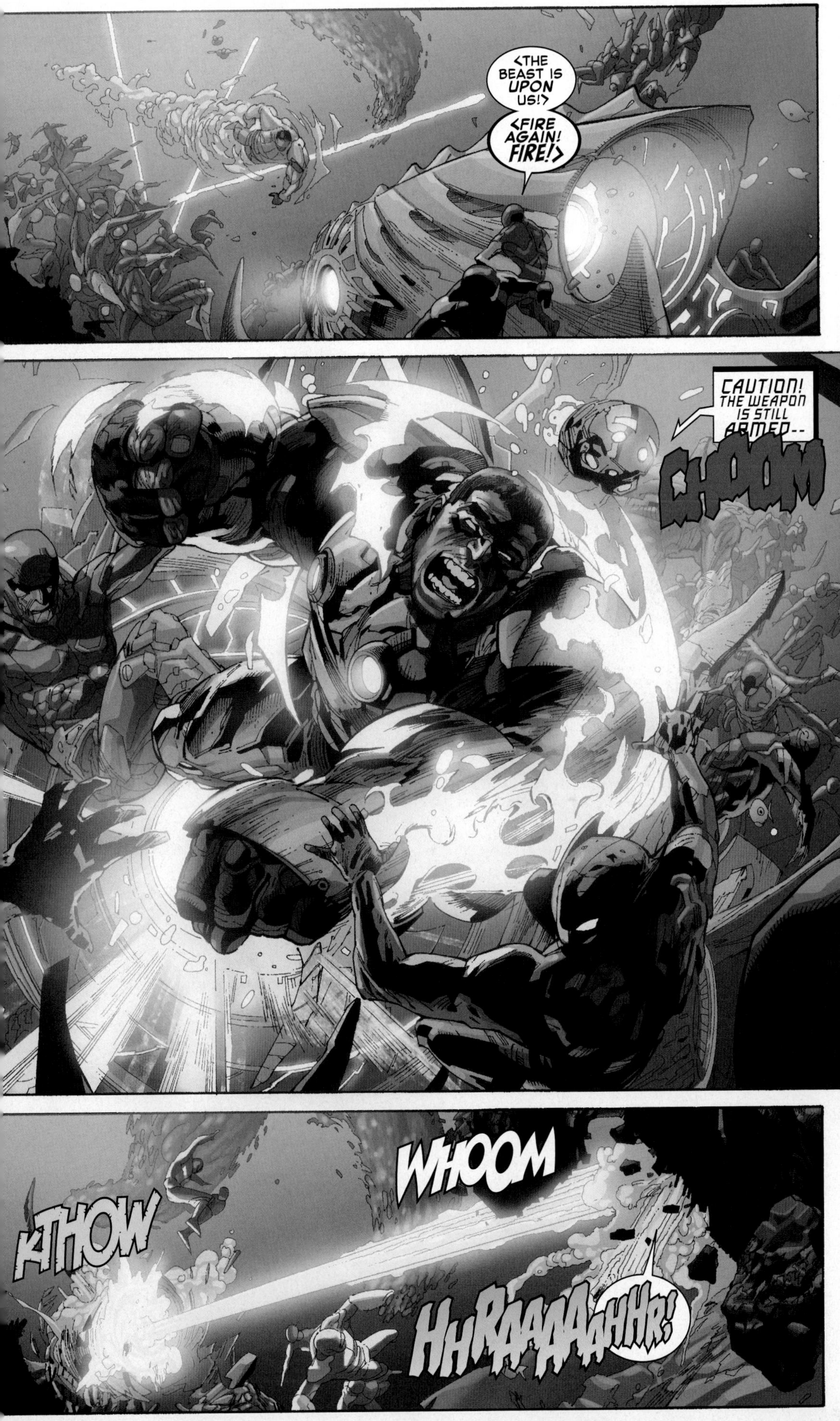
<THE BEAST IS UPON US!>
<FIRE AGAIN! FIRE!>
CAUTION! THE WEAPON IS STILL ARMED--
CHOOM
WHOOM
KTHOW
HHRAAAAAHHR!

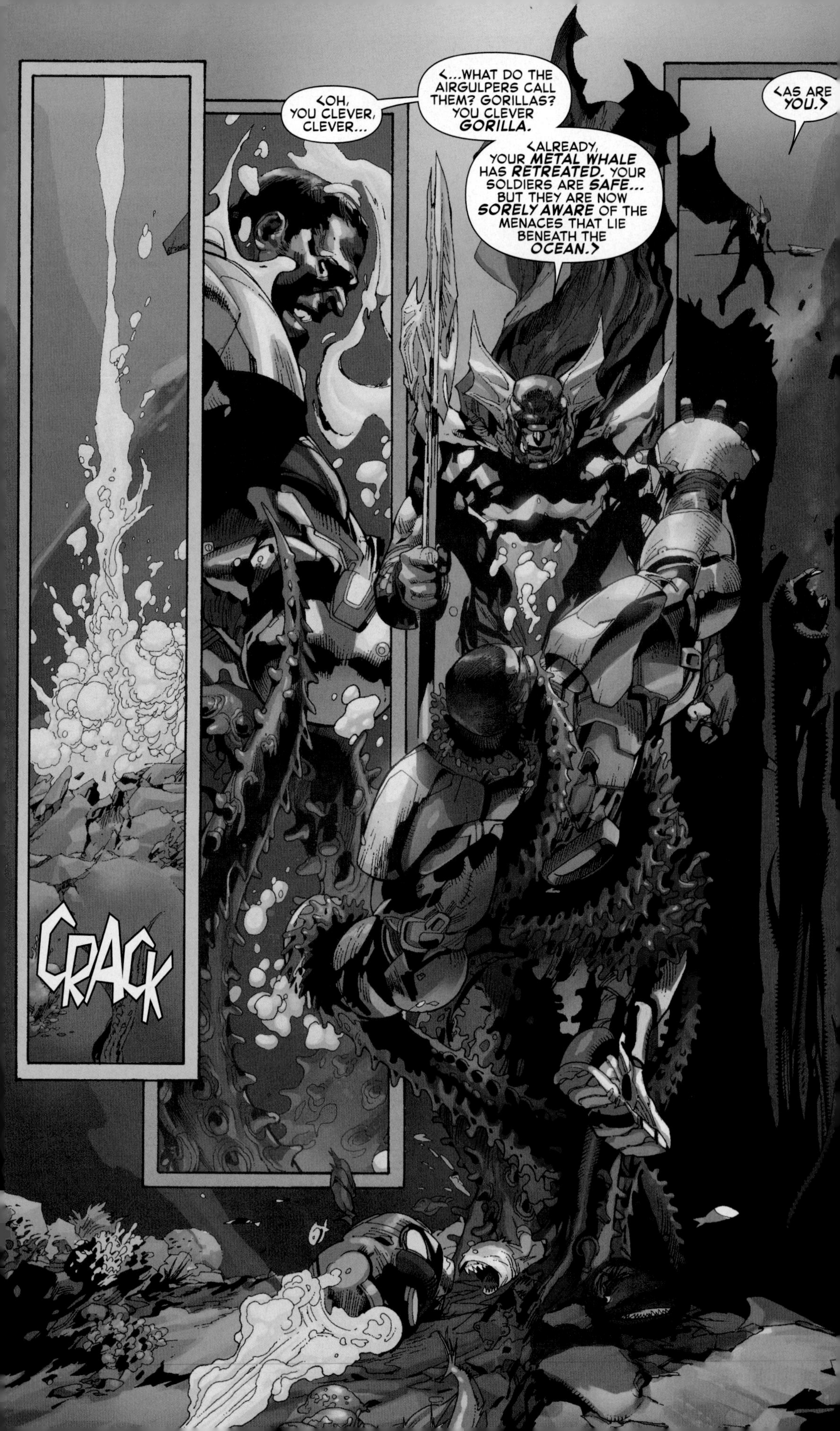

<OH, YOU CLEVER, CLEVER...
<...WHAT DO THE AIRGULPERS CALL THEM? GORILLAS? YOU CLEVER GORILLA.
<ALREADY, YOUR METAL WHALE HAS RETREATED. YOUR SOLDIERS ARE SAFE... BUT THEY ARE NOW SORELY AWARE OF THE MENACES THAT LIE BENEATH THE OCEAN.>
<AS ARE YOU.>
CRACK

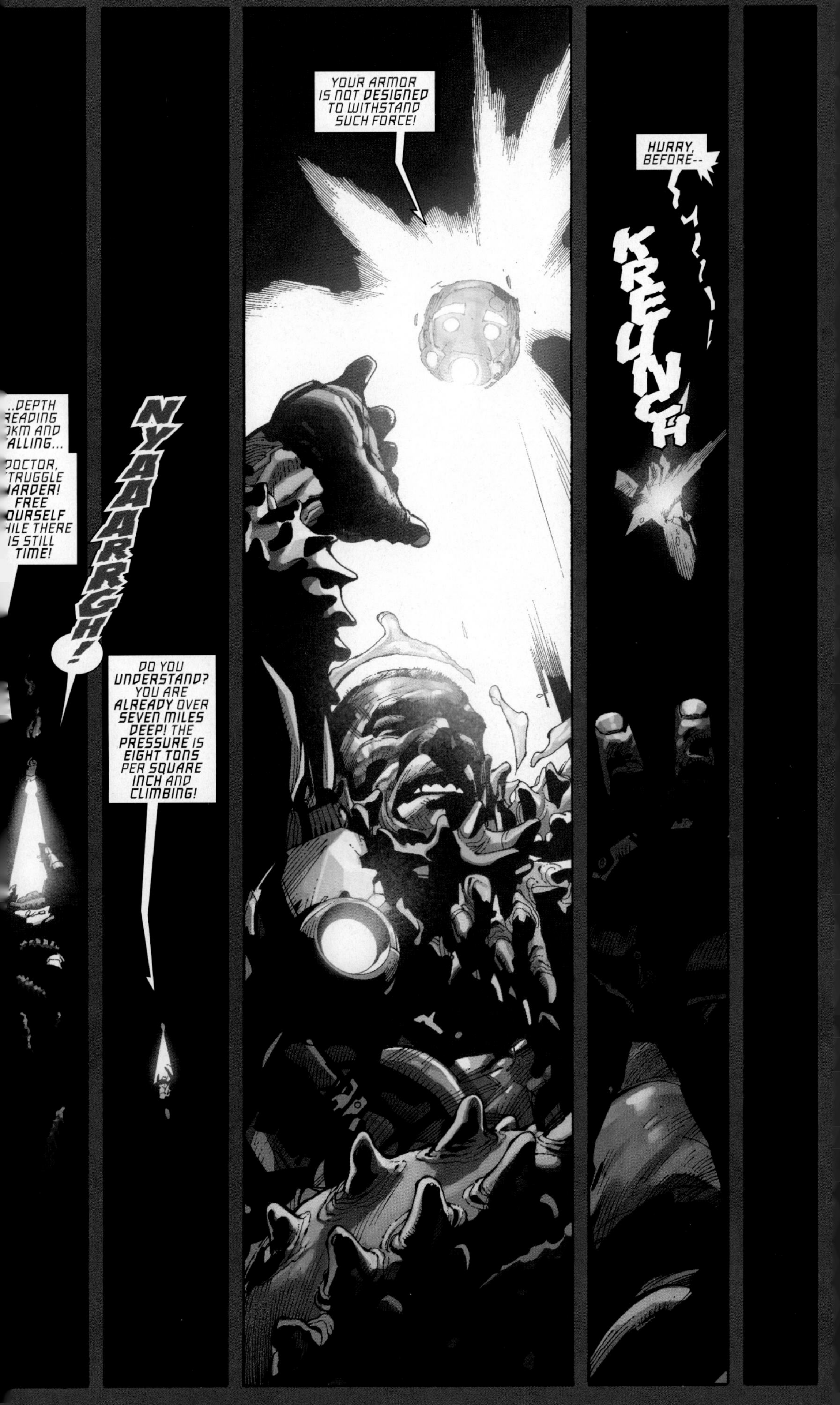
..DEPTH
DOCTOR,
HARDER!
FREE
IS STILL
TIME!
NYAAAARRGH!
DO YOU UNDERSTAND? YOU ARE ALREADY OVER SEVEN MILES DEEP! THE PRESSURE IS EIGHT TONS PER SQUARE INCH AND CLIMBING!
YOUR ARMOR IS NOT DESIGNED TO WITHSTAND SUCH FORCE!
HURRY, BEFORE--
KREUNCH

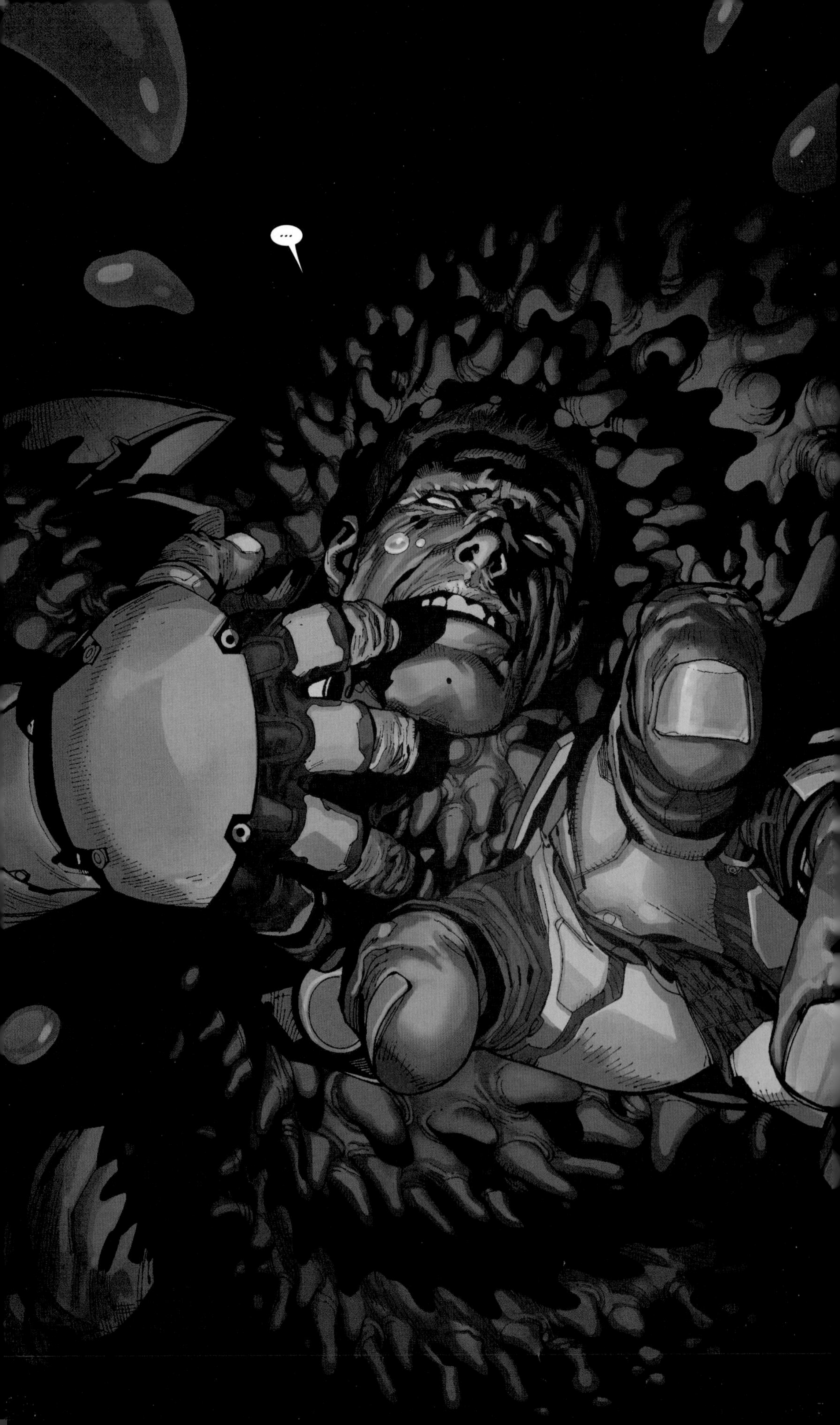
...

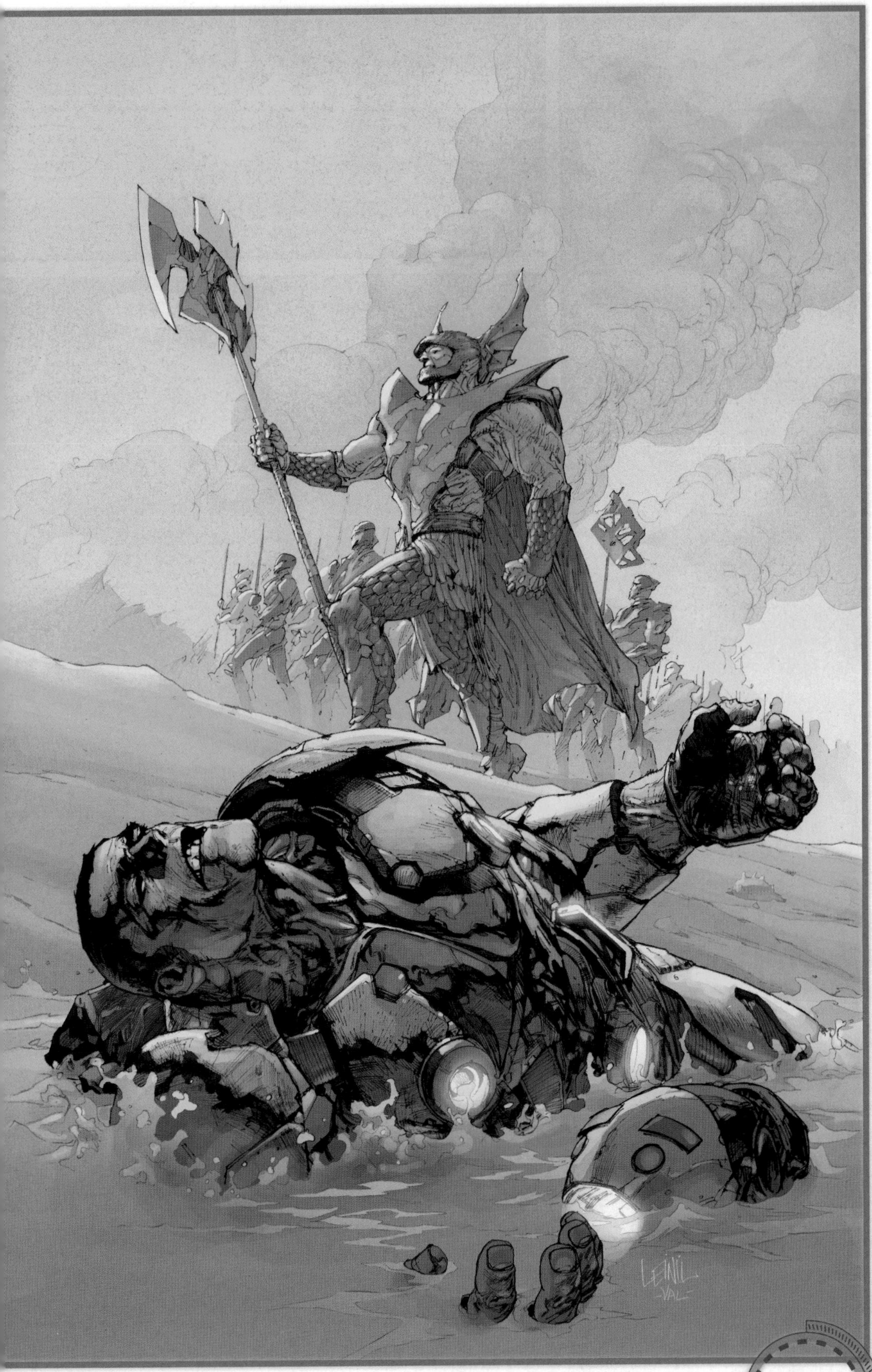
LEINIL
VAL

05

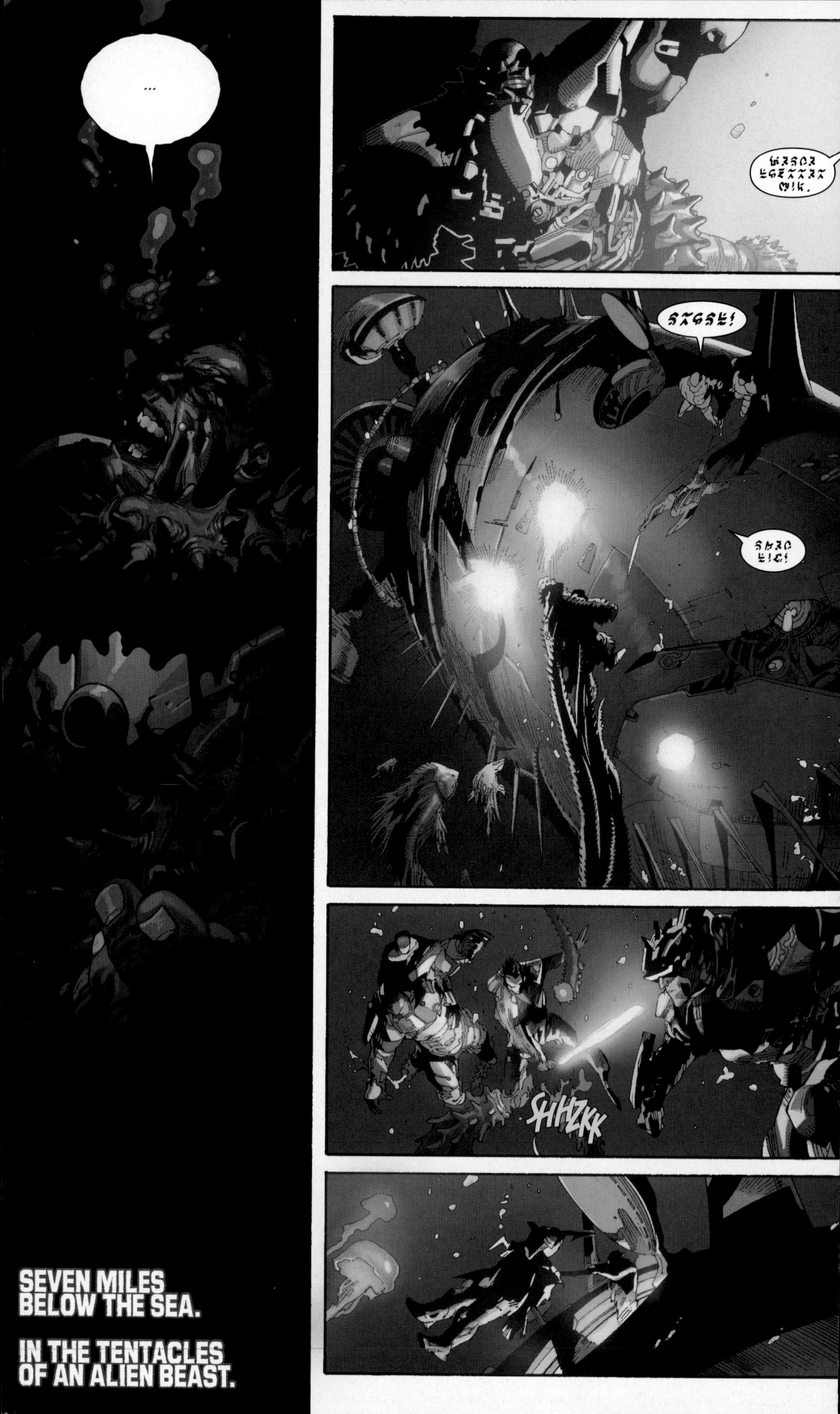
...
SHHZKK
SEVEN MILES BELOW THE SEA.
IN THE TENTACLES OF AN ALIEN BEAST.

<ADMIRAL, WE ARE TAKING ON WATER AT A SIGNIFICANT RATE!>*

THE CHINESE MEGA-SUB, THE DREADNOUGHT.

* TRANSLATED FROM CHINESE.

<THEN RADIO S.H.I.E.L.D.-PACIFIC! TELL THEM WE'VE BEEN FORCED TO SURFACE!>

<SURFACE? SIR, WHAT IS TO STOP ATTUMA FROM ATTACKING AGAIN? AND HAVE YOU FORGOTTEN BANNER? DO WE SIMPLY ABANDON HIM?>

<WE MUST, ADMIRAL. DREADNOUGHT REQUIRES IMMEDIATE REPAIR.>

<SIR, IN HUMANITY'S NAME--->

<IF YOU FEEL SO STRONGLY, LIN, ASSEMBLE A CREW AND TAKE A SUB OUT. TRACK ATTUMA'S MOVEMENTS--DISCREETLY-- AND REMAIN ALERT FOR BANNER.>

<AND LIN--->

<--DO NOT LET YOUR SHIP BE SEEN BY ATTUMA...>

<...OR BY THE HULK.>

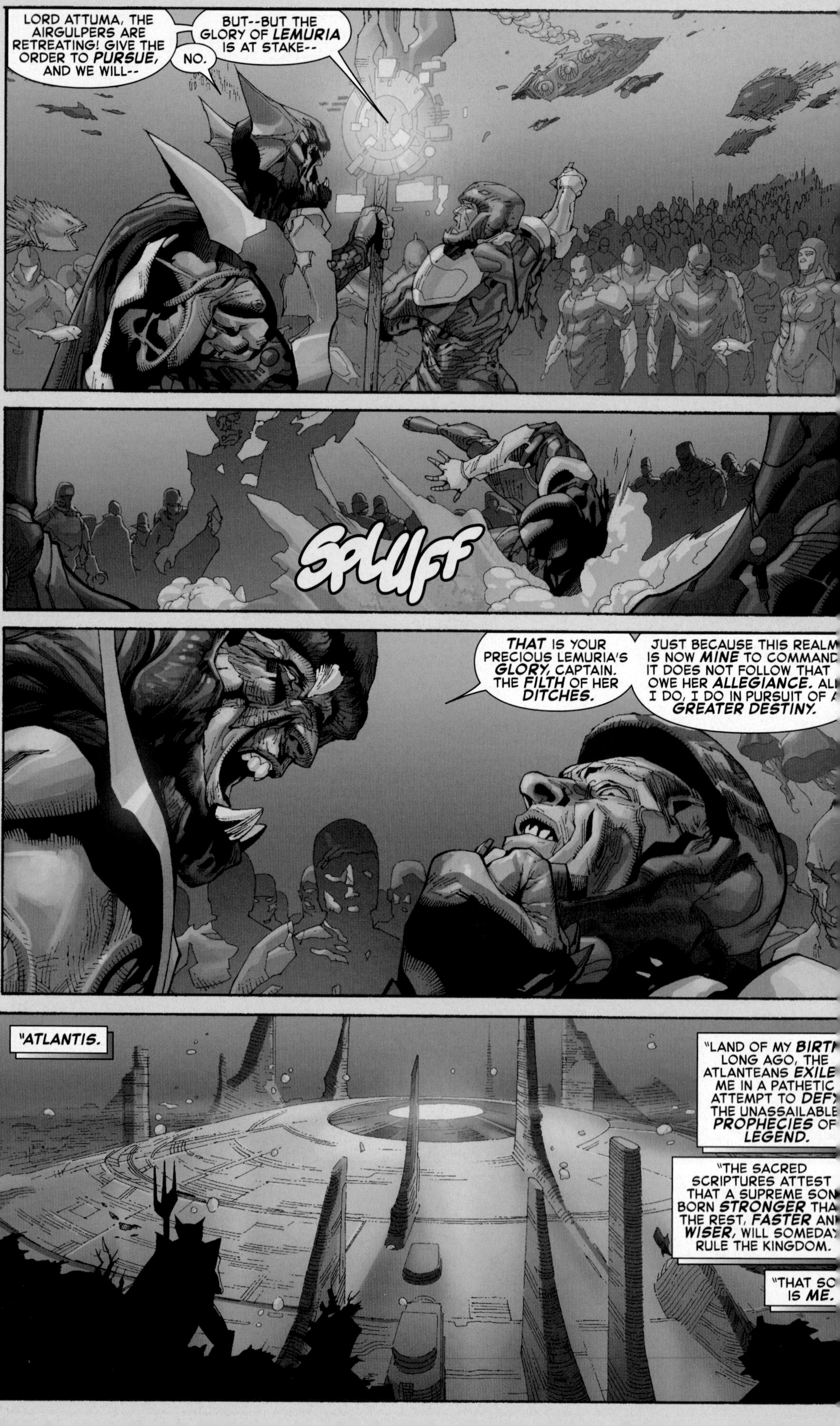
LORD ATTUMA, THE AIRGULPERS ARE RETREATING! GIVE THE ORDER TO PURSUE, AND WE WILL--
NO.
BUT--BUT THE GLORY OF LEMURIA IS AT STAKE--
SPLUFF
THAT IS YOUR PRECIOUS LEMURIA'S GLORY, CAPTAIN. THE FILTH OF HER DITCHES.
JUST BECAUSE THIS REALM IS NOW MINE TO COMMAND IT DOES NOT FOLLOW THAT OWE HER ALLEGIANCE. AL I DO, I DO IN PURSUIT OF GREATER DESTINY.
"ATLANTIS.
"LAND OF MY BIRT LONG AGO, THE ATLANTEANS EXILE ME IN A PATHETIC ATTEMPT TO DEF THE UNASSAILABLE PROPHECIES OF LEGEND.
"THE SACRED SCRIPTURES ATTEST THAT A SUPREME SON BORN STRONGER THA THE REST, FASTER AN WISER, WILL SOMEDA RULE THE KINGDOM.
"THAT SO IS ME.

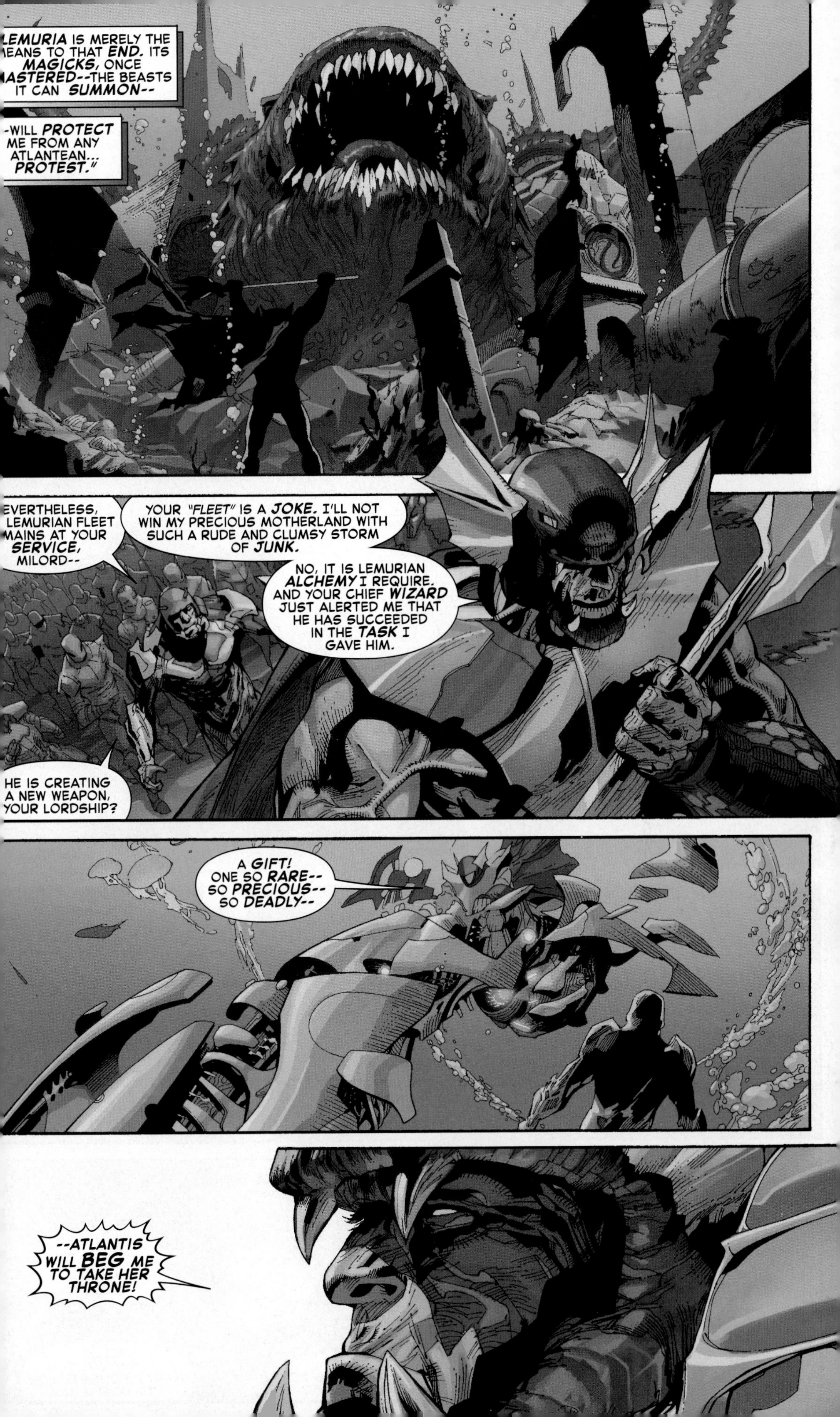

LEMURIA IS MERELY THE MEANS TO THAT END. ITS MAGICKS, ONCE MASTERED--THE BEASTS IT CAN SUMMON--
-WILL PROTECT ME FROM ANY ATLANTEAN... PROTEST."
EVERTHELESS, LEMURIAN FLEET MAINS AT YOUR SERVICE, MILORD--
YOUR "FLEET" IS A JOKE. I'LL NOT WIN MY PRECIOUS MOTHERLAND WITH SUCH A RUDE AND CLUMSY STORM OF JUNK.
NO, IT IS LEMURIAN ALCHEMY I REQUIRE. AND YOUR CHIEF WIZARD JUST ALERTED ME THAT HE HAS SUCCEEDED IN THE TASK I GAVE HIM.
HE IS CREATING A NEW WEAPON, YOUR LORDSHIP?
A GIFT! ONE SO RARE--SO PRECIOUS--SO DEADLY--
--ATLANTIS WILL BEG ME TO TAKE HER THRONE!

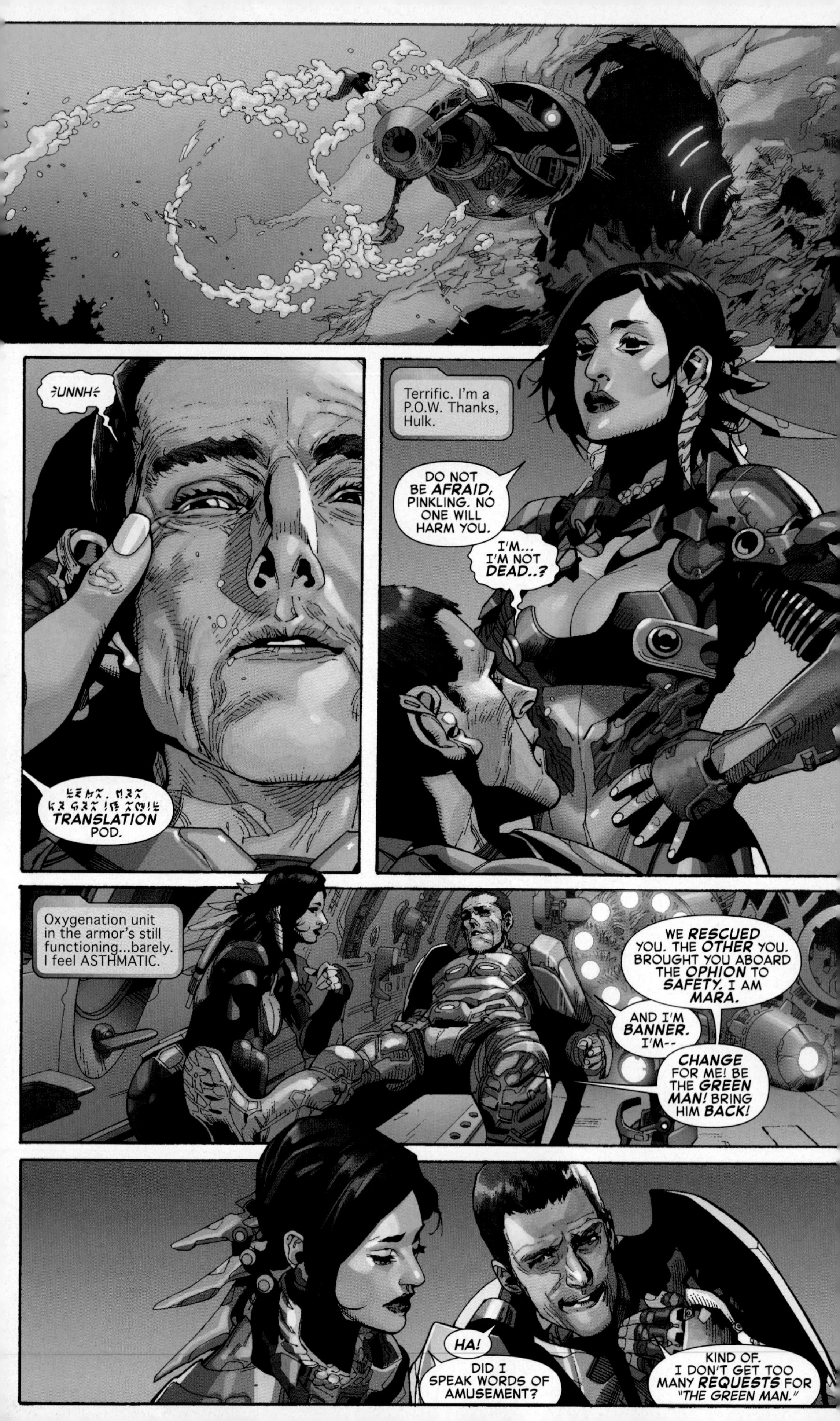
UNNH
TRANSLATION POD.
Terrific. I'm a P.O.W. Thanks, Hulk.
DO NOT BE AFRAID, PINKLING. NO ONE WILL HARM YOU.
I'M... I'M NOT DEAD..?
Oxygenation unit in the armor's still functioning...barely. I feel ASTHMATIC.
WE RESCUED YOU. THE OTHER YOU. BROUGHT YOU ABOARD THE OPHION TO SAFETY. I AM MARA.
AND I'M BANNER. I'M--
CHANGE FOR ME! BE THE GREEN MAN! BRING HIM BACK!
HA!
DID I SPEAK WORDS OF AMUSEMENT?
KIND OF. I DON'T GET TOO MANY REQUESTS FOR "THE GREEN MAN."

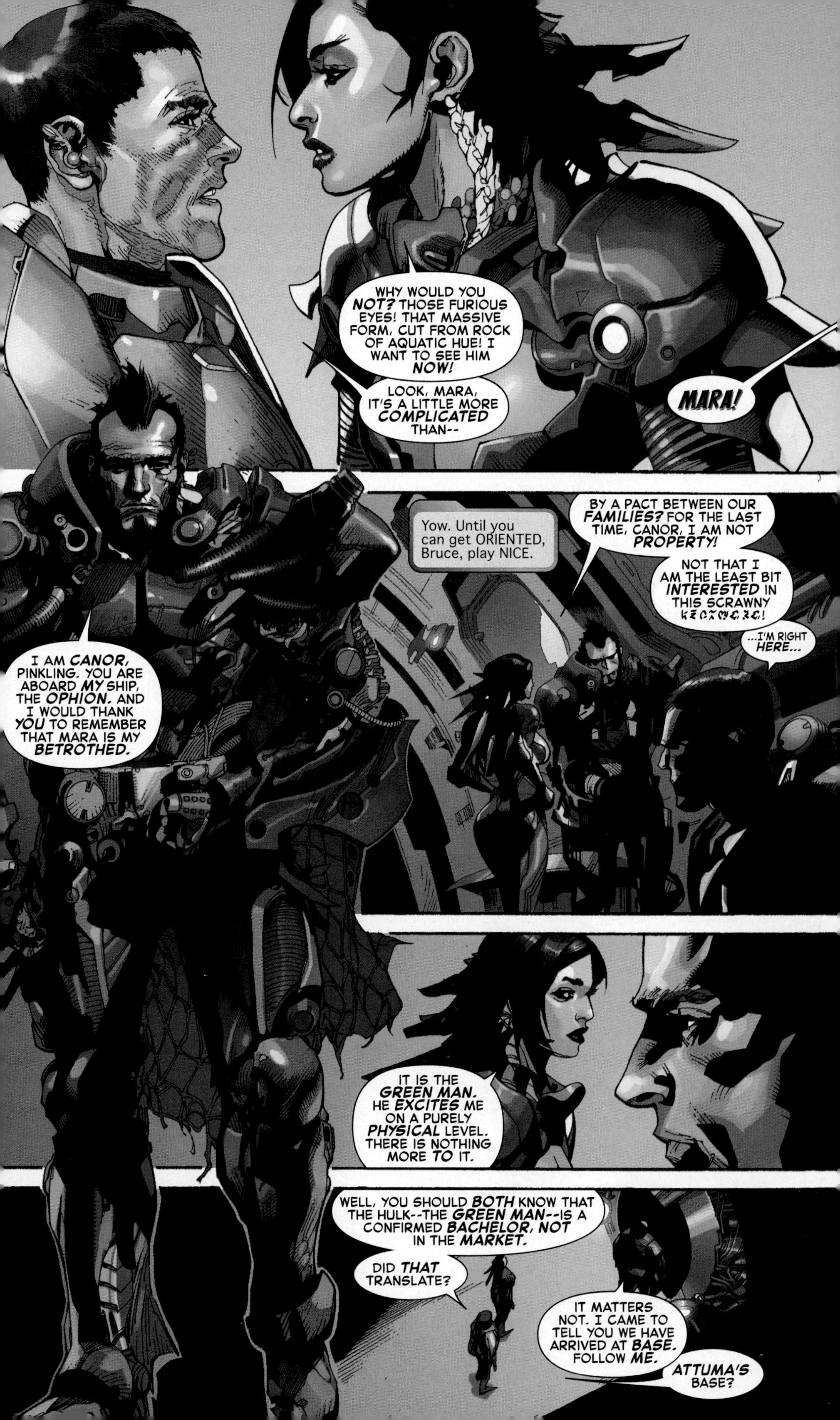
WHY WOULD YOU NOT? THOSE FURIOUS EYES! THAT MASSIVE FORM, CUT FROM ROCK OF AQUATIC HUE! I WANT TO SEE HIM NOW!
LOOK, MARA, IT'S A LITTLE MORE COMPLICATED THAN--
MARA!
I AM CANOR, PINKLING. YOU ARE ABOARD MY SHIP, THE OPHION. AND I WOULD THANK YOU TO REMEMBER THAT MARA IS MY BETROTHED.
Yow. Until you can get ORIENTED, Bruce, play NICE.
BY A PACT BETWEEN OUR FAMILIES? FOR THE LAST TIME, CANOR, I AM NOT PROPERTY!
NOT THAT I AM THE LEAST BIT INTERESTED IN THIS SCRAWNY
...I'M RIGHT HERE...
IT IS THE GREEN MAN. HE EXCITES ME ON A PURELY PHYSICAL LEVEL. THERE IS NOTHING MORE TO IT.
WELL, YOU SHOULD BOTH KNOW THAT THE HULK--THE GREEN MAN--IS A CONFIRMED BACHELOR, NOT IN THE MARKET.
DID THAT TRANSLATE?
IT MATTERS NOT. I CAME TO TELL YOU WE HAVE ARRIVED AT BASE. FOLLOW ME.
ATTUMA'S BASE?

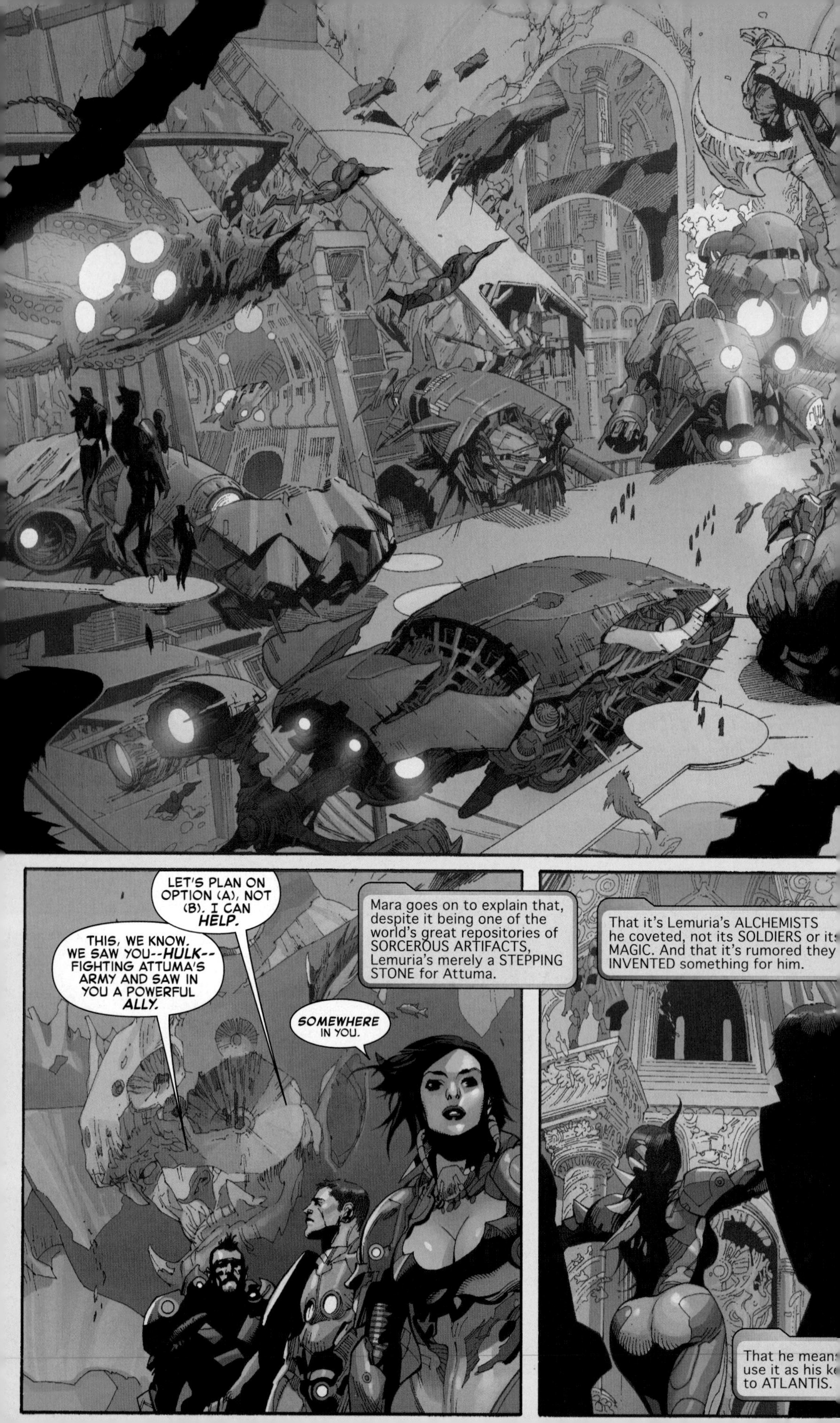

LET'S PLAN ON OPTION (A), NOT (B). I CAN HELP.
THIS, WE KNOW. WE SAW YOU--HULK--FIGHTING ATTUMA'S ARMY AND SAW IN YOU A POWERFUL ALLY.
SOMEWHERE IN YOU.
Mara goes on to explain that, despite it being one of the world's great repositories of SORCEROUS ARTIFACTS, Lemuria's merely a STEPPING STONE for Attuma.
That it's Lemuria's ALCHEMISTS he coveted, not its SOLDIERS or it
MAGIC. And that it's rumored they INVENTED something for him.
That he mean
use it as his k
to ATLANTIS.

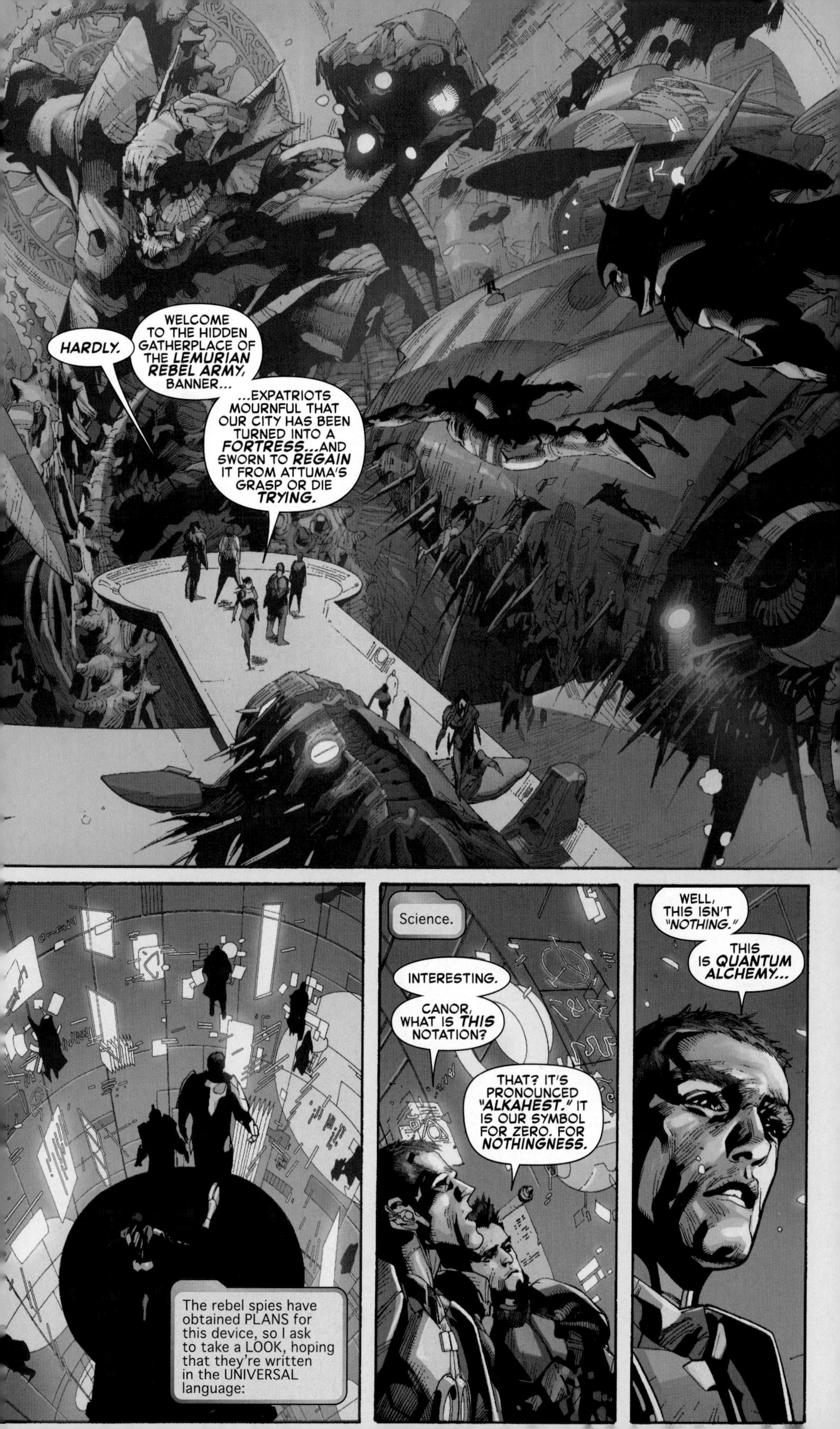
WELCOME TO THE HIDDEN GATHERPLACE OF THE LEMURIAN REBEL ARMY, BANNER...
HARDLY.
...EXPATRIOTS MOURNFUL THAT OUR CITY HAS BEEN TURNED INTO A FORTRESS...AND SWORN TO REGAIN IT FROM ATTUMA'S GRASP OR DIE TRYING.
The rebel spies have obtained PLANS for this device, so I ask to take a LOOK, hoping that they're written in the UNIVERSAL language:
Science.
INTERESTING.
CANOR, WHAT IS THIS NOTATION?
THAT? IT'S PRONOUNCED "ALKAHEST." IT IS OUR SYMBOL FOR ZERO. FOR NOTHINGNESS.
WELL, THIS ISN'T "NOTHING."
THIS IS QUANTUM ALCHEMY...

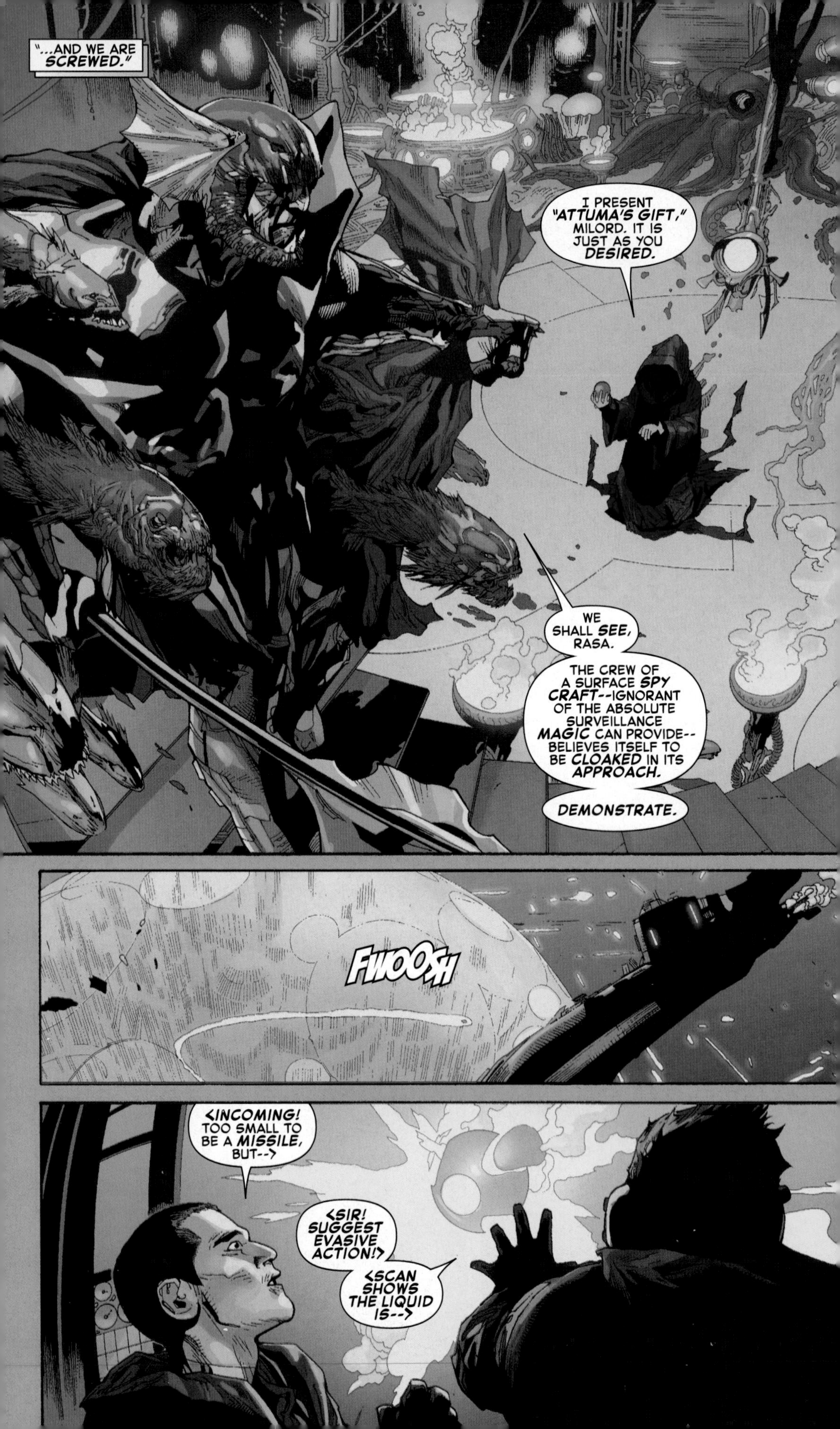
"...AND WE ARE SCREWED."
I PRESENT "ATTUMA'S GIFT," MILORD. IT IS JUST AS YOU DESIRED.
WE SHALL SEE, RASA.
THE CREW OF A SURFACE SPY CRAFT--IGNORANT OF THE ABSOLUTE SURVEILLANCE MAGIC CAN PROVIDE--BELIEVES ITSELF TO BE CLOAKED IN ITS APPROACH.
DEMONSTRATE.
FWOOSH
<INCOMING! TOO SMALL TO BE A MISSILE, BUT-->
<SIR! SUGGEST EVASIVE ACTION!>
<SCAN SHOWS THE LIQUID IS-->

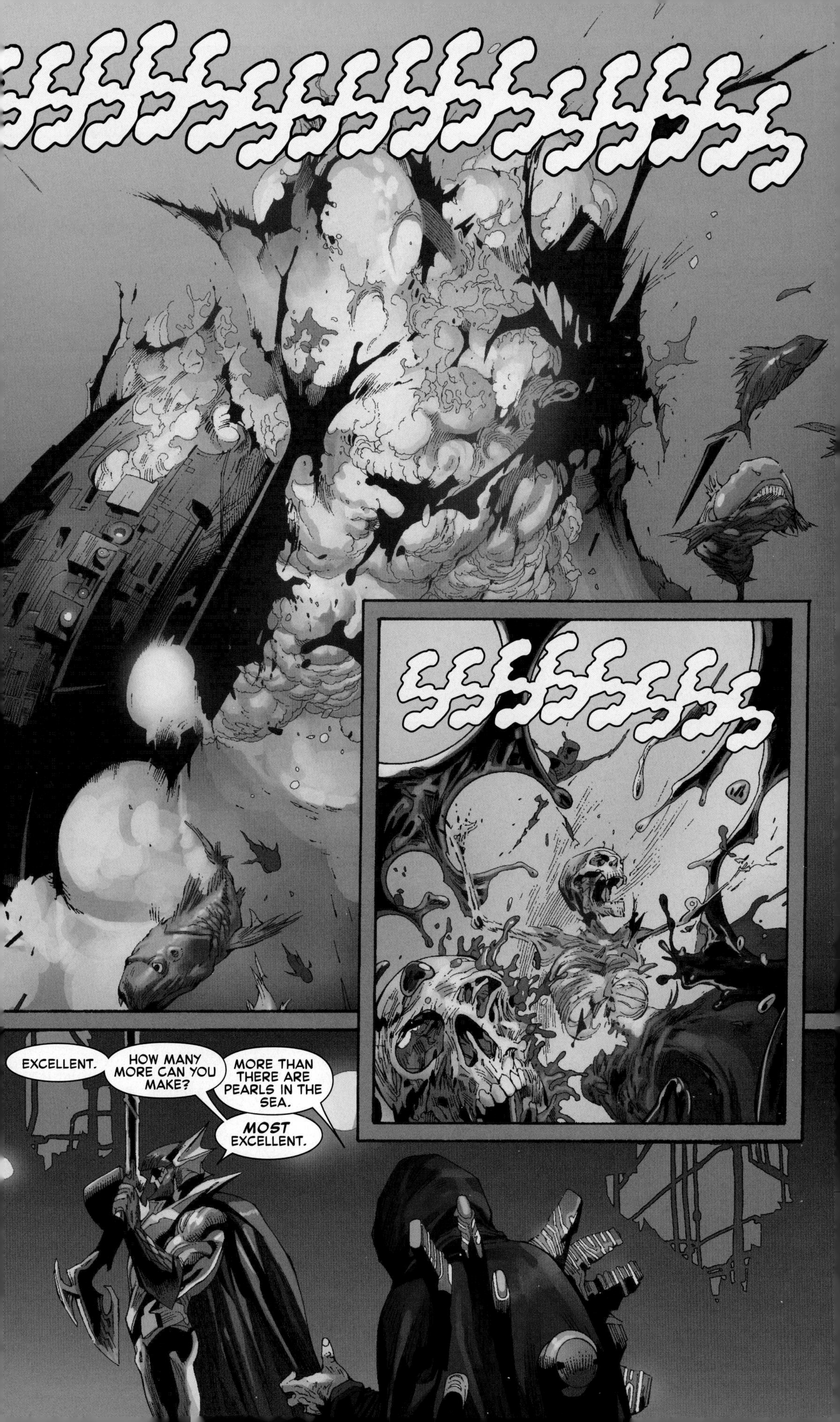
SSSSSSSSSSSSSSSSSHHHHHHHH
SSSSSSHHHH
EXCELLENT.
HOW MANY MORE CAN YOU MAKE?
MORE THAN THERE ARE PEARLS IN THE SEA.
MOST EXCELLENT.

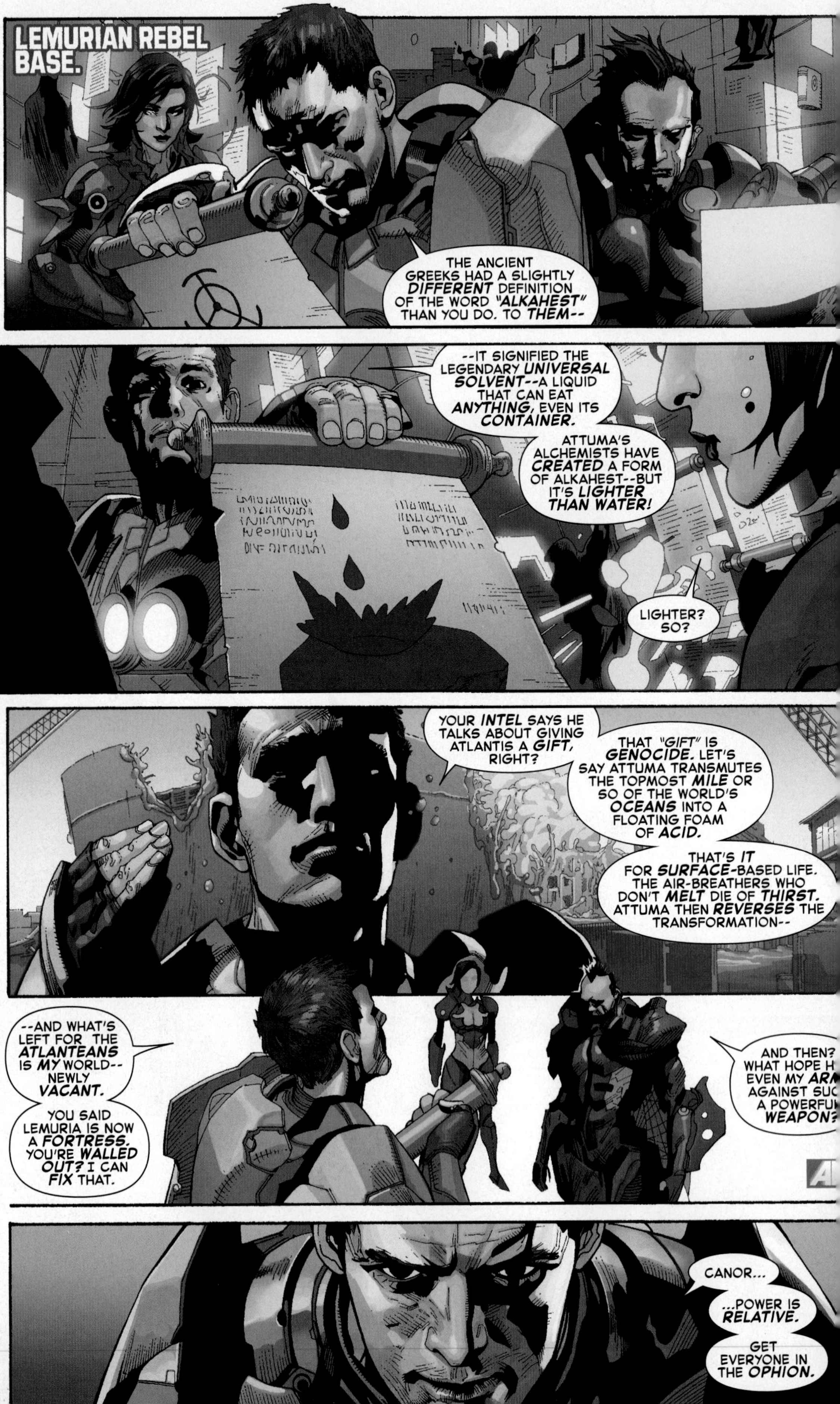
LEMURIAN REBEL BASE.
THE ANCIENT GREEKS HAD A SLIGHTLY DIFFERENT DEFINITION OF THE WORD "ALKAHEST" THAN YOU DO. TO THEM--
--IT SIGNIFIED THE LEGENDARY UNIVERSAL SOLVENT--A LIQUID THAT CAN EAT ANYTHING, EVEN ITS CONTAINER.
ATTUMA'S ALCHEMISTS HAVE CREATED A FORM OF ALKAHEST--BUT IT'S LIGHTER THAN WATER!
LIGHTER? SO?
YOUR INTEL SAYS HE TALKS ABOUT GIVING ATLANTIS A GIFT, RIGHT?
THAT "GIFT" IS GENOCIDE. LET'S SAY ATTUMA TRANSMUTES THE TOPMOST MILE OR SO OF THE WORLD'S OCEANS INTO A FLOATING FOAM OF ACID.
THAT'S IT FOR SURFACE-BASED LIFE. THE AIR-BREATHERS WHO DON'T MELT DIE OF THIRST. ATTUMA THEN REVERSES THE TRANSFORMATION--
--AND WHAT'S LEFT FOR THE ATLANTEANS IS MY WORLD--NEWLY VACANT.
YOU SAID LEMURIA IS NOW A FORTRESS. YOU'RE WALLED OUT? I CAN FIX THAT.
AND THEN? WHAT HOPE H EVEN MY AR AGAINST SUC A POWERFU WEAPON?
CANOR...
...POWER IS RELATIVE.
GET EVERYONE IN THE OPHION.

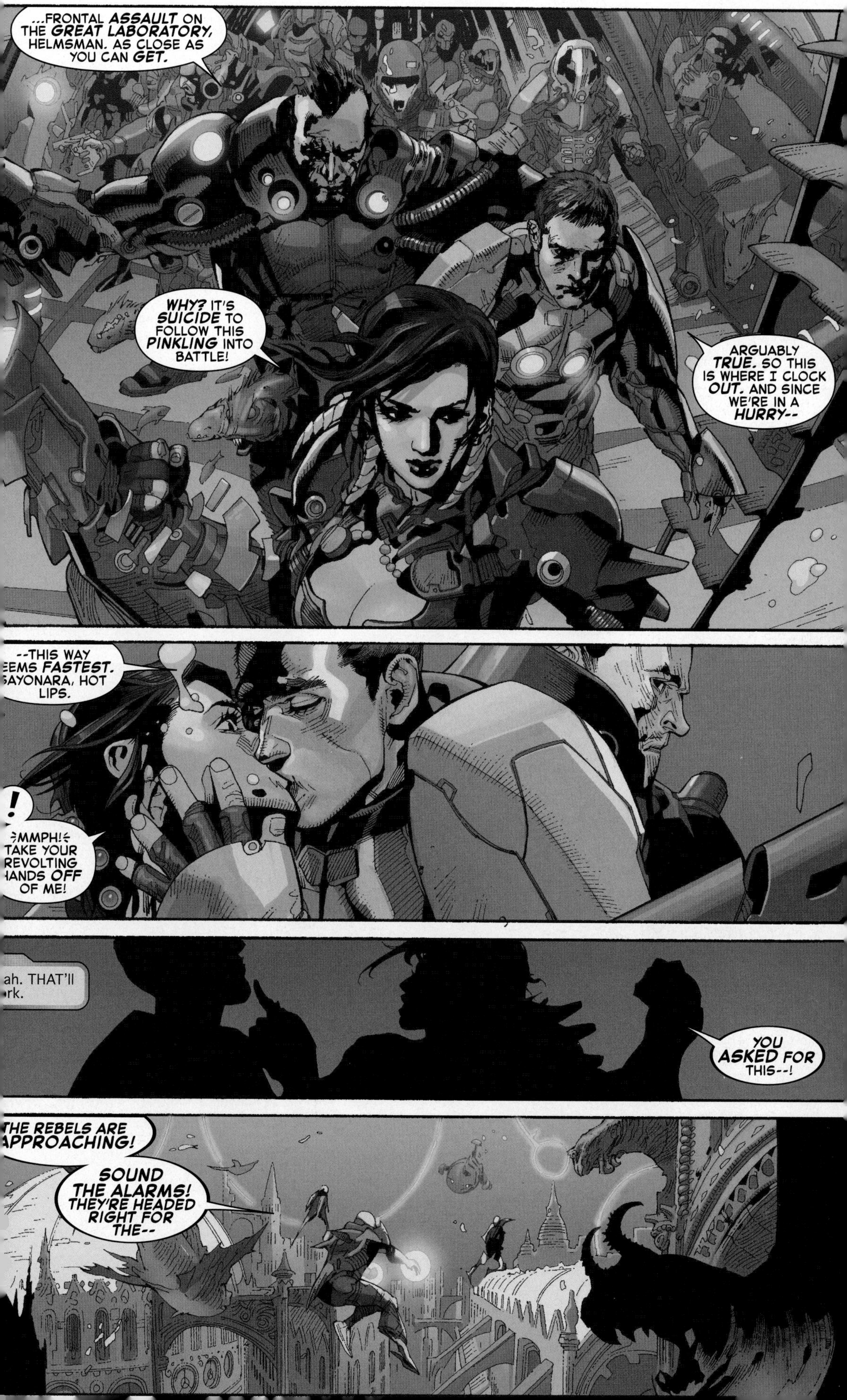
...FRONTAL ASSAULT ON THE GREAT LABORATORY, HELMSMAN. AS CLOSE AS YOU CAN GET.
WHY? IT'S SUICIDE TO FOLLOW THIS PINKLING INTO BATTLE!
ARGUABLY TRUE. SO THIS IS WHERE I CLOCK OUT. AND SINCE WE'RE IN A HURRY--
--THIS WAY EEMS FASTEST. AYONARA, HOT LIPS.
!
MMPH! TAKE YOUR REVOLTING ANDS OFF OF ME!
ah. THAT'll rk.
YOU ASKED FOR THIS--!
THE REBELS ARE APPROACHING!
SOUND THE ALARMS! THEY'RE HEADED RIGHT FOR THE--

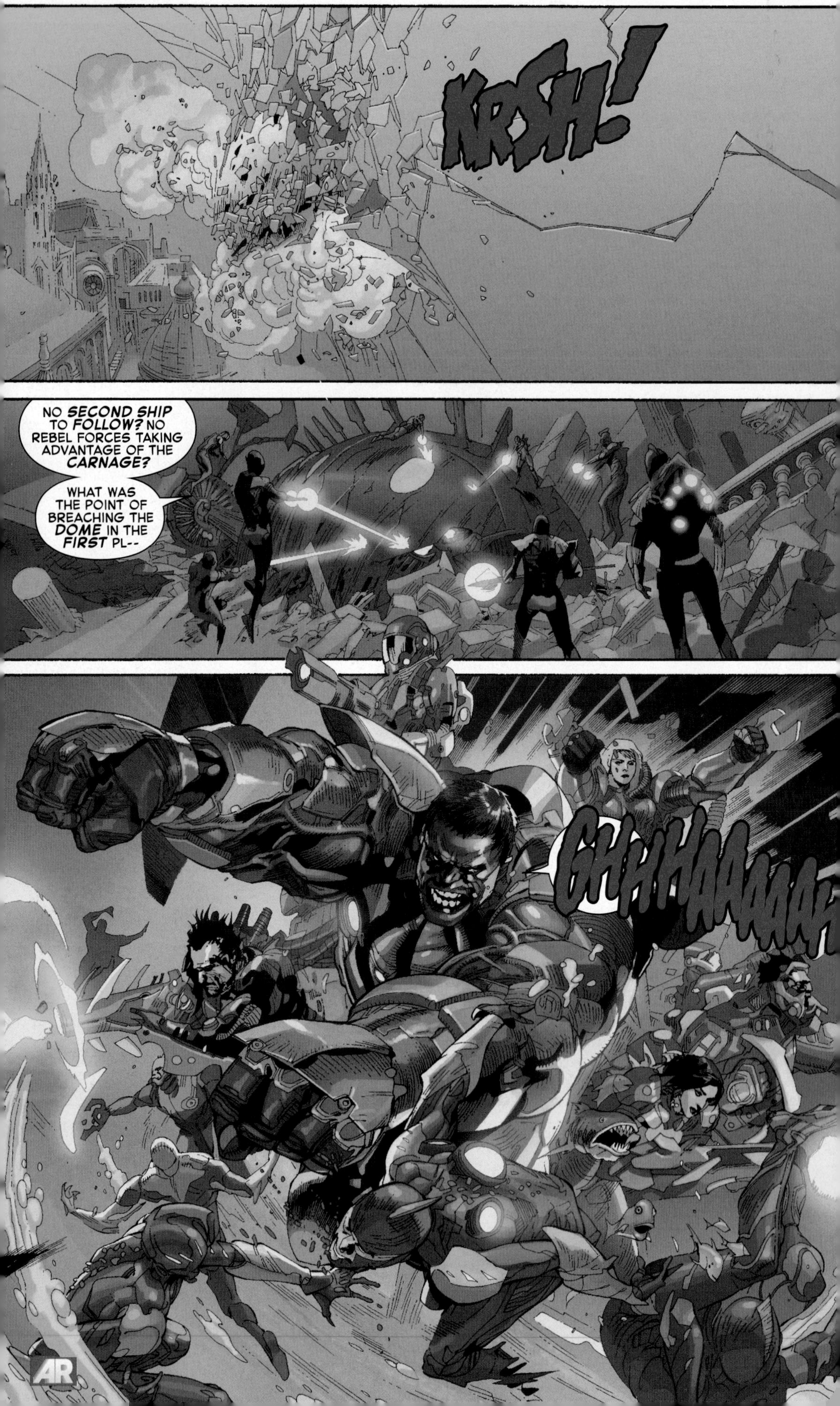
KRSH!
NO SECOND SHIP TO FOLLOW? NO REBEL FORCES TAKING ADVANTAGE OF THE CARNAGE?
WHAT WAS THE POINT OF BREACHING THE DOME IN THE FIRST PL--
GHHHAAAAAAH

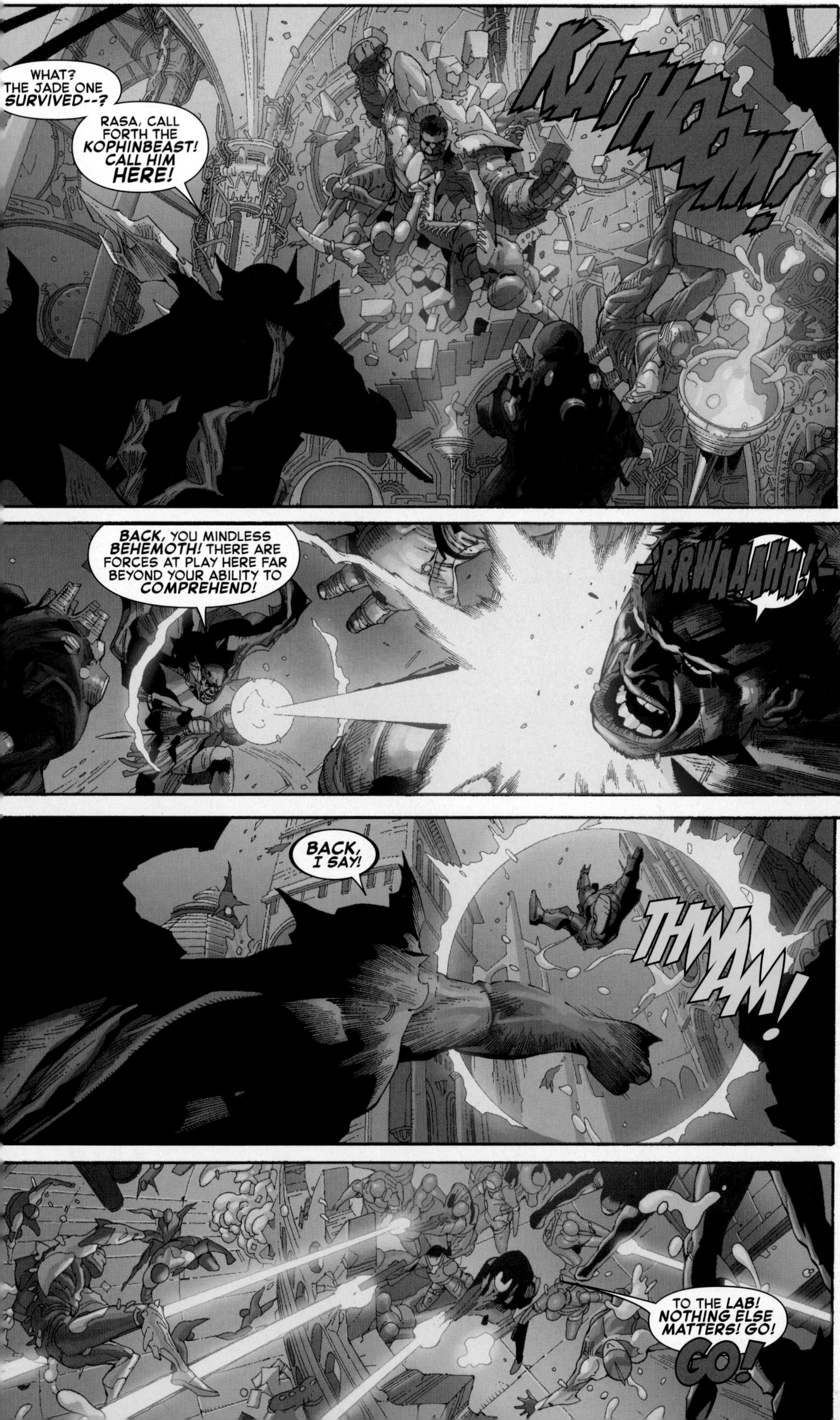
WHAT? THE JADE ONE SURVIVED--?
RASA, CALL FORTH THE KOPHINBEAST! CALL HIM HERE!
KATHOOM!
BACK, YOU MINDLESS BEHEMOTH! THERE ARE FORCES AT PLAY HERE FAR BEYOND YOUR ABILITY TO COMPREHEND!
RRWAAAHH!
BACK, I SAY!
THWAM!
TO THE LAB! NOTHING ELSE MATTERS! GO! GO!

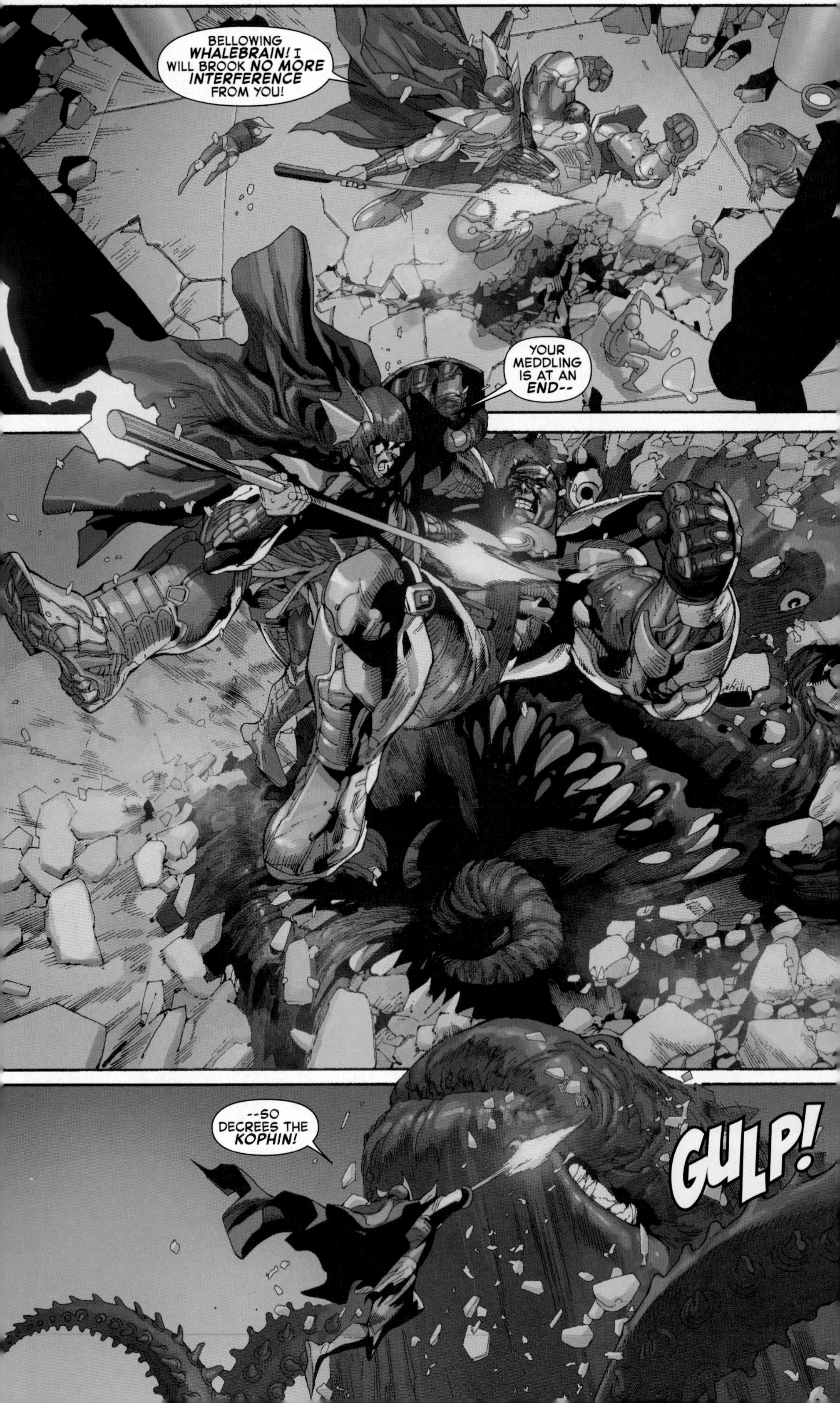
BELLOWING WHALEBRAIN! I WILL BROOK NO MORE INTERFERENCE FROM YOU!
YOUR MEDDLING IS AT AN END--
--SO DECREES THE KOPHIN!
GULP!

ATTUMA'S MEN CANNOT *HOLD* US!

IT IS NOT HIS *WARRIORS* WE MUST *FEAR,* CANOR--

--IT IS ATTUMA, *HIMSELF!* THE *GREEN MAN* WAS OUR DEFENSE AGAINST *HIM*--

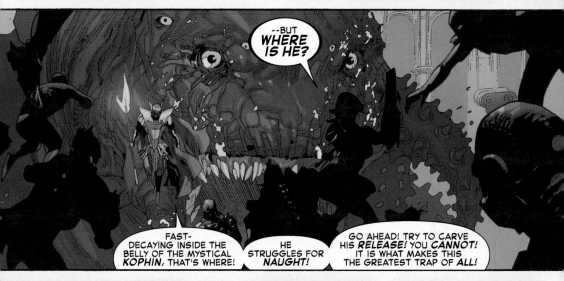

--BUT *WHERE IS HE?*

FAST-DECAYING INSIDE THE BELLY OF THE MYSTICAL *KOPHIN,* THAT'S WHERE!

HE STRUGGLES FOR *NAUGHT!*

GO AHEAD! TRY TO CARVE HIS *RELEASE!* YOU *CANNOT!* IT IS WHAT MAKES THIS THE GREATEST TRAP OF *ALL!*

THE HIDE OF THE *KOPHIN* IS MAGICALLY *IMPENETRABLE!* *NOTHING* CAN TEAR *THROUGH* IT! NO--

--THING--

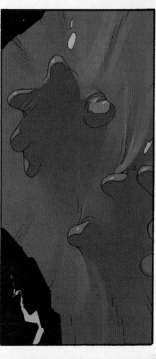

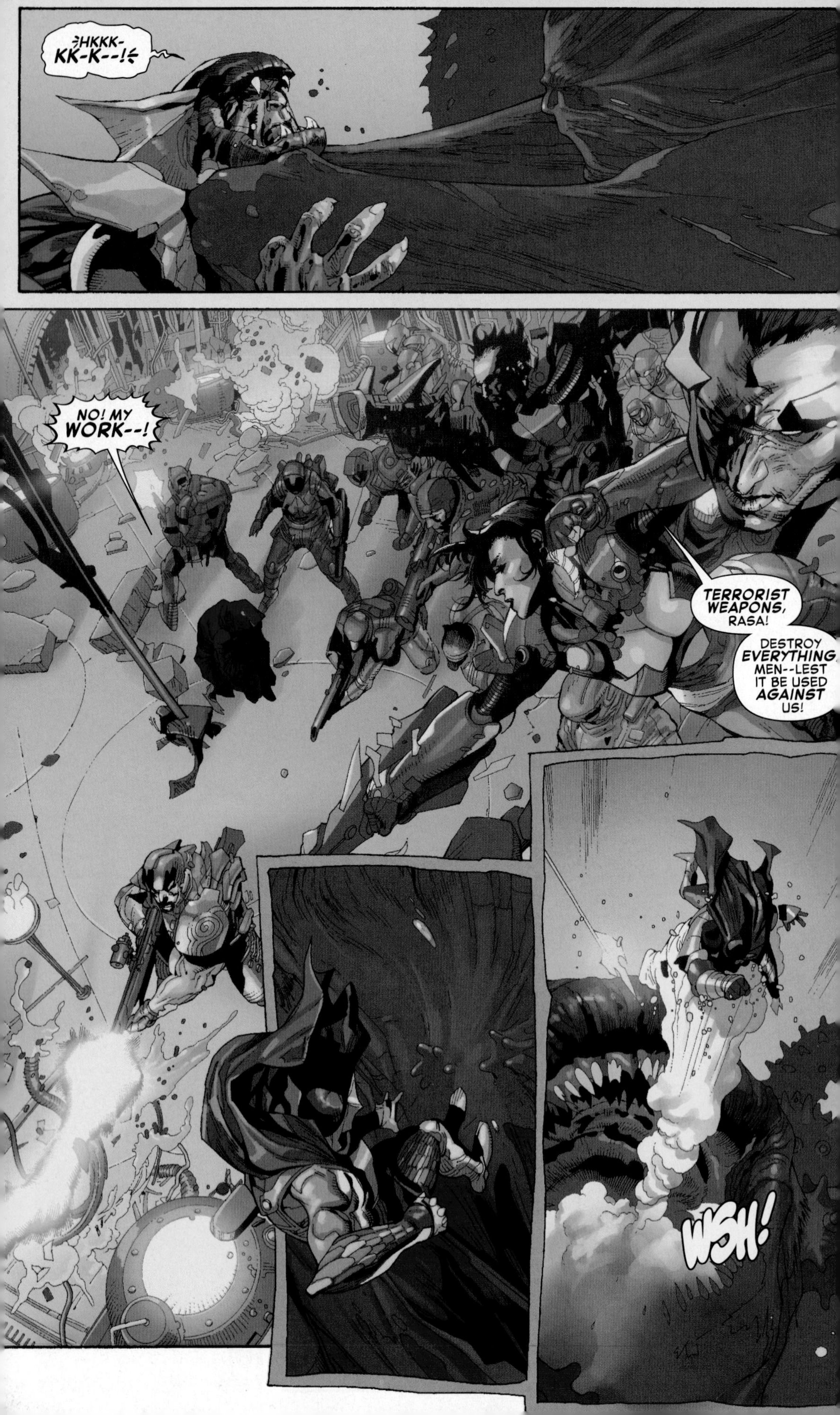

HKKK-KK-K--!
NO! MY WORK--!
TERRORIST WEAPONS, RASA!
DESTROY EVERYTHING, MEN--LEST IT BE USED AGAINST US!
WSH!

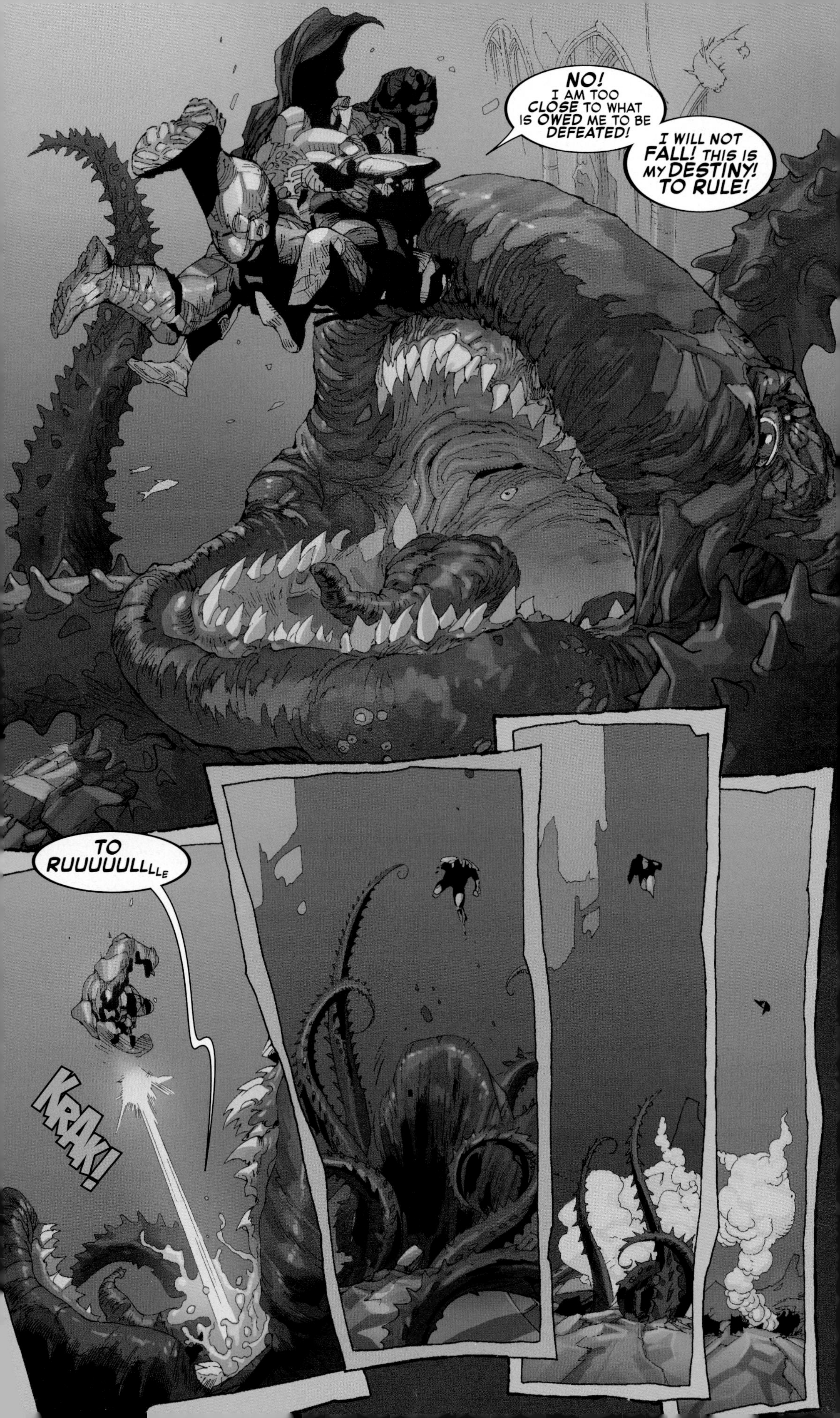
NO! I AM TOO CLOSE TO WHAT IS OWED ME TO BE DEFEATED!
I WILL NOT FALL! THIS IS MY DESTINY! TO RULE!
TO RUUUUULLLLLE
KRAK!

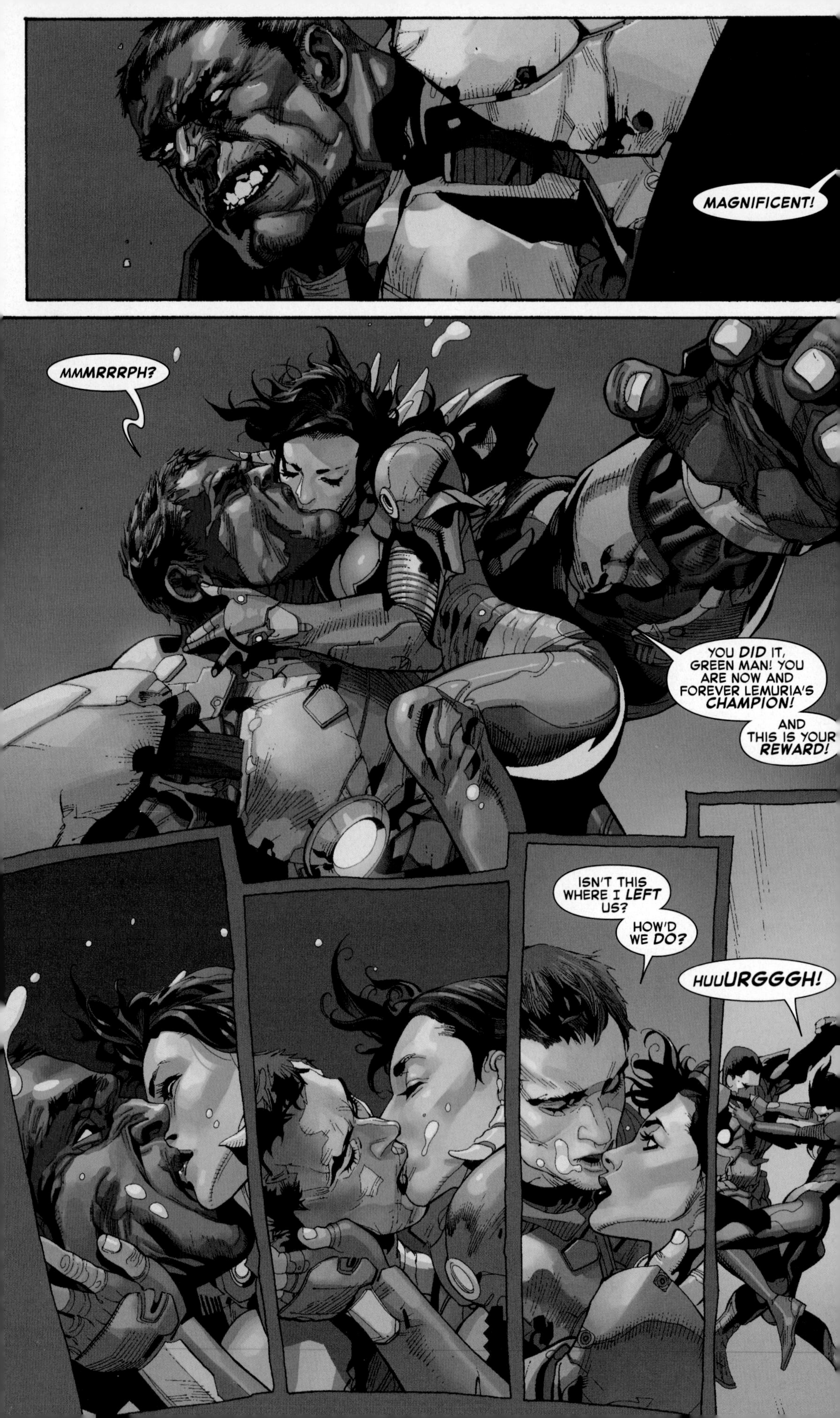
MAGNIFICENT!
MMMRRRPH?
YOU DID IT, GREEN MAN! YOU ARE NOW AND FOREVER LEMURIA'S CHAMPION!
AND THIS IS YOUR REWARD!
ISN'T THIS WHERE I LEFT US?
HOW'D WE DO?
HUUURGGGH!

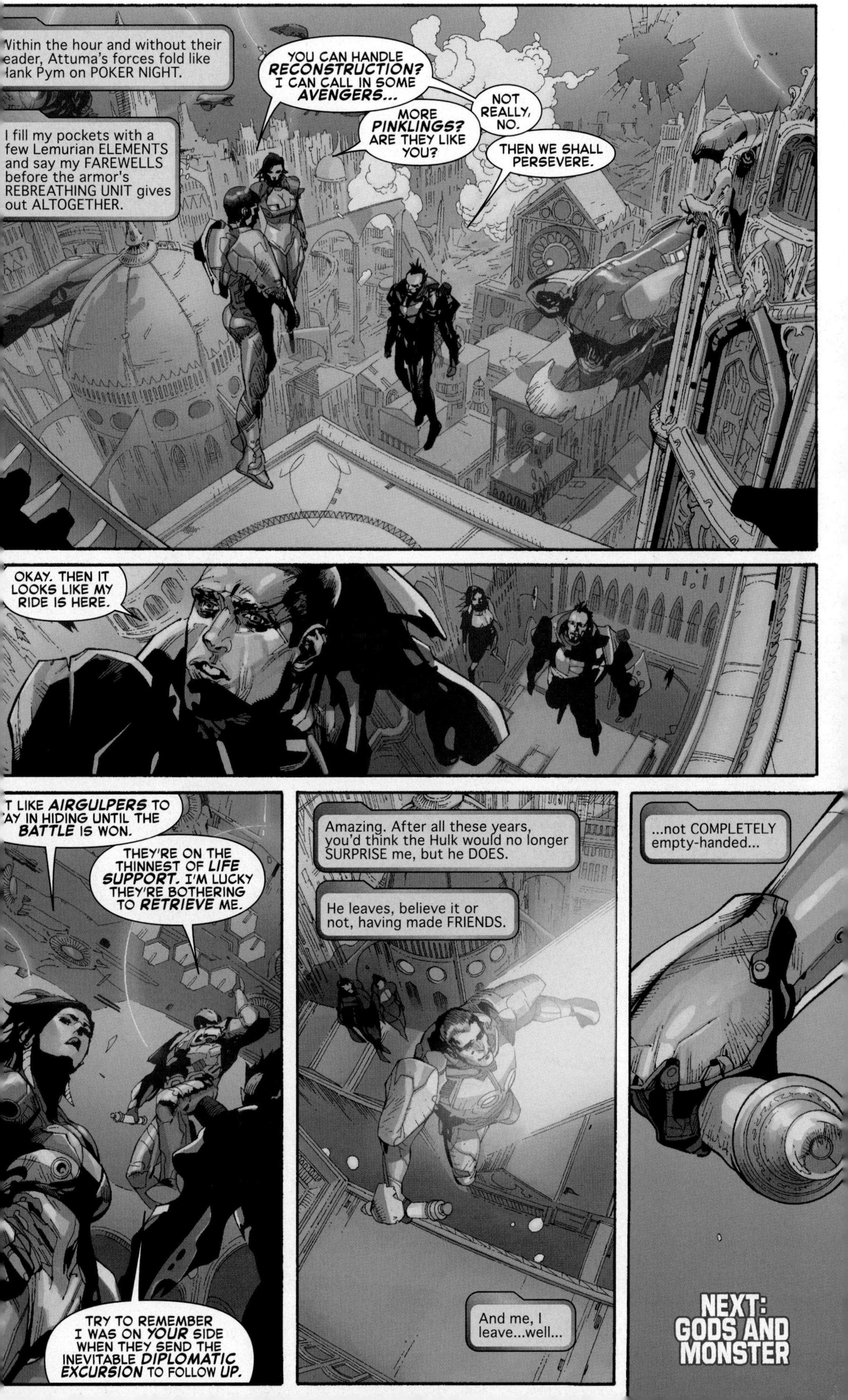

Within the hour and without their leader, Attuma's forces fold like Hank Pym on POKER NIGHT.
YOU CAN HANDLE RECONSTRUCTION? I CAN CALL IN SOME AVENGERS...
NOT REALLY, NO.
MORE PINKLINGS? ARE THEY LIKE YOU?
THEN WE SHALL PERSEVERE.
I fill my pockets with a few Lemurian ELEMENTS and say my FAREWELLS before the armor's REBREATHING UNIT gives out ALTOGETHER.
OKAY. THEN IT LOOKS LIKE MY RIDE IS HERE.
T LIKE AIRGULPERS TO AY IN HIDING UNTIL THE BATTLE IS WON.
THEY'RE ON THE THINNEST OF LIFE SUPPORT. I'M LUCKY THEY'RE BOTHERING TO RETRIEVE ME.
TRY TO REMEMBER I WAS ON YOUR SIDE WHEN THEY SEND THE INEVITABLE DIPLOMATIC EXCURSION TO FOLLOW UP.
Amazing. After all these years, you'd think the Hulk would no longer SURPRISE me, but he DOES.
He leaves, believe it or not, having made FRIENDS.
And me, I leave...well...
...not COMPLETELY empty-handed...
NEXT: GODS AND MONSTER

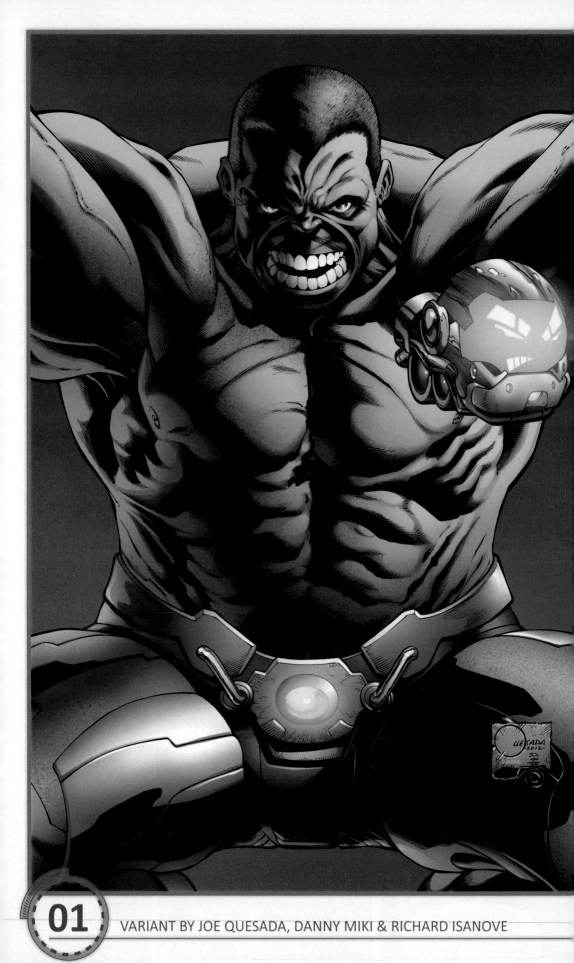

01 VARIANT BY JOE QUESADA, DANNY MIKI & RICHARD ISANOVE

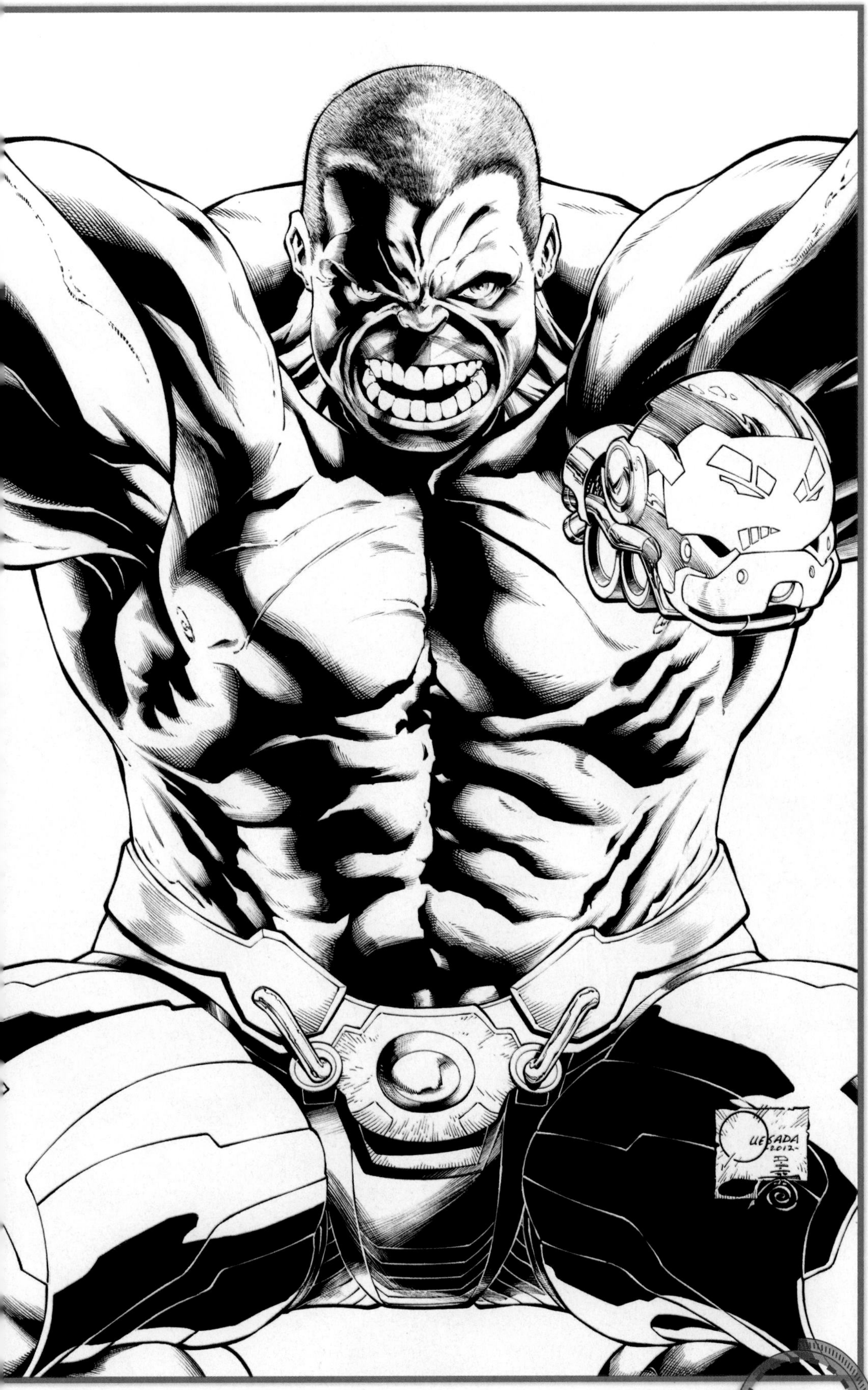
QUESADA 2012

SKETCH VARIANT BY JOE QUESADA & DANNY MIKI

01

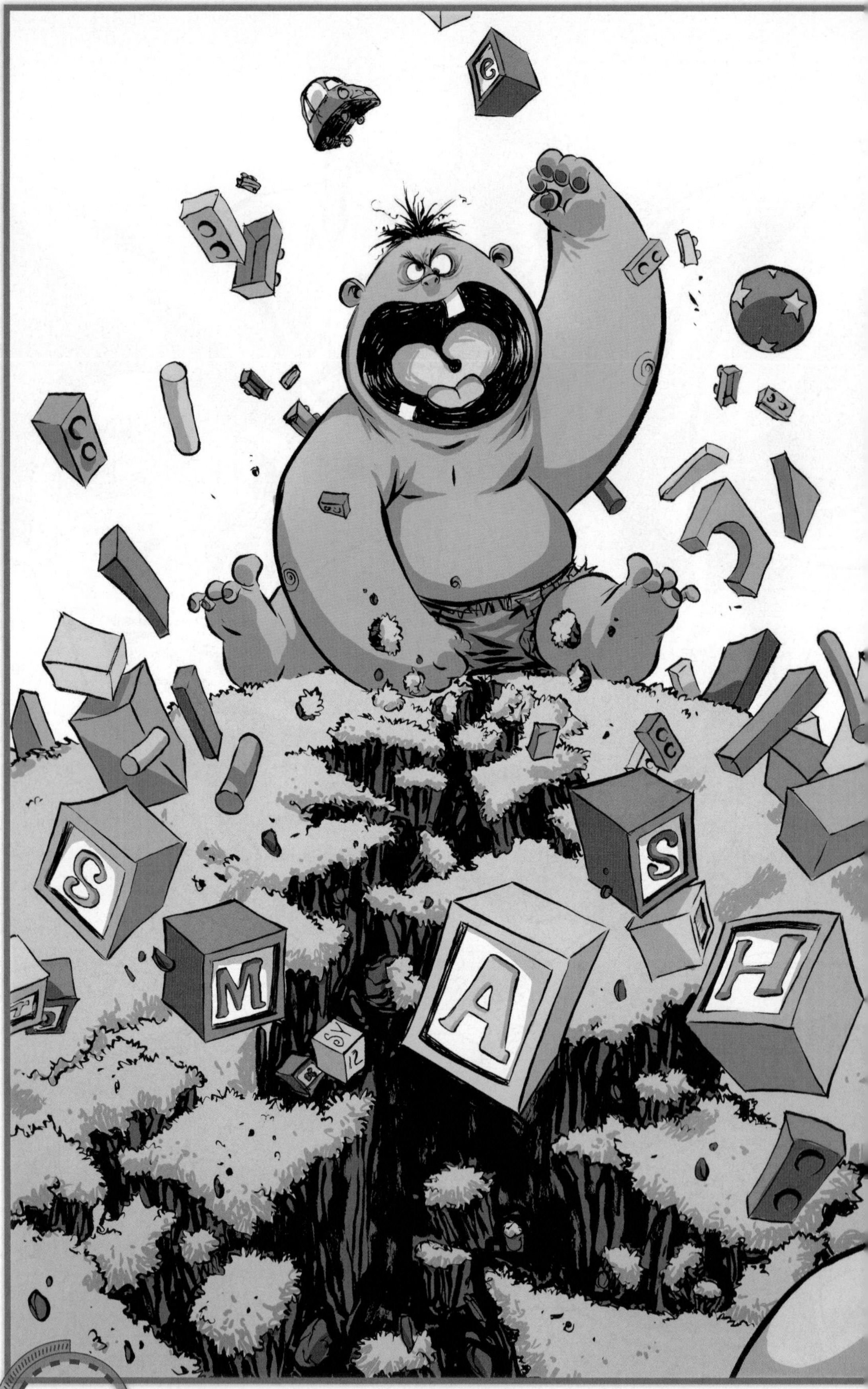
S
M
A
S
H

01 VARIANT BY SKOTTIE YOUNG

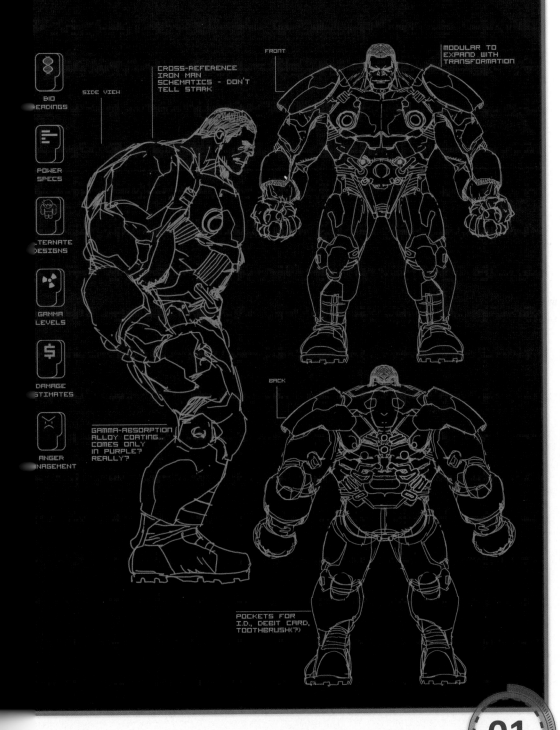

BIO
READINGS

POWER
SPECS

ALTERNATE
DESIGNS

GAMMA
LEVELS

DAMAGE
ESTIMATES

ANGER
MANAGEMENT

SIDE VIEW

CROSS-REFERENCE
IRON MAN
SCHEMATICS - DON'T
TELL STARK

FRONT

MODULAR TO
EXPAND WITH
TRANSFORMATION

GAMMA-ABSORPTION
ALLOY COATING...
COMES ONLY
IN PURPLE?
REALLY?

BACK

POCKETS FOR
I.D., DEBIT CARD,
TOOTHBRUSH(?)

VARIANT BY LEINIL FRANCIS YU

01

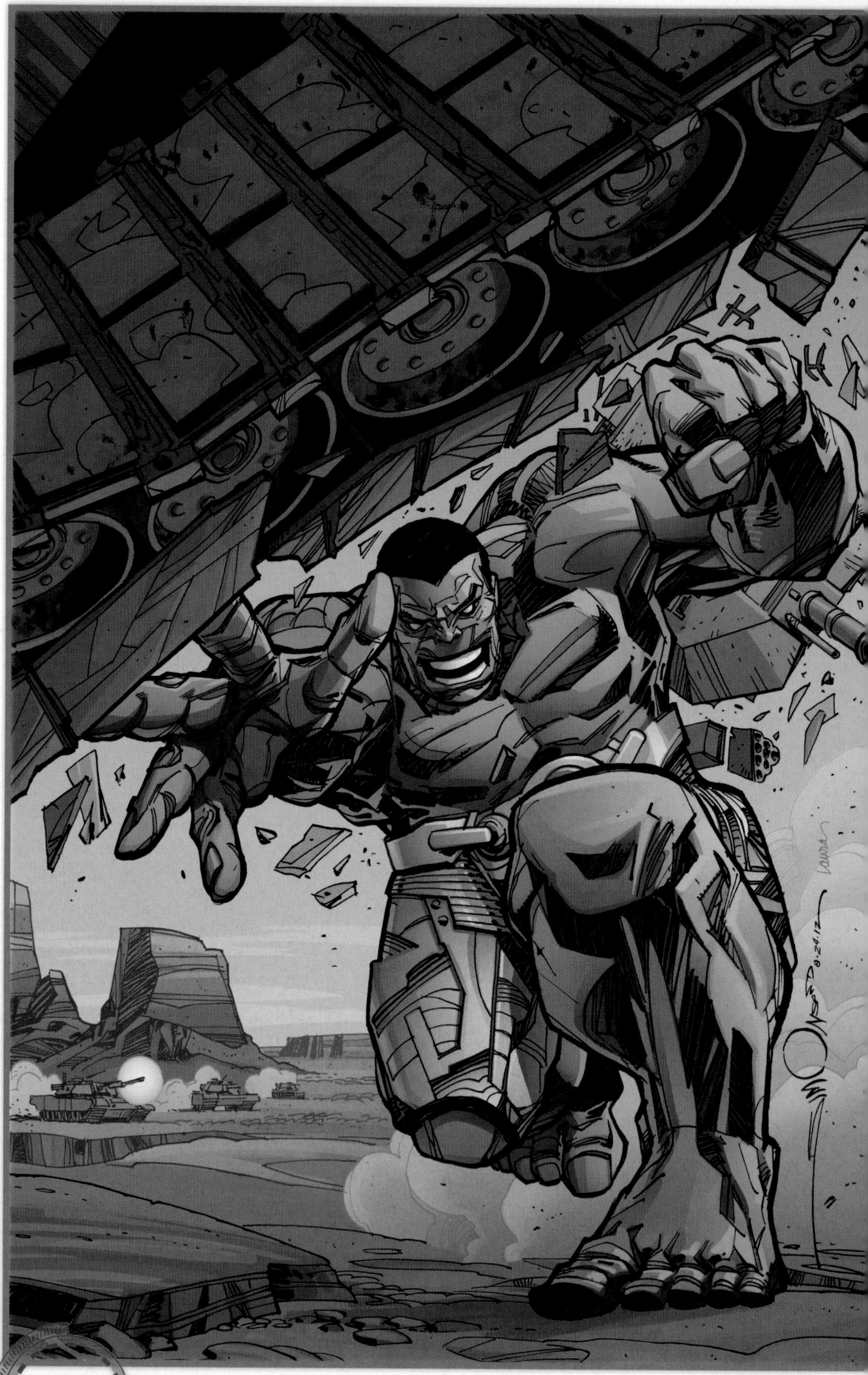

01 VARIANT BY WALTER SIMONSON & LAURA MARTIN

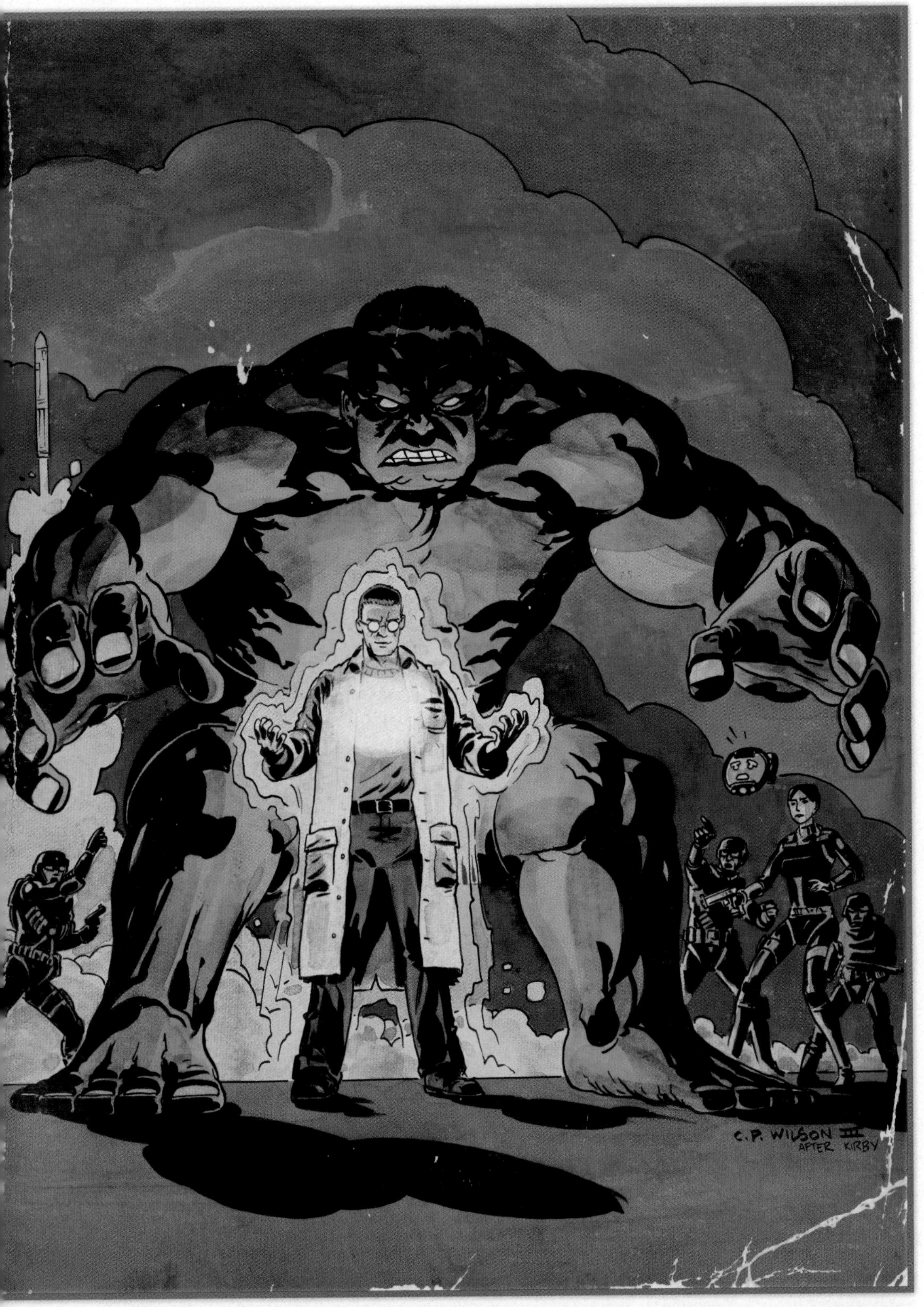
C.P. WILSON III
AFTER KIRBY

PHANTOM VARIANT BY C.P. WILSON III

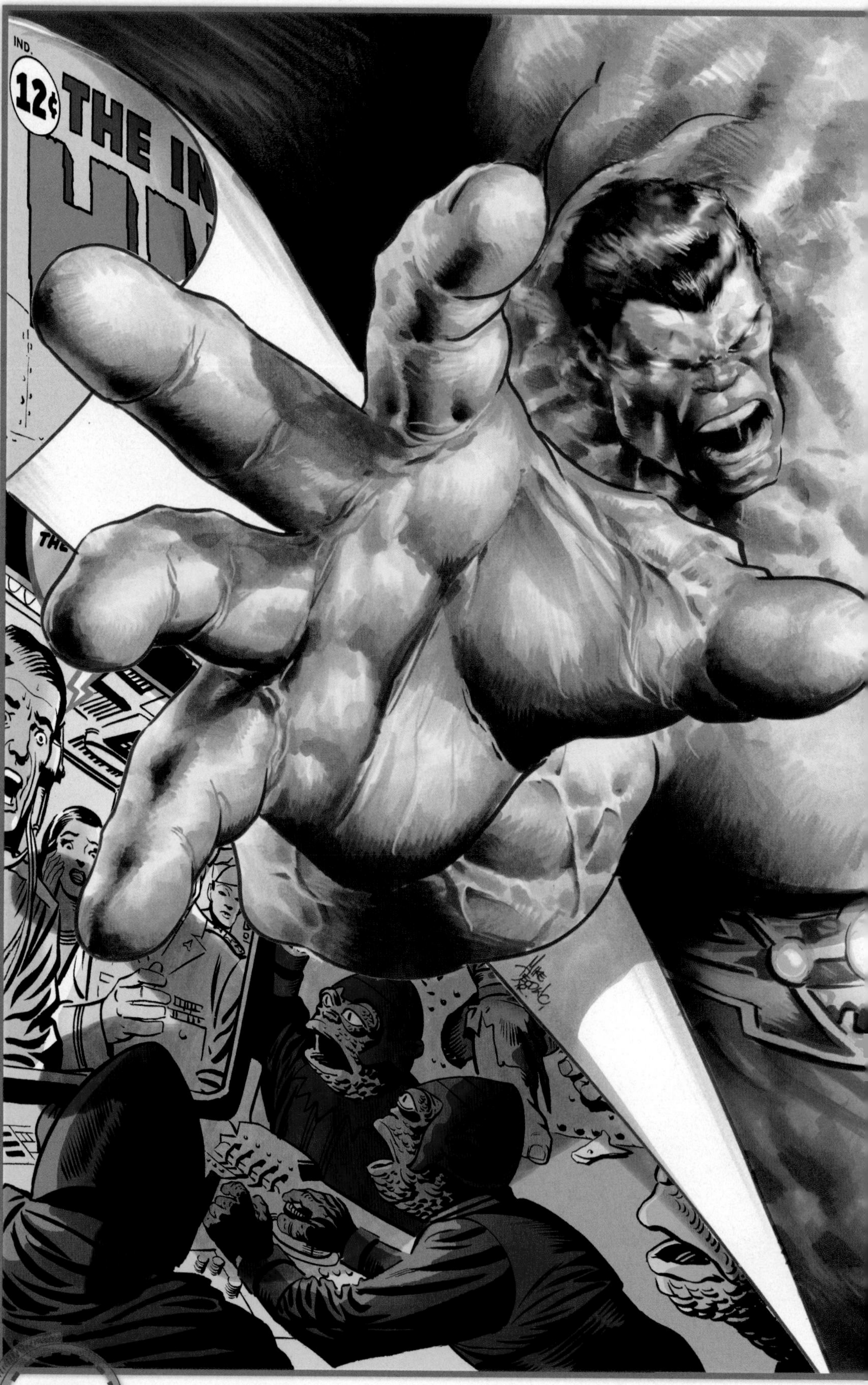
IND.
12¢
THE IN

02 VARIANT BY MIKE DEODATO & RAIN BEREDO

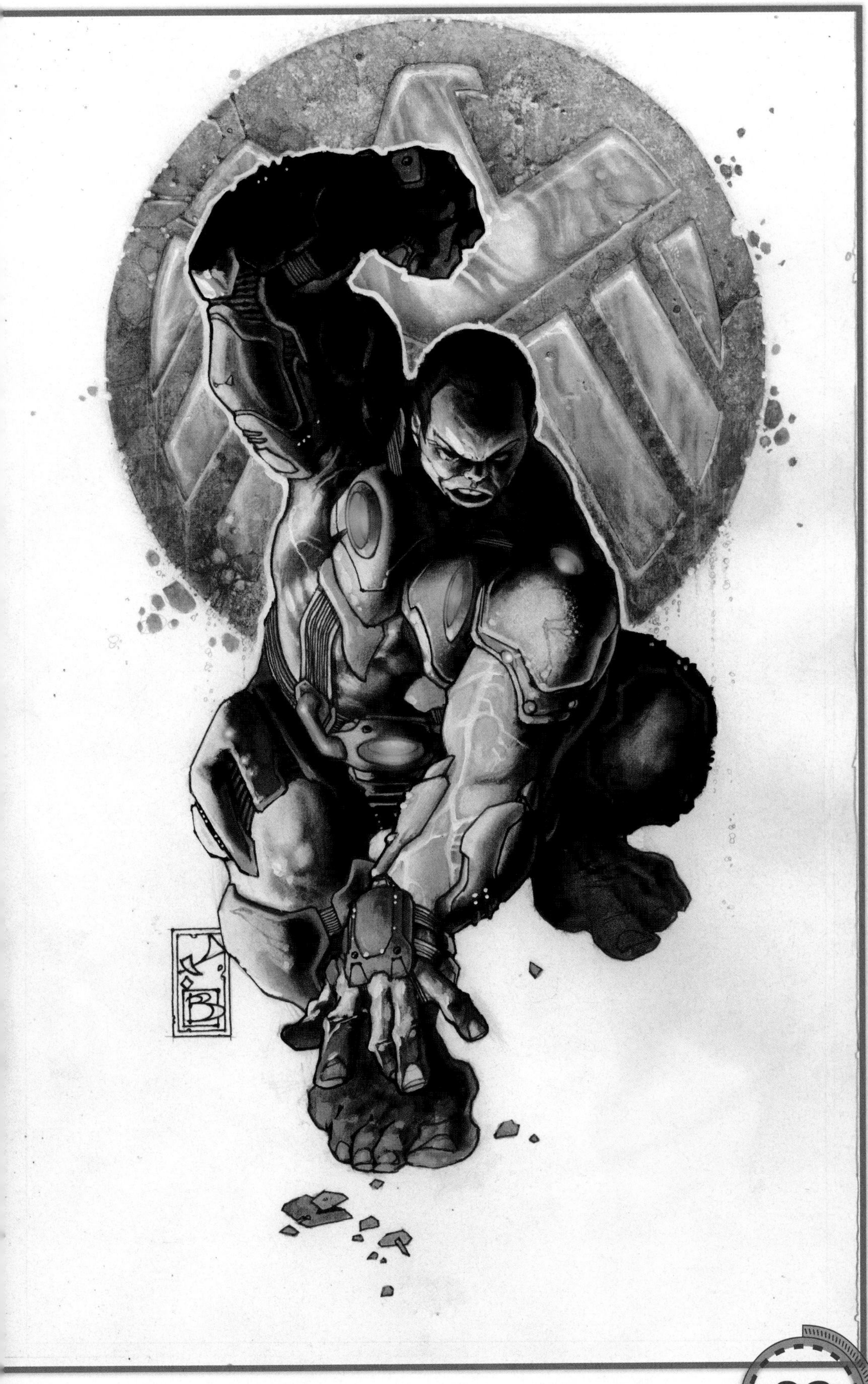

VARIANT BY SIMONE BIANCHI

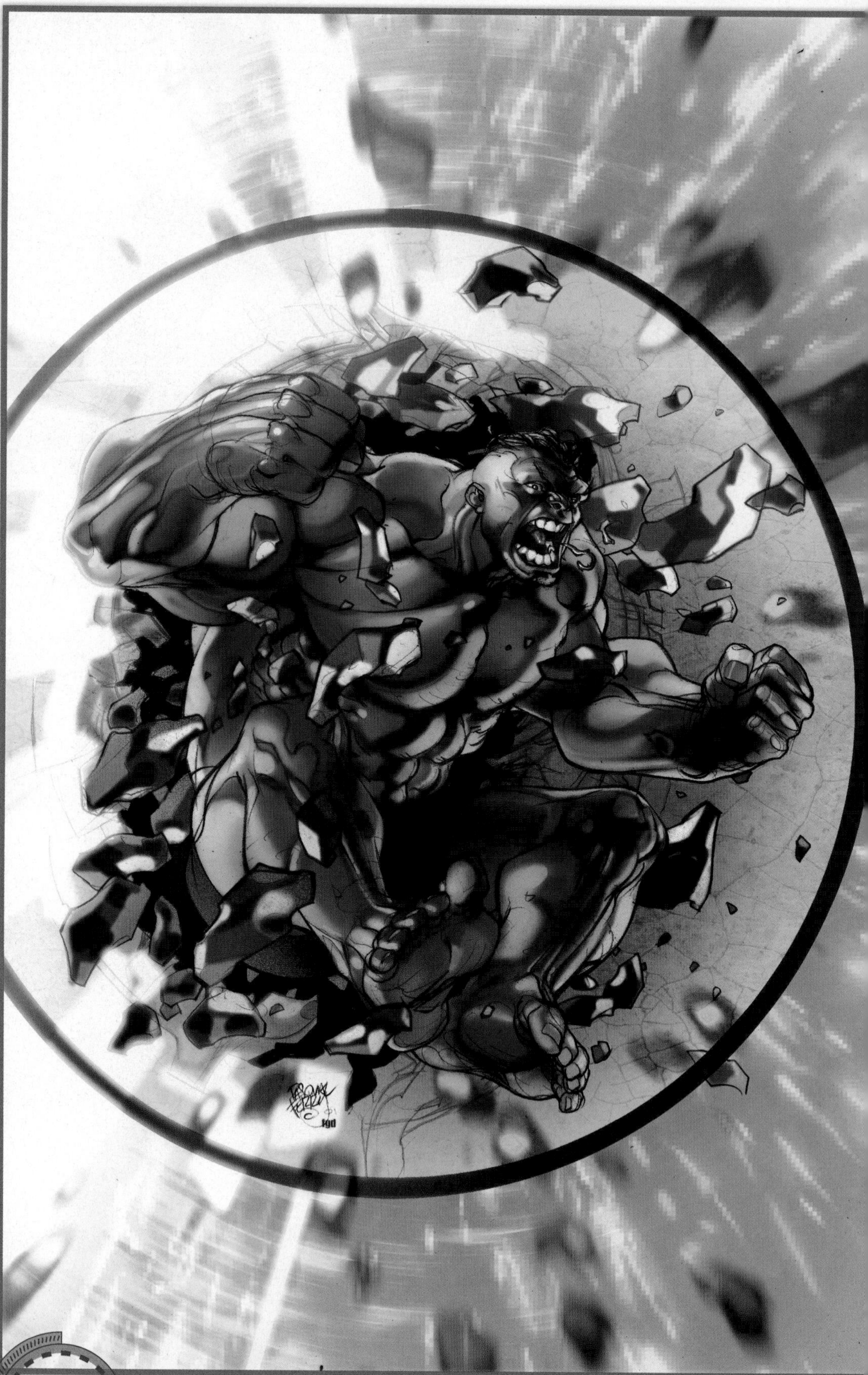

04 VARIANT BY PASQUAL FERRY & FRANK D'ARMATA

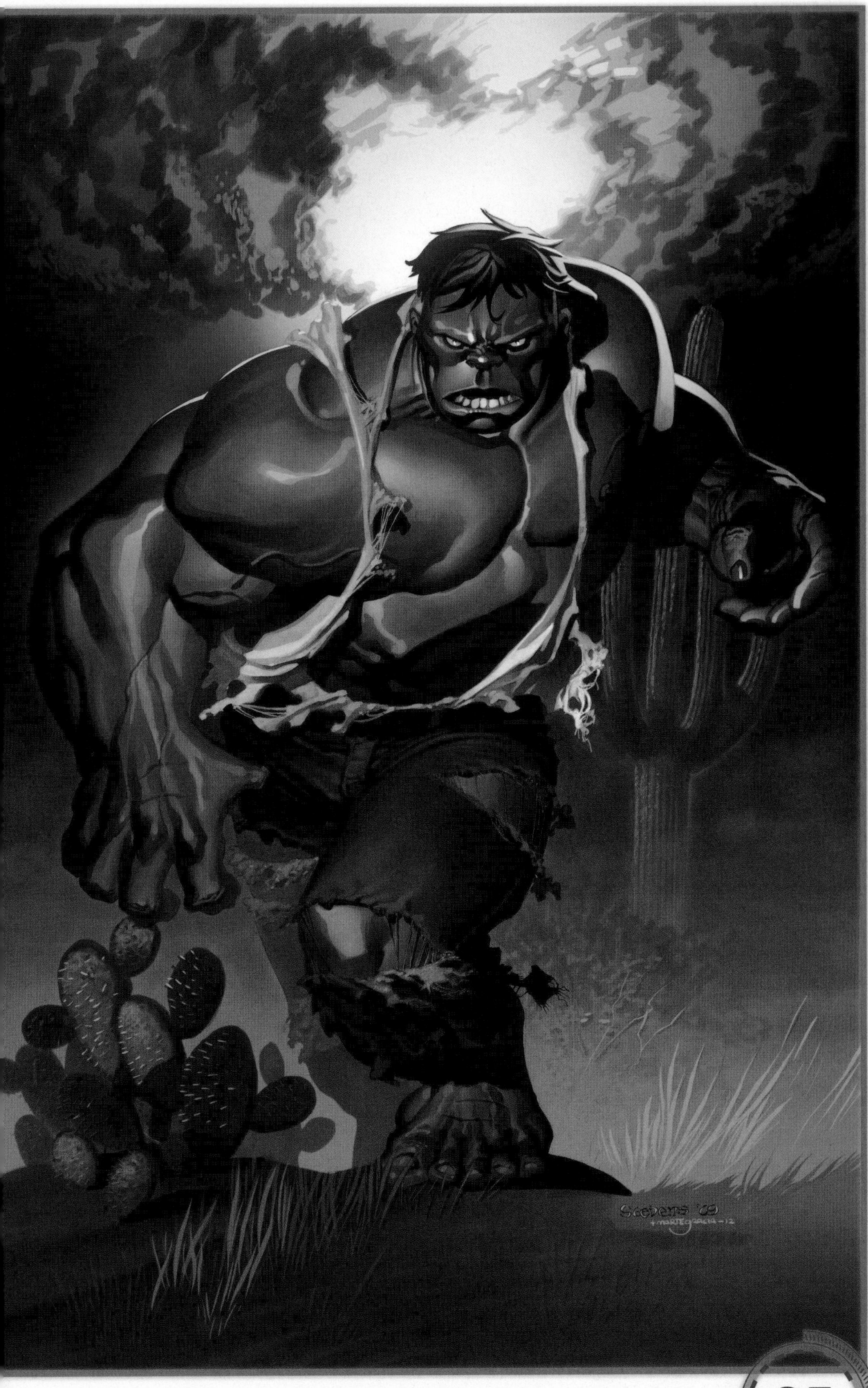

VARIANT BY CHRIS STEVENS & MARTE GRACIA

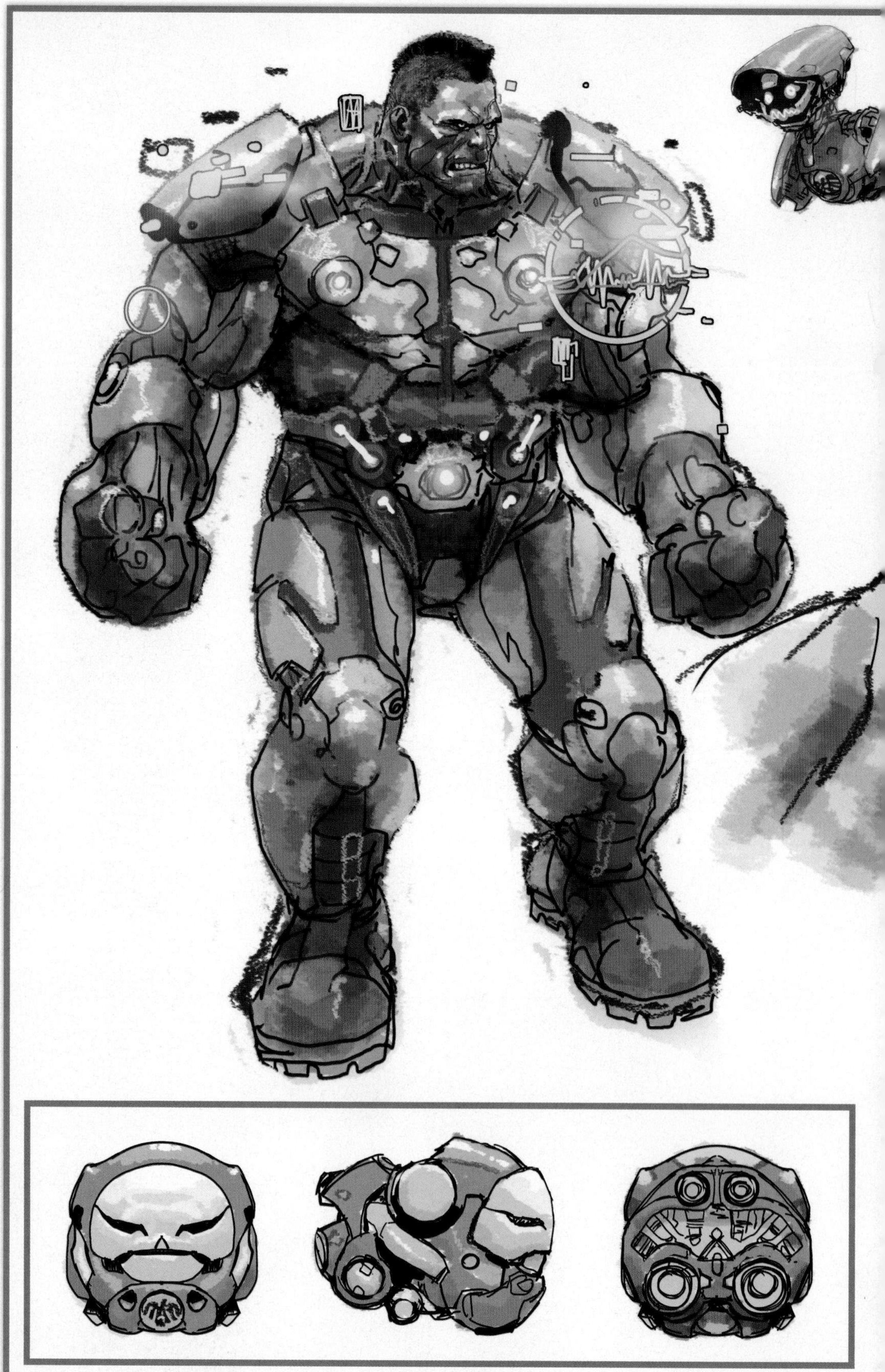

HULK AND R.O.B. CHARACTER STUDIES BY LEINIL FRANCIS YU

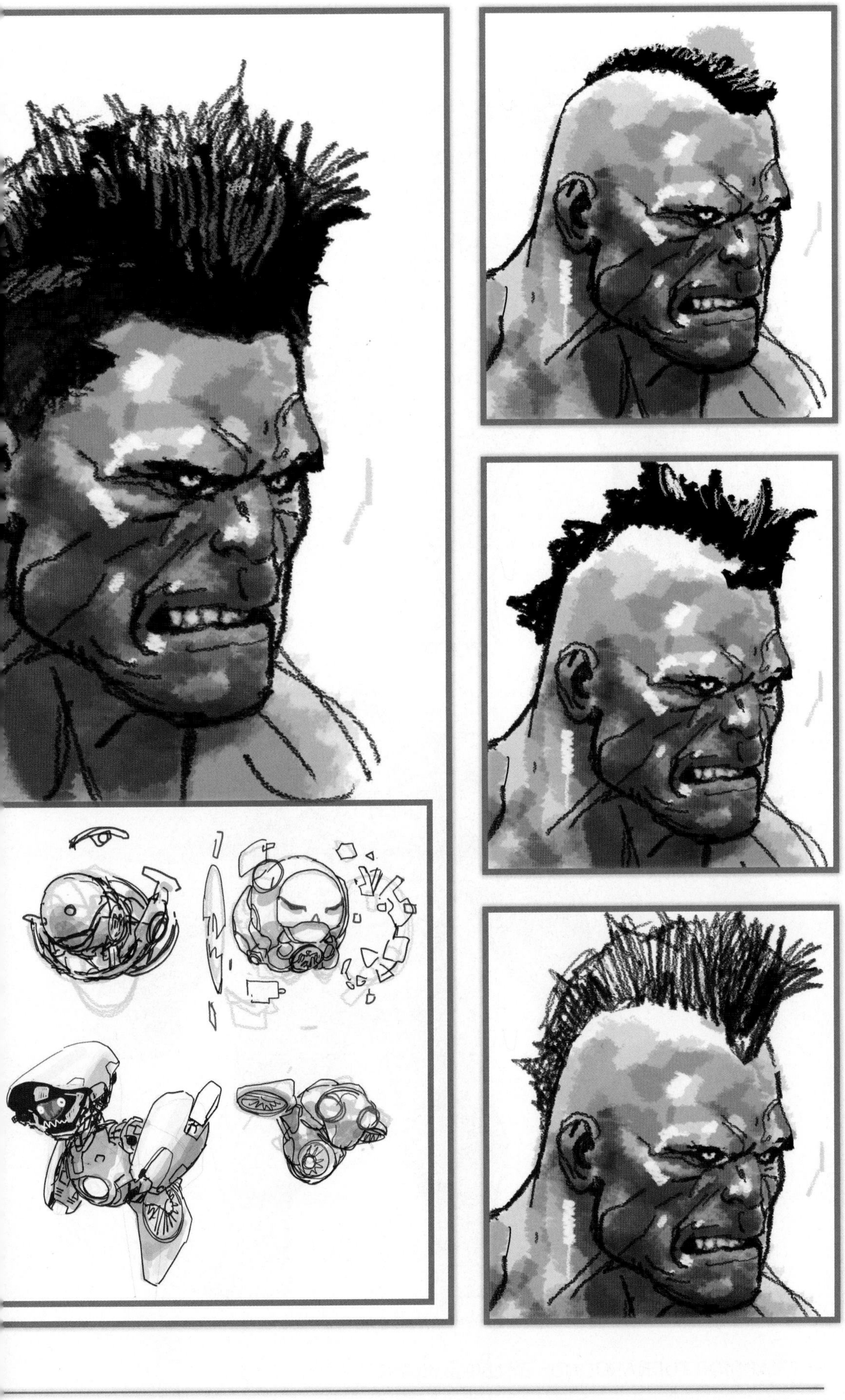

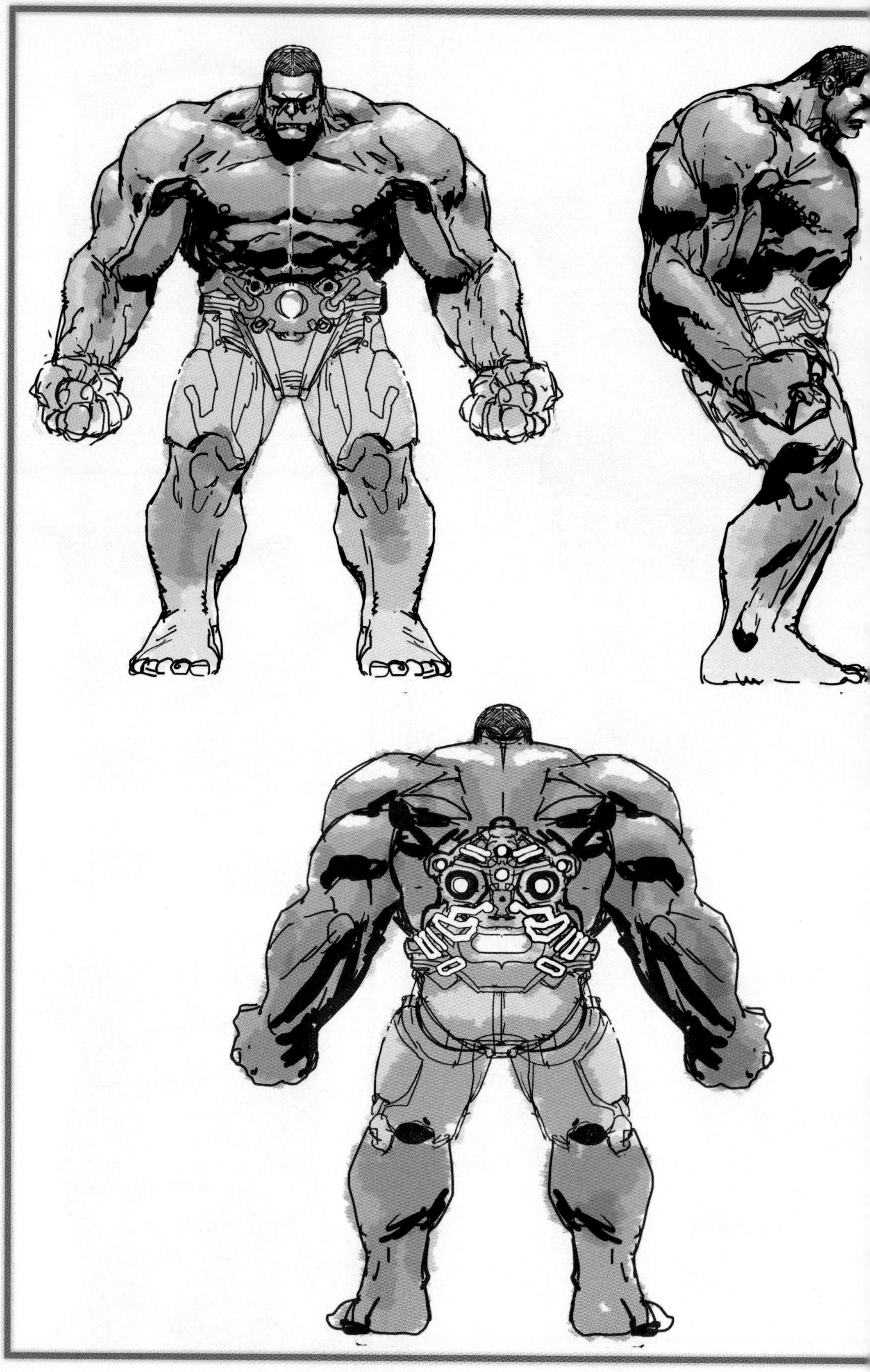

HULK ARMOR TURNAROUNDS BY LEINIL FRANCIS YU

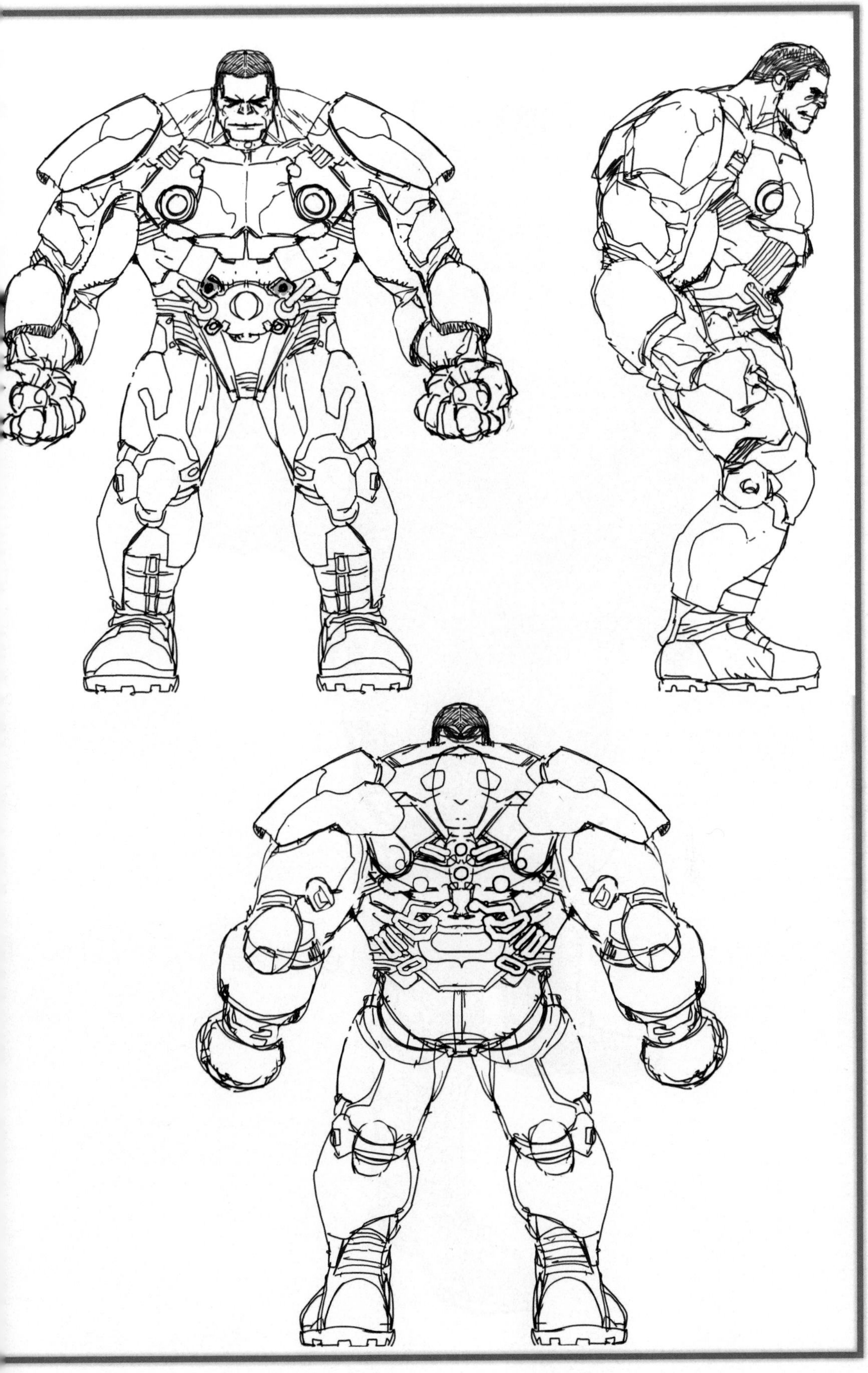

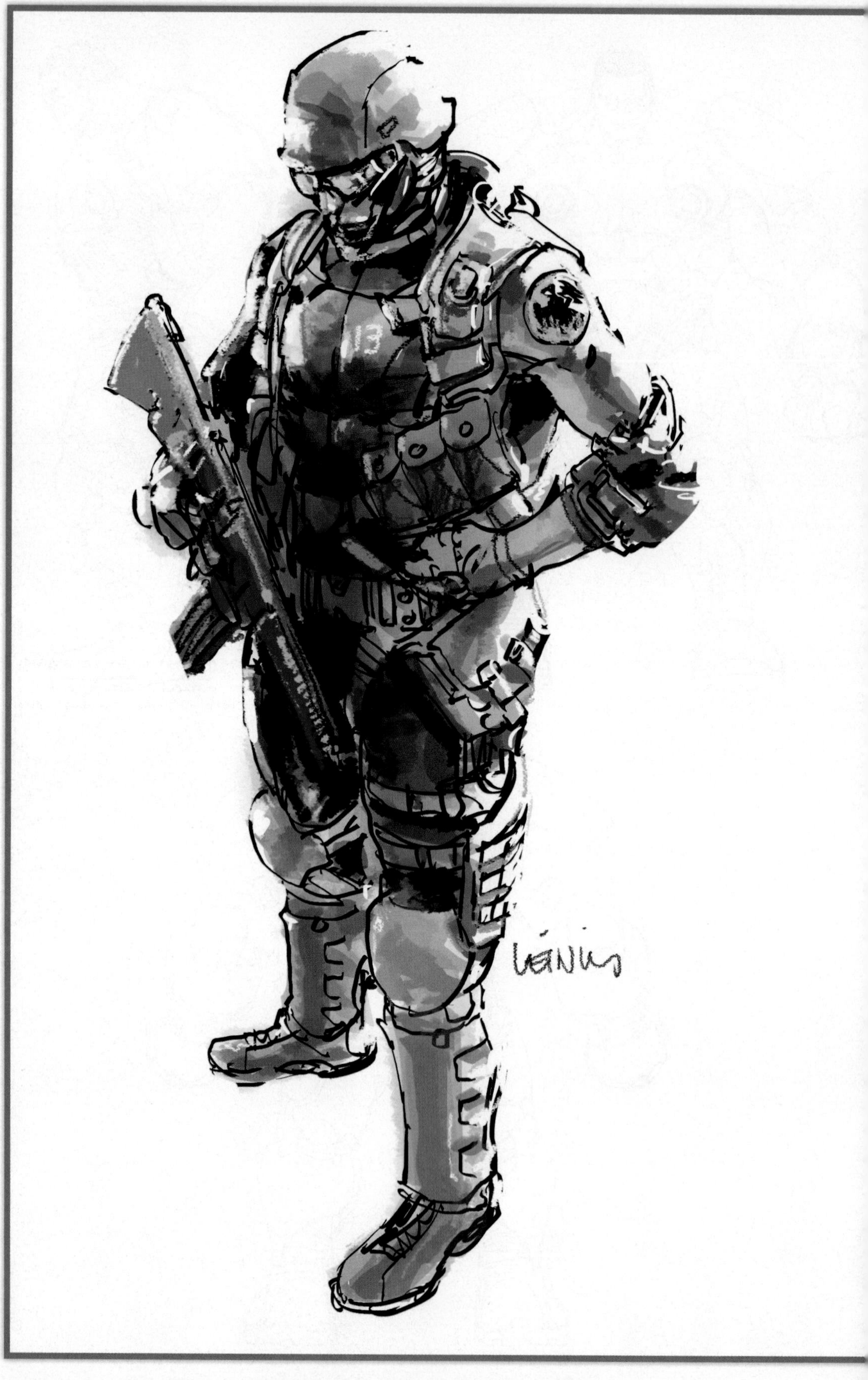

S.H.I.E.L.D. SOLDIER CHARACTER STUDY BY LEINIL FRANCIS YU

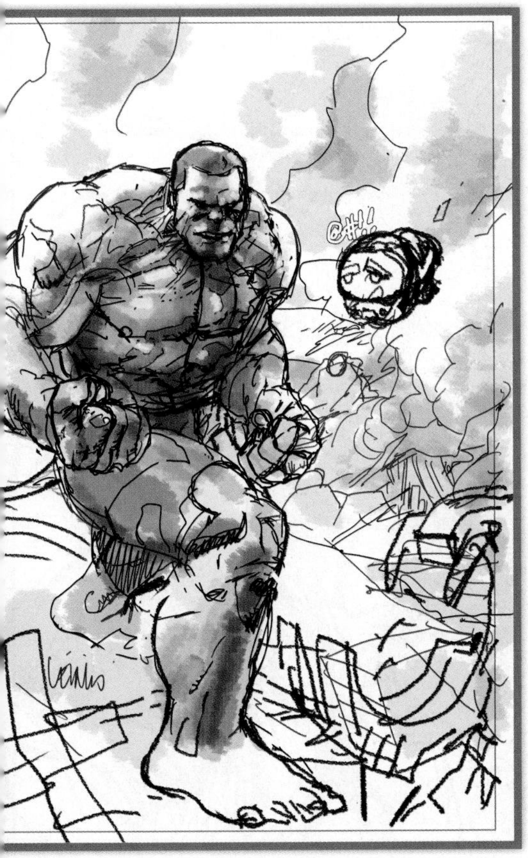

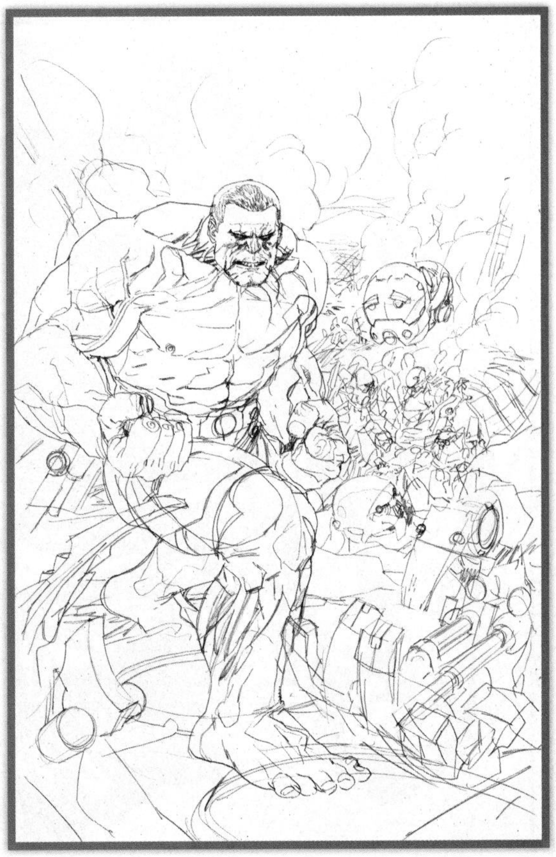

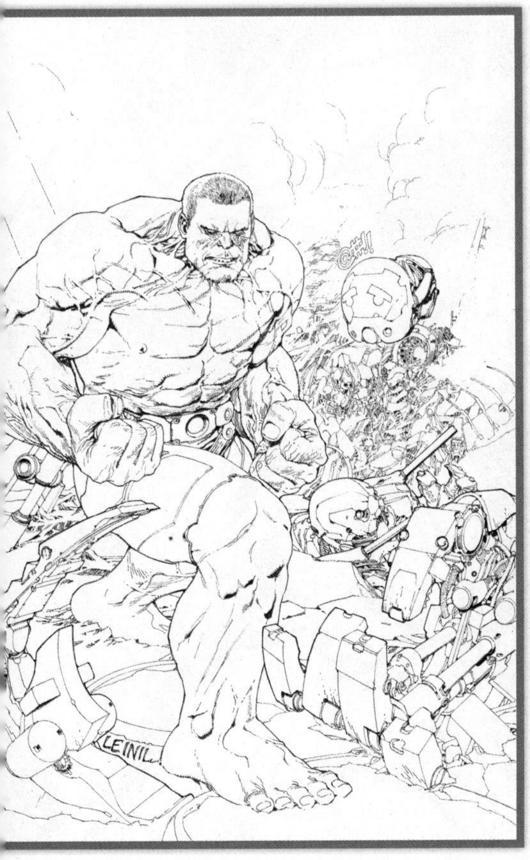
LEINIL

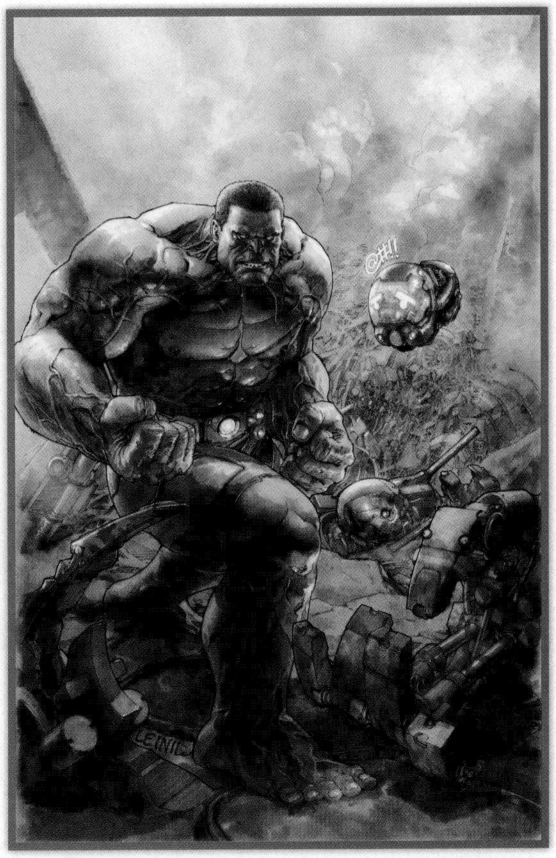
LEINIL

ISSUE #1 COVER ART PROCESS BY LEINIL FRANCIS YU

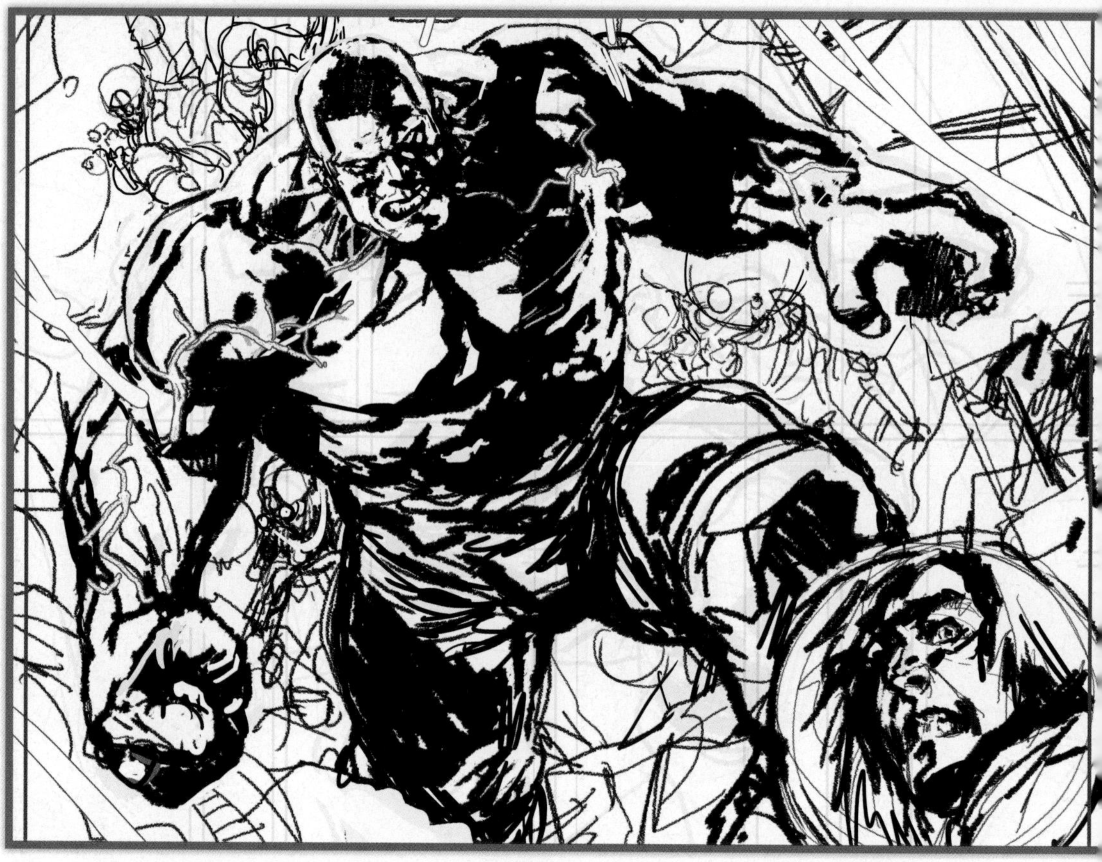

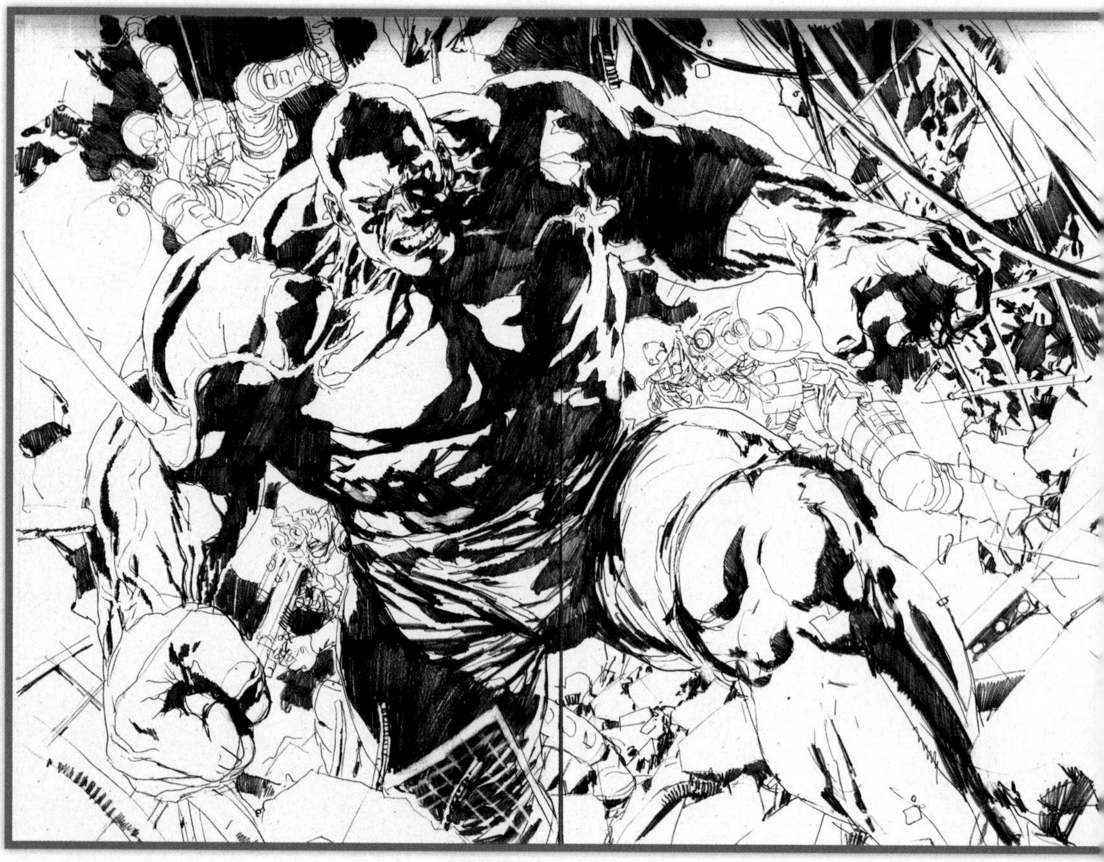

ISSUE #1, PAGES 12-13 ART PROCESS

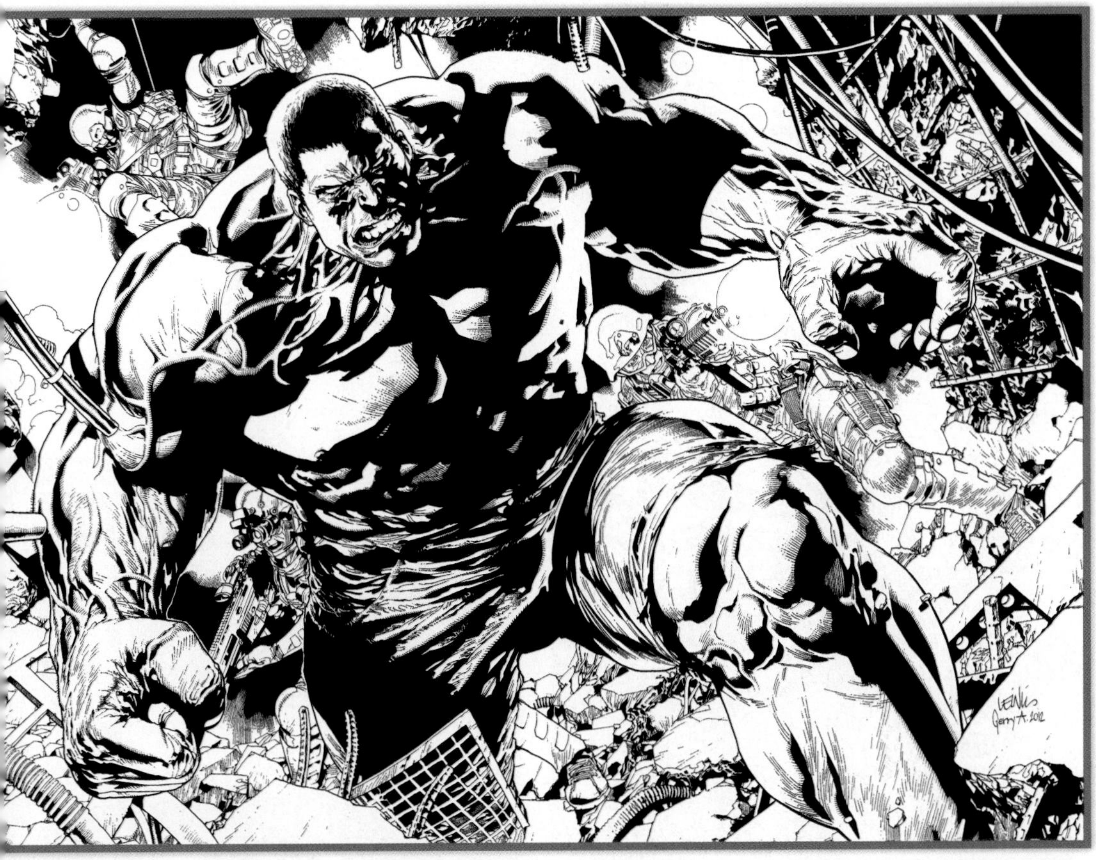

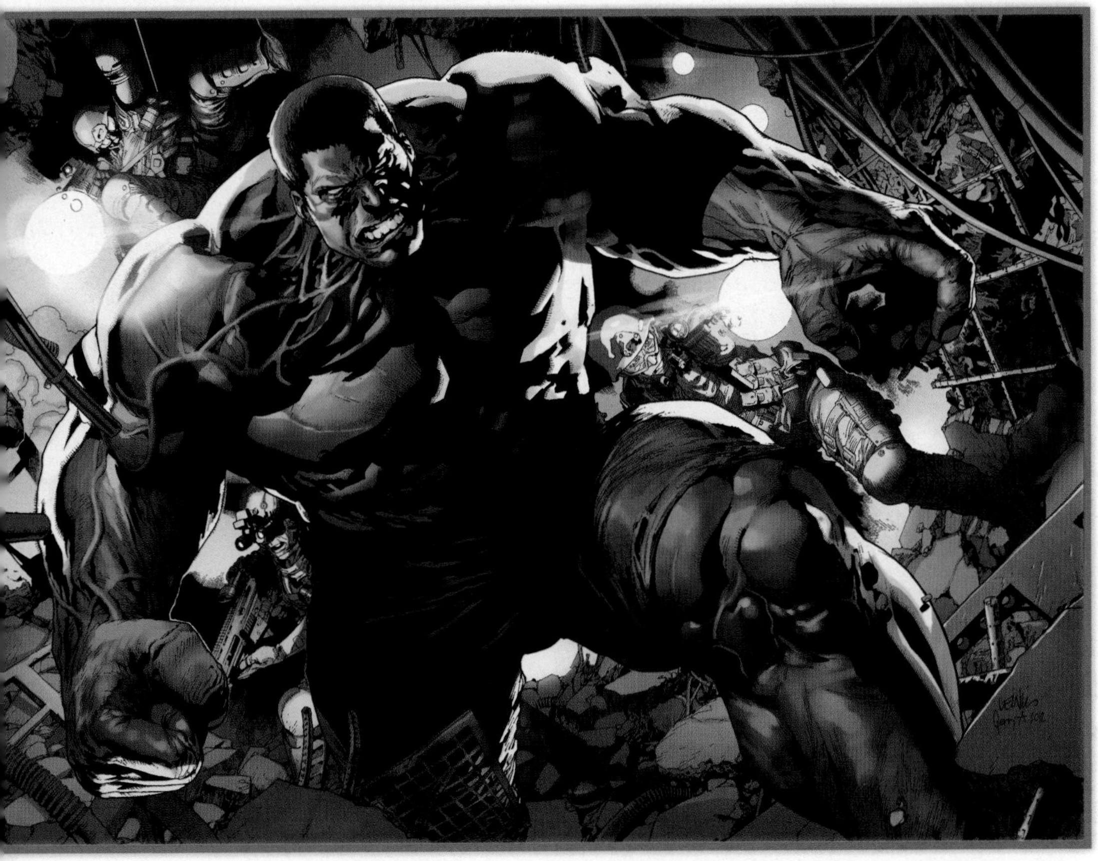

BY LEINIL FRANCIS YU, GERRY ALANGUILAN & SUNNY GHO

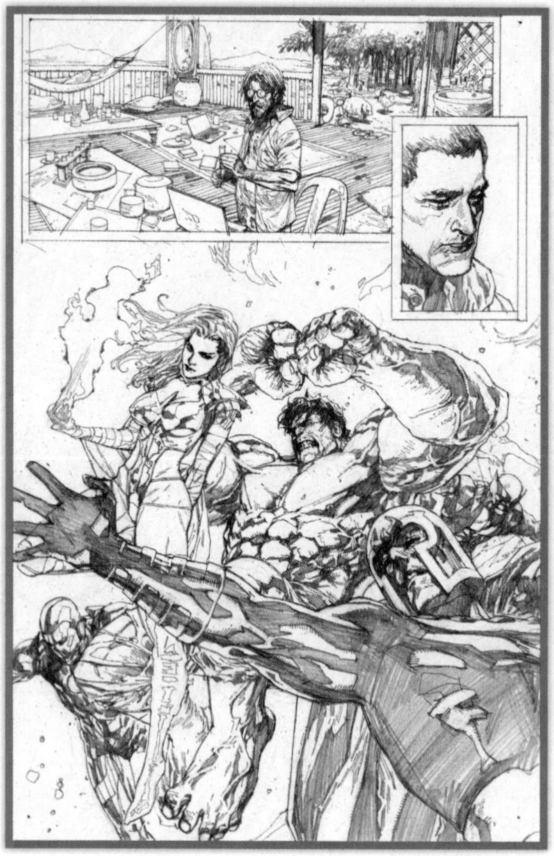

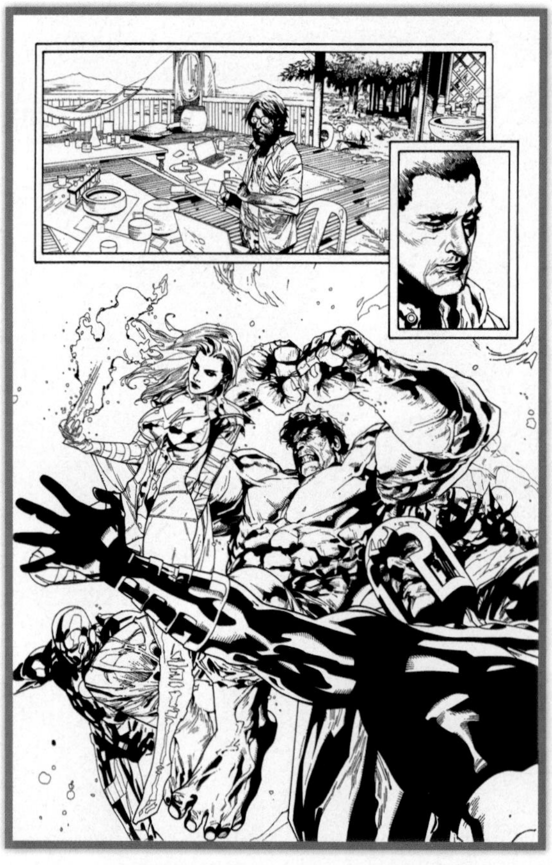

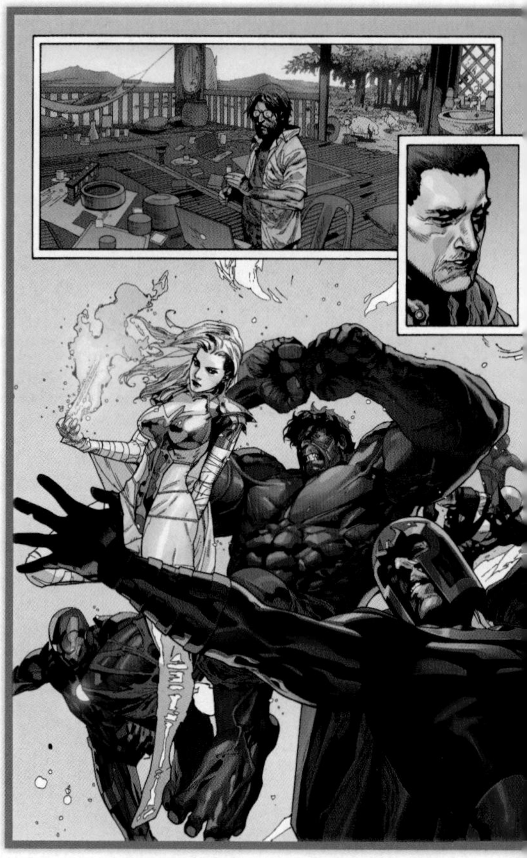

ISSUE #1, PAGE 5 ART PROCESS BY LEINIL FRANCIS YU, GERRY ALANGUILAN & SUNNY GH

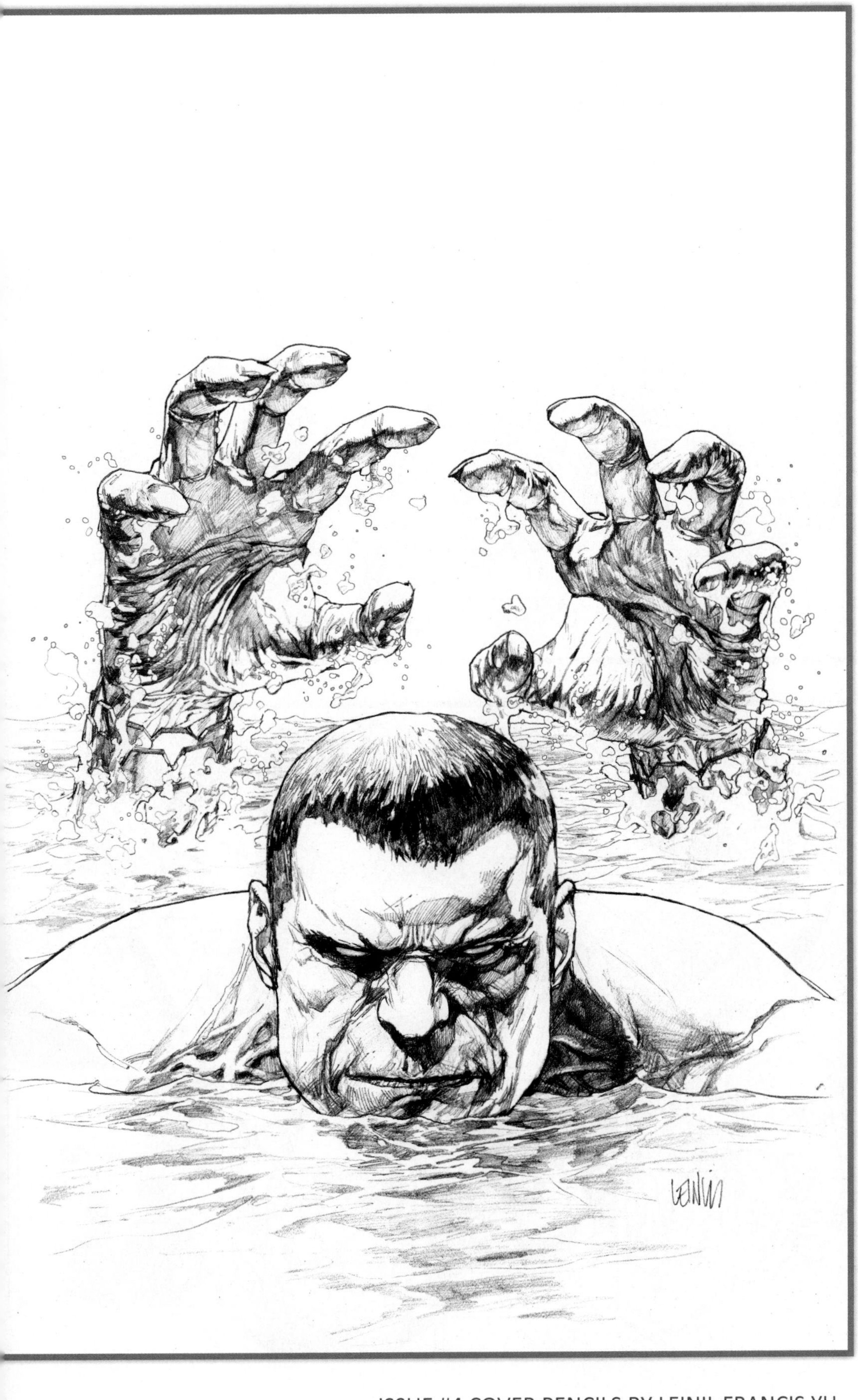

ISSUE #4 COVER PENCILS BY LEINIL FRANCIS YU

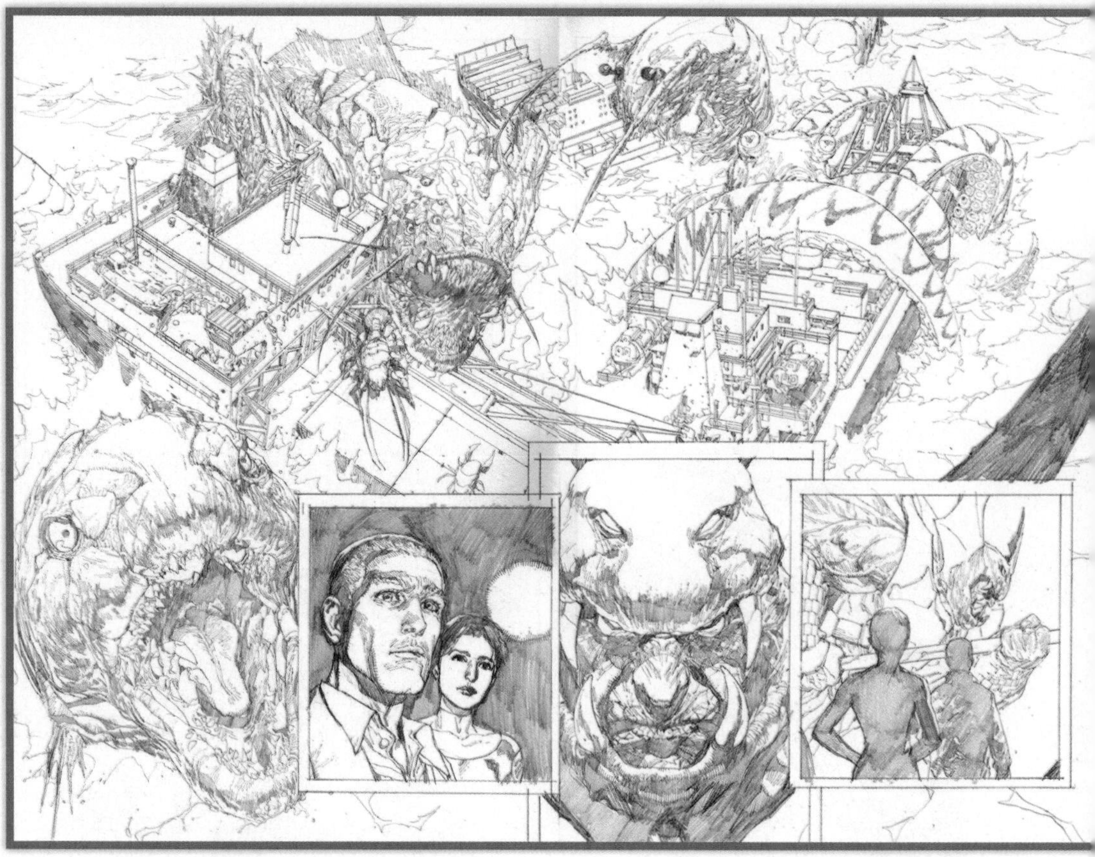

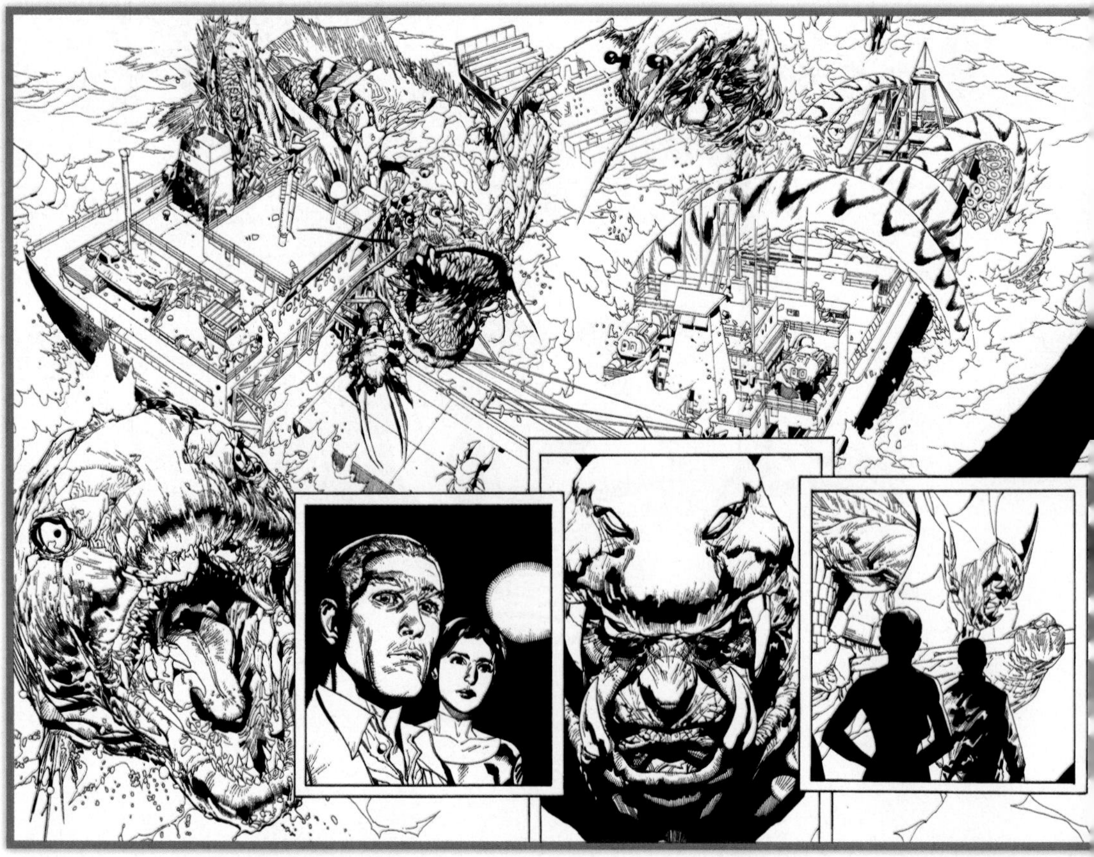

ISSUE #4, PAGES 8-9 ART PROCESS

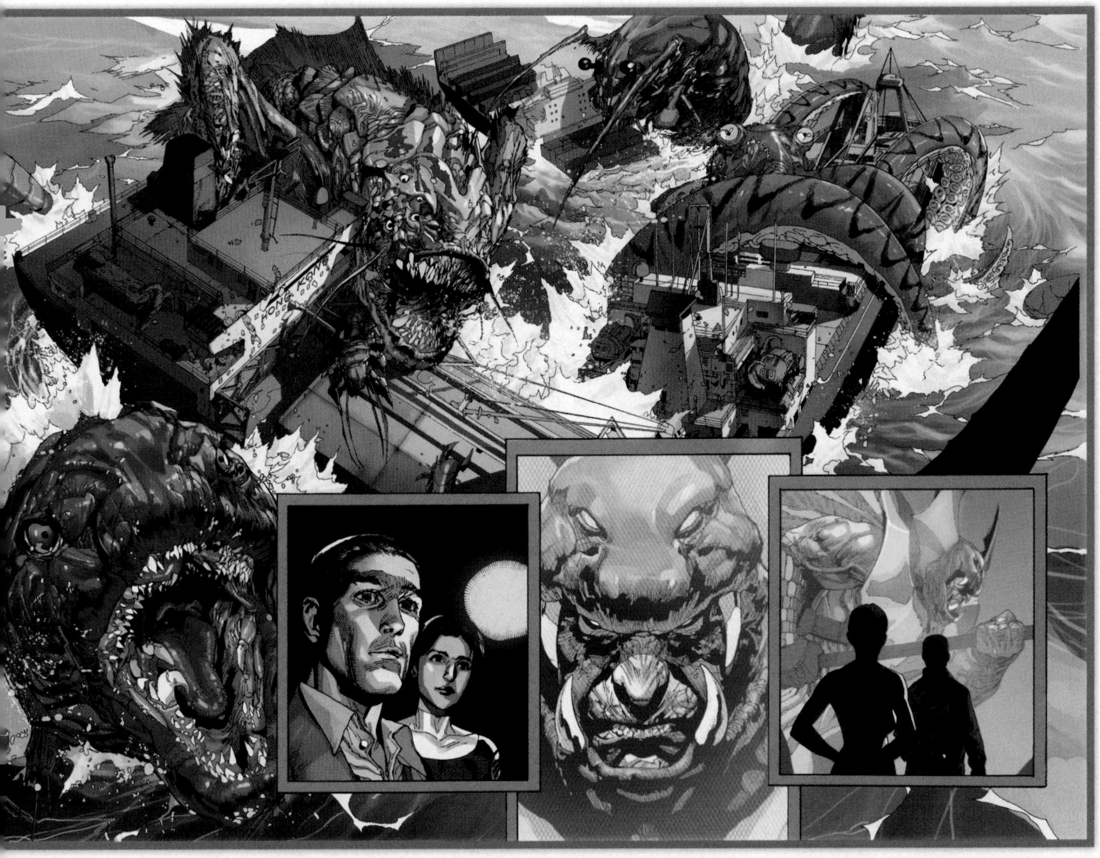
HONG KONG

BY LEINIL FRANCIS YU, GERRY ALANGUILAN & SUNNY GHO

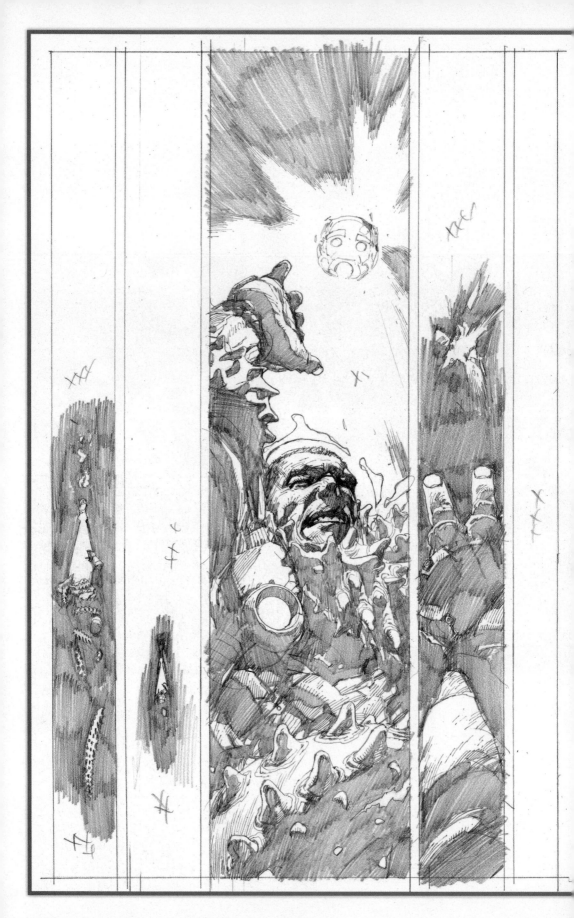

ISSUE #4, PAGE 19 ART PROCESS

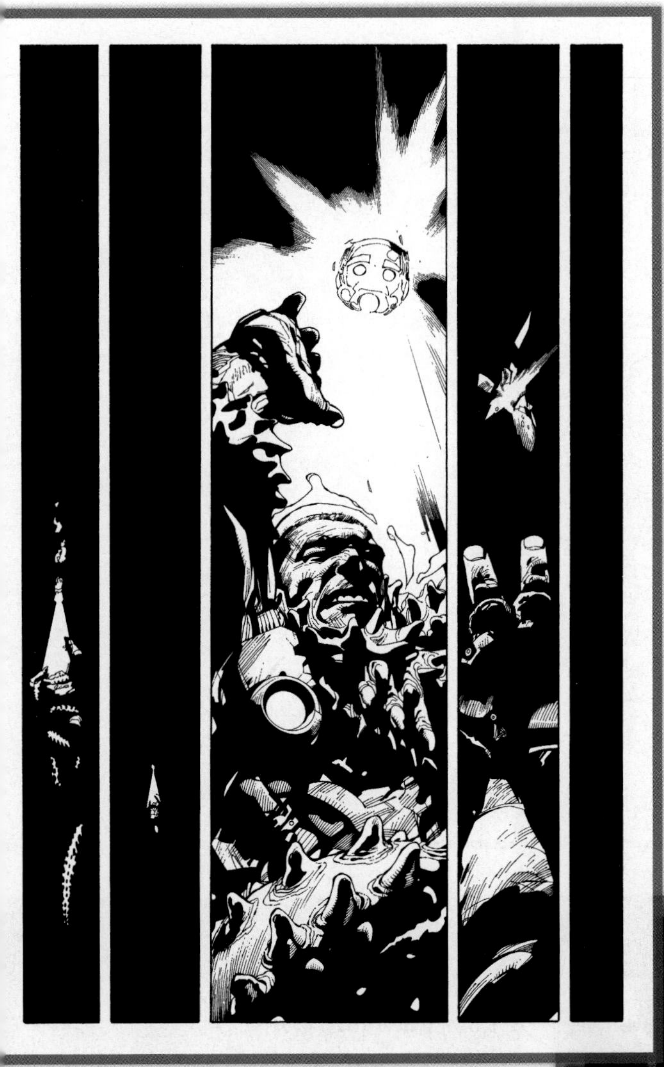

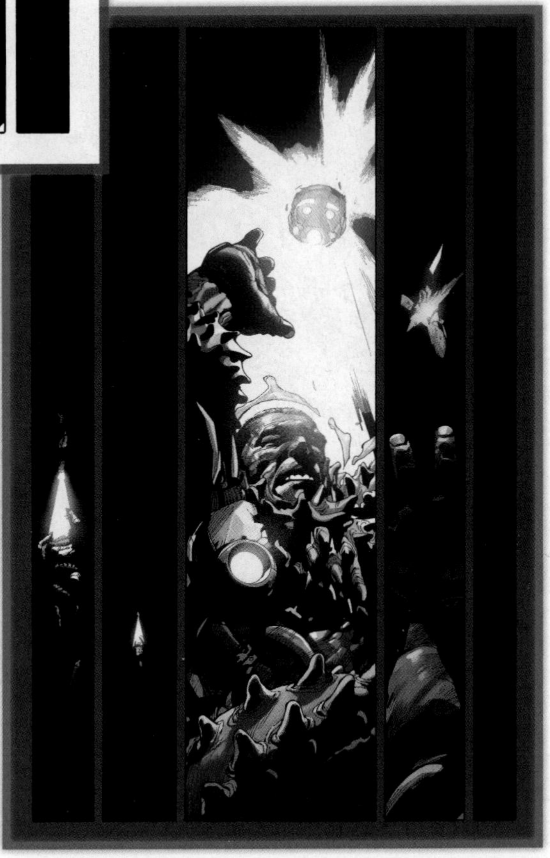

BY LEINIL FRANCIS YU, GERRY ALANGUILAN & SUNNY GHO

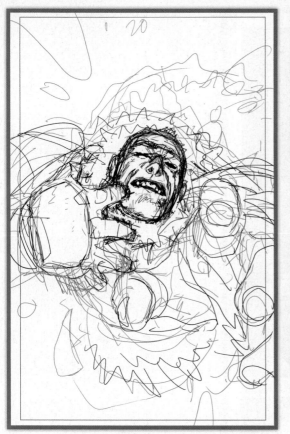

ISSUE #4, PAGE 20 ART PROCESS BY LEINIL FRANCIS YU, GERRY ALANGUILAN & SUNNY GH

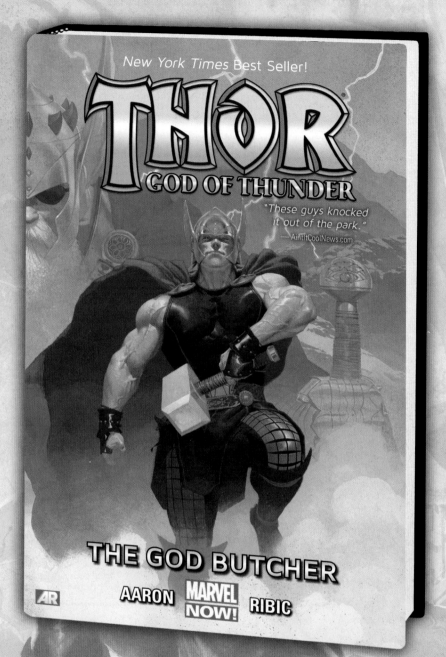

TO ACCESS THE FREE *MARVEL AUGMENTED REALITY APP* THAT ENHANCES AND CHANGES THE WAY YOU EXPERIENCE COMIC

1. **Download the app for free via marvel.com/ARapp**
2. **Launch the app on your camera-enabled Apple iOS® or Android™ device***
3. **Hold your mobile device's camera o any cover or panel with the AR grap**
4. **Sit back and see the future of comics in action!**

***Available on most camera-enabled Apple iOS® and Android™ devices. Content subject to change and availability.**

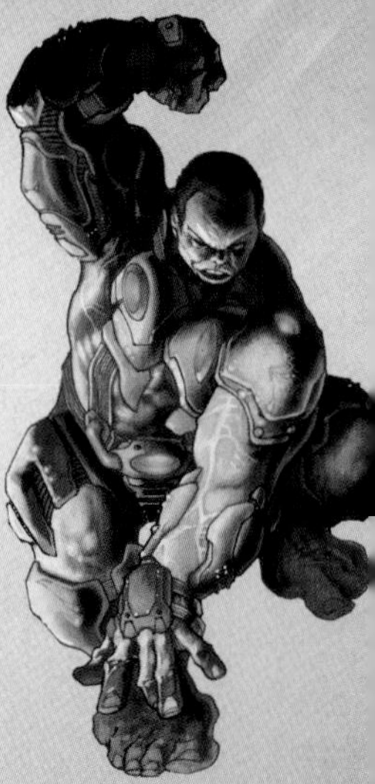

INDESTRUCTIBLE HULK

AR INDEX